A PACIFIST AT WAR

*Russell Chambers
Bury Place
London WC1*

A PACIFIST AT WAR

Letters and Writings of
BERTRAND RUSSELL
1914-1918

Edited by Nicholas Griffin

SPOKESMAN
Nottingham

NOTE

The letters in this volume are taken from Part I of *The Selected Letters of Bertrand Russell, Volume 2, The Public Years, 1914-1970,* edited by Nicholas Griffin (Routledge, 2001). In reprinting them here I have taken the opportunity to correct a number of small errors as well as to supply some information that was not available when the letters were first edited. Most of the errors were pointed out to me by Sheila Turcon, who also supplied much of the missing information. She has worked very thoroughly through both sides of the Colette O'Niel correspondence and I am extremely grateful to her for allowing me to make use of the results of her research.

N.G.

First published 2001 by Routledge as 'War (1914-1918)', part of *The Selected Letters of Bertrand Russell*

This edition plus addtions first published 2014
By Spokesman
Russell House, Bulwell Lane, Nottingham NG6 0BT, England

© 2014 The Bertrand Russell Peace Foundation Ltd by agreement with McMaster University and Routledge; Nicholas Griffin for selection and editorial matter; McMaster University for illustrations.

Typeset in Bembo

All rights reserved. No part of this book may be reprinted or reproduced or utilised in any form or by any electronic, mechanical or other means, now known or hereafter invented, including photocopying and recording, or in any information storage or retrieval system, without permission in writing.

British Library Cataloguing in Publication Data
A catalogue record for this book is available from the British Library

ISBN 978 0 85124 837 0

Printed in Nottingham by Russell Press Ltd (www.russellpress.com)

CONTENTS

Introduction 7

Part I: Letters 13

Part II: Writings 193

Bertrand Russell in 1916

Colette O'Niel in 1916

Ottoline Morrell

INTRODUCTION

'The period from 1910 to 1914 was a time of transition', Russell tells us at the beginning of the second volume of his *Autobiography*. 'My life before 1910 and my life after 1914 were as sharply separated as Faust's life before and after he met Mephistopheles.' Before 1910 Russell's life was that of an independent scholar working on the most abstruse topics in mathematical logic and the foundations of mathematics. It was a time of extraordinary achievement. His work during the two decades before the war had transformed philosophy no less radically than Einstein's work in the same period had transformed physics. Few, if any, other philosophers can match Russell's intellectual fertility during these two astonishing decades. The crowning achievement of this period was *Principia Mathematica*, published in three magisterial volumes between 1910 and 1913 and the product of a ten-year collaboration with Russell's friend and former teacher, Alfred North Whitehead. This was a book like no other. Written largely in the language of symbolic logic (by the second volume, English words appear sparingly), it sought to show how all mathematical concepts could be defined in logical terms and how the theorems of classical mathematics could be derived from logical first principles. In terms of size, complexity, difficulty of subject matter, and the unfamiliar abstraction of its approach, it was probably the most daunting book ever written. Coming after a long series of other contributions, it established Russell's pre-eminence in philosophy. Even as it was being published, Russell was already turning his attention to other branches of philosophy: theory of knowledge and the philosophy of matter. And in 1912 he evinced skills in a new direction by writing an enduringly successful introduction to philosophy, *The Problems of Philosophy*. It remains in print to this day and continues to introduce new generations of students to philosophy. Russell referred to it as his 'shilling shocker'; it was not at all the sort of work one might have expected from an author of *Principia Mathematica*. World-wide academic recognition was just beginning. Early in 1914 Russell had spent a term at Harvard as a visiting professor and the university hoped he might accept a permanent position there. And in the same year, plans were being made for him to visit the University of Göttingen in Germany, then the leading centre for mathematics in the world. On the eve of war, Russell could have looked back on two decades of startling intellectual achievement; and looked forward to a spectacular academic career.

In 1910, as the first volume of *Principia* came from the press, Russell's main work on the philosophy of mathematics was finished and his fame as a philosopher just beginning. In the same year, he got a job. Russell's parents had died when he was young and his share of their estate had been held in trust until he came of age in 1893. It was not a large fortune, but Russell's needs were modest – even frugal – and his inheritance was large enough to support him. He was not, however, in favour of inherited wealth unless it was used for some important end which might not be achieved without it. This he took the writing of *Principia* to be. But when *Principia* was finished, he decided he should earn his own living and, in 1910, he took up a five-year lectureship in logic and the principles of mathematics at Trinity College, Cambridge. This was his first sustained experience of university teaching and Russell was eager to spread the word about symbolic logic which, he hoped, would transform the practice of philosophy. His position, however, was not a regular Trinity lectureship, which would have carried with it a Fellowship at the College, but a special appointment designed to promote teaching and research in Russell's particular field of expertise. At the time, this did not seem to matter very much, but the fact that Russell's lectureship came up for renewal in the middle of the war and that he did not have a Fellowship will play an important role in our story.

Russell's private life also changed during this period of transition. His first marriage, to Alys Pearsall Smith, had begun to fall apart in 1901 after seven relatively happy and tranquil years. The crisis had been precipitated by a semi-mystical experience Russell had in which he had seemed to find revealed the terrible loneliness of individual human life, a loneliness which he thought could only be overcome by the most intense and passionate love. His marriage had been affectionate, harmonious, amicable, and productive – many who knew them had even thought of it as a model of a new type of marriage, in which both partners were free to pursue their differing interests, an ideal balance of mutual affection and independent activity. The trouble, as Russell now saw it, was that this relationship lacked the emotional intensity which alone could make life bearable. Moreover, it became clear, after a year of much hope and some effort, that the more passionate relationship he now desired was not possible with Alys, who had no temperament for the more operatic role in which Bertie now wished to cast her. From 1902 their marriage was effectively dead, though they continued to live together in increasing bitterness and despair. In 1910 Russell's new lectureship at Trinity also led to domestic changes, for it required him to live in Cambridge during term. After the first term, Alys did not accompany him to Cambridge, so that, while they were still together during the vacations, they were for the first time living apart for much of the year. A much more serious change, however, occurred the following year when Russell, in rapid succession, got to know and fell in love with Lady Ottoline Morrell, the flamboyant hostess of the Bloomsbury group. Colourful, extravagant and romantic, Ottoline was the very antithesis of Alys's Quaker plainness. Opera was not beyond her range – indeed, it seemed her natural element. Emotionally, as her biographer, Miranda Seymour, emphasized, she lived life on the grand scale, and in principle, at any rate, was fully prepared to live up to Russell's ideal of a love which could make life bearable. This was the passionate, life-transforming love affair of which he had dreamed.

Swept away by his emotions, Bertie immediately told Alys and separated from her. He also proposed that Ottoline leave her husband, Philip (a Liberal MP), and her young daughter, Julian, to live with him. Ottoline's head was cooler and she refused. Indeed, she was cooler than Bertie about the entire affair. She soon became alarmed at the overwhelming intensity of Russell's emotions, and vexed by the relentless persistence with which she found herself pursued. She was, moreover, by no means so strongly attracted to him sexually as he was to her. Bertie struggled for the next three years to come to terms with these underlying facts – never very successfully, for as soon as he started to pull away from Ottoline, her interest in him would revive. It seems, in fact, that Ottoline was excited more by the idea of an affair with him than by the reality. She was happy to be the muse, confidante and comforter of a great philosopher, but for her this role involved a certain remoteness from daily contact and ordinary life which Russell found hard to cope with. Happy or not, Bertie's affair with Ottoline began a profound change in him: 'Ottoline had a very great influence upon me, which was almost wholly beneficial' he wrote in his *Autobiography*.

> She laughed at me when I behaved like a don or a prig, and when I was dictatorial in conversation. She gradually cured me of the belief that I was seething with appalling wickedness which could only be kept under by iron self-control. She made me less self-centred, and less self-righteous. Her sense of humour was very great, and I became aware of the danger of arousing it unintentionally. She made me much less of a Puritan, and much less censorious than I had been. And of course the mere fact of happy love after the empty years made everything easier. (*Autobiography*, vol. i, p. 205).

It was not, however, Lady Ottoline who played Mephistopheles to Russell's Faust according to Russell's account in the second volume of his *Autobiography*, but World War I. The outbreak of the First World War in August 1914 dramatically changed almost everything in Russell's life. It was the War that made him a public figure and ensured that henceforth philosophy would only occasionally prevail over politics for his attention. Russell had always been political; he was, in fact, born into politics. His family had an important place in the radical wing of the

Liberal aristocracy. His grandfather had twice been prime minister, and his grandmother, who brought him up after his parents' deaths, groomed him for high political office. The American philosopher, George Santayana, who was a close friend of Russell's brother, said that she was preparing him to be prime minister, and given the family's place in the Liberal establishment, it was not an absurd ambition. It is hard to imagine Russell as a successful party politician, but throughout his life his political commitments were profound and his political activism intense. His first book had been on politics (*German Social Democracy*, 1896) and even during the writing of *Principia* he had taken time off for political campaigns: in favour of free trade in 1904 and, much more extensively, in support of women's suffrage in 1906-10. He had regularly campaigned in British elections, usually in support of the Liberals, and had once stood for election himself as a women's suffrage candidate. But it was not until the First World War that politics came to dominate his life.

Unlike so many, who went enthusiastically to war in the summer of 1914, he knew the War would be a disaster. Nor did he share the general British opinion that Germany was entirely responsible. He thought the secret diplomacy of the Liberal administration under Sir Edward Grey, which had entangled Britain in a series of alliances to defend continental countries against aggression, shared a good deal of the responsibility. He had, moreover, no doubts at all that it was his public duty to oppose the War:

> I never had a moment's doubt as to what I must do. I have at times been paralyzed by scepticism, at times I have been cynical, at other times indifferent, but when the War came I felt as if I heard the voice of God. I knew it was my business to protest, however futile protest might be. My whole nature was involved. As a lover of truth, the national propaganda of all the belligerent nations sickened me. As a lover of civilization, the return to barbarism appalled me. As a man of thwarted parental feeling, the massacre of the young wrung my heart. I hardly supposed that much good would come of opposing the War, but I felt that for the honour of human nature those who were not swept off their feet should show that they stood firm. (*Autobiography*, vol. ii, pp. 17-18)

The War made Russell a popular figure among pacifists and those on the left who were opposed to it, but it made him *persona non grata* with the Government, including many of his erstwhile allies in the Liberal establishment (though not with Ottoline and her husband, who remained staunchly supportive of the pacifists). The costs of opposing the War were high. The government fined him, confiscated his passport, placed him under surveillance, banned him from certain parts of the country, and eventually jailed him. He was viciously attacked in print and in person and, on at least one occasion, physically assaulted. He lost his job at Cambridge, his academic career, and many of his former friends. During the War he was dependent on his brother for providing him a place to live and when it ended he was broke, jobless, and exhausted. None of this caused him to waver for a moment in his unrelenting opposition.

The outbreak of war was a public crisis in Russell's life that he rose to with dignity and courage. Simultaneously with it there occurred a private crisis which he handled far less impressively. In the spring of 1914 he had travelled to America primarily to lecture for a term at Harvard. When his Harvard lectures were over he travelled on to the Midwest to give more lectures. One of his stops was Chicago where he stayed at the home of Dr. E. Clark Dudley, an eminent surgeon, at the invitation of Dudley's daughter, Helen, who had visited Bertie and Alys years before. In Chicago he found Helen unexpectedly interesting. She wrote poetry and plays and felt stifled by the lack of literary society in Chicago. Russell was a sympathetic audience for her woes and his visit offered her a chance of escape. After one night together they had decided that she would accompany her father on a visit to England during the summer and she would stay on with Bertie after her father returned to America. Although Bertie told her (without mentioning Ottoline by name) that he was in love with a woman from whom he could not break, they still thought they might live together, have children and even get married if Bertie could obtain a divorce.

Bertie's affair with Ottoline had been in an unsatisfactory state for so long that he could hardly be blamed for taking an interest in another woman. Bertie, of course, was still passionately in love with Ottoline, but he desperately wanted children and daily companionship and neither of these was possible with her. Their sexual relationship was strained by Ottoline's reluctance and Bertie's ardour, and just before he returned from the US she had written to him asking that their relationship henceforth be Platonic. Bertie thought, no doubt naively, that children and daily companionship would be possible with Helen, while Ottoline could be elevated to the position of muse and inspirer. Moreover, satisfactory sexual relations with Helen would help him avoid making unwelcome demands on Ottoline. Ottoline had even suggested that he have a relationship with another woman. In principle, all seemed well. As a rational adjustment of means to ends, the scheme had much to commend it. Unfortunately, it took little account of the emotional needs of the three people involved, and it began to unravel as soon as Bertie got back to England.

Ottoline tried to be generous when she learnt the news and wrote several letters to Bertie saying that she didn't want to stand in his way and hoping that he would be happy with Helen. But any such outcome was made impossible by Ottoline's changed attitude to Bertie now there was a competitor for his affections. No more was heard of her request for a Platonic relationship; regular meetings were resumed, often at Ottoline's request; her letters became longer and more affectionate. Poor Helen had little chance, on either side of the Atlantic, of competing with a revival of Ottoline's affection. It seems clear, moreover, that Bertie in Chicago had let his emotions run away with him. He may not have given Helen to understand that he was more in love with her than he thought himself to be at the time. But it is clear that she had come to think that he was more in love with her than he discovered himself to be once he'd returned to England. In his *Autobiography* (vol. i, p. 213) Russell says 'the shock of the war killed my passion for her'. The outbreak of war, which had thrown Ottoline and Bertie together, did change the plans Russell made in Chicago in one important practical respect: if he was to be effective in opposing the war he could not afford to live openly with a woman who was not his wife, even getting a divorce would be dangerous. For Russell, brought up to put public duty before private happiness, this would have been an important consideration. None the less, it is hard to avoid the suspicion that, in this case, public duty was used as an excuse for getting rid of a private entanglement which now threatened his all-important relationship with Ottoline. When the war broke out, Helen was already *en route* to England. The scene was set for both private and public tragedy.

PART I
LETTERS

WEDNESDAY NEXT.
CORN EXCHANGE, CAMBRIDGE.
Removed thereto from Trinity College, Cambridge, under a Distress levied for non-payment of a fine under the Defence of the Realm (Consolidation) Regulations, 1914.

The Furnishings of the College Rooms
of the
Honble. Bertrand Russell, M.A., F.R.S.,
Including:
CHIPPENDALE 6-LEGGED SETTEE,
SUPERIOR TURKEY CARPETS and RUGS,
Walnut Kneehole Writing Table, 6 Large Bookcases, Antique Mahogany Pembroke Table, Coromandel Wood Tea Caddy, mounted with 10 painted medallions, upwards of 100 OZS. of PLATE, Plated Articles, Gentleman's Gold Watch and Chain.

COLUMBIA UNIVERSITY
BUTLER GOLD MEDAL,
awarded to Bertrand Russell, 1915.
LIBRARY
of upwards of
1,500 VOLUMES of BOOKS,
Royal Society Proceedings and Transactions, 1908-14; London Mathematical Society Proceedings, Vols 4—15; Blake's Works, ed. Ellis and Yeats, 3 Vols., 1893; Cambridge Modern History, Vols. 3—7; Bentham's Works, ed. J. Bowring, 11 Vols., 1843; Berkeley's Works, 4 Vols., 1877; Baldwin's Dictionary of Philosophy and Psychology, 1901-5; Hobbes' Complete Works, ed. Sir W. Molesworth, 16 Vols., 1839-45; Revue de Metaphysique et de Morale, 1893-1914; Mathematical and Philosophical Works, Poetical Works, &c., &c

To be Sold by Auction by
Messrs. Catling and Son,
AT the CORN EXCHANGE, on WEDNESDAY NEXT, JULY 26th, 1916, at 3.30 in the Afternoon precisely.
On View Morning of Sale.
Further Particulars of the AUCTIONEERS, 6, St. Andrew's-street, Cambridge.

An advertisement sent to Russell's Cambridge colleague, F M Cornford, announcing the auction of Russell's belongings on 26 July 1916 for non-payment of a fine under the Defence of the Realm (Consolidation) Regulations 1914 (see p80).

THE OUTBREAK OF WAR IN AUGUST 1914 took Russell by surprise. He was in Cambridge on Sunday, 2 August when he came upon John Maynard Keynes hurrying to borrow a motorcycle on which to rush up to London: the government had called on him for urgent financial advice. It was only then that Russell realized that war was about to break out. 'Looking back', he wrote, 'it seems extraordinary that one did not realize more clearly what was coming.' But he had 'found it impossible to believe that Europe would be so mad as to plunge into war' (*Autobiography*, vol. ii, p. 15).

None the less, he had been concerned about the international situation. At the end of July he helped organize a petition of 61 Cambridge dons urging that Britain remain neutral in the event of a Continental war. (It was published in the *Manchester Guardian* on 3 August, the day Germany declared war on France.) The wide support in Cambridge for British neutrality was not untypical of the country as a whole: a number of liberal and left-wing organizations declared in favour of neutrality at this time. It was not then known that secret British undertakings to France made neutrality impossible. In any case, support for British neutrality collapsed quickly on 4 August when Germany attacked France through neutral Belgium.

Once war broke out out, it was difficult to know what to do to oppose it. With great difficulty Russell managed to get a letter condemning it published in the Liberal journal, *The Nation*, in which he frequently published before the war (see *Collected Papers*, vol. xiii, pp. 6-9). H. W. Massingham, the editor, printed it only because he had promised to do so before the war was declared and then with his own disclaimer printed afterwards. After this, the Liberal press was entirely closed to Russell until some Liberal organs broke ranks with the government over conscription in 1916. Once war was declared, it was evident that those opposed to it were too few and too weak to have any hope of limiting the fighting. Instead, Russell turned to longer-term schemes which might serve, once peace has been restored, to make futures wars less likely.

One organization of this kind was the Union of Democratic Control (UDC). Its aims were to place foreign policy under tighter parliamentary control (thereby eliminating, it was hoped, the secret diplomacy that had embroiled Britain in a Continental conflict), to secure peace in Europe through an international League with powers of arbitration, to reduce armaments, and to ensure that territorial changes were carried out by plebiscite. (Some of its policies bore fruit after the war in The League of Nations.) The UDC was founded at a meeting on 10 August at which Russell was present. Although he was very pessimistic about its chances, he endorsed its programme and worked hard for its success.

Most of Russell's friends and colleagues (including those closest to him and those whom he had hitherto regarded as political allies) supported the government's policy after Germany invaded Belgium. Alfred and Evelyn Whitehead, for example, his oldest and closest friends, supported the war and this difference cast a chill on their friendship, which was never quite the same afterwards. Of all those close to him, only Ottoline and Philip Morrell were wholeheartedly opposed to the war. Philip gained Bertie's admiration as one of the few MPs who braved a very hostile House of Commons to speak against war in the debate on 3 August, thereby ending any hope he might have had of political advancement. Russell had gone to London for the debate, but the public gallery was packed and he could not get a seat. Instead, he spent the evening wandering through the cheering crowds round Trafalgar Square and discovering to his horror that ordinary people were delighted by the prospect of war. The isolation that the war imposed on Russell and the Morrells threw Bertie and Ottoline together. They needed each other's support now more than ever and during the early months of the war they became closer than they had been for a long time.

1   [To Ottoline Morrell]   [Trinity College]
                                              [5 August 1914]
                                              Wednesday evening

My Dearest

We are terribly alone in this dreadful world. I have been home ten minutes, and have had a letter from Mrs Whitehead in favour of war, and a talk with Prof. Hobson,[1] who got most of the signatures to our manifesto,[2] but has gone over completely because of Belgium. One can only suffer and wait. But I do see the point of view of those who believe in the war, and it is a comfort, because it makes it easy not to hate them. And I think at the very last it could not be helped; but until the very last it could have been. Dearest it was a comfort being with you. I felt so deeply one with you. I don't know how I could have borne it if we had been divided.

Now that nothing can be done one must try to live as quietly as possible, away from fever. I shall try to work. But if you find out anything I can do, please let me know. Jaurès[3] is happier than we who remain.

Your
    B.

---

1 Ernest William Hobson (1856–1933), Sadleirian Professor of Mathematics at Cambridge.
2 The letter to the *Manchester Guardian* in support of neutrality. See *Papers*, vol. xiii, p. 482.
3 Jean Jaurès (1859–1914), leader of the French socialists and one of the few on the French left who had remained a pacifist as the war approached. He had been assassinated on 31 July.

Bertie's troubles, however, were not confined to the war. On 8 August Helen Dudley was expected to arrive in England with her father. It seems that Russell had made some attempt to dissuade her from coming, but she did not take the hint, and she could hardly have foreseen how the war would affect their plans. It had been intended that she should stay with Bertie after her father returned to America, but if Bertie was to retain any political influence it would hardly have been possible for him to live openly with a woman who was not his wife. Helen's father thought it would be best if Helen returned with him. But this was unwelcome both to Helen, who continued to hope that a relationship with Bertie might still be possible, and to Bertie, who continued to think that a stay in London would further her literary career and who also feared for her state of mind if both her literary and her romantic hopes were shattered too abruptly. The problem, then, was to find somewhere she could stay. The situation was obviously difficult, and it is hard to see how a happy outcome might have been devised at this stage. Bertie's unease was compounded by the fact that, as appears from the next letter, he had not fully explained his relation with Ottoline to Helen. In America he had told Helen, without mentioning Ottoline by name, that he had a relationship with someone from whom he would not break. It is difficult to imagine, as events unfolded over the next few weeks, quite what Helen understood his relationship to Ottoline to be.

[To Ottoline Morrell] [34 Russell Chambers[1]] 2
[12 August 1914]
Wednesday night

My Darling

I cannot tell you all that your love is to me in these days – it is *much* more to me than ever before – today I felt an absolute fullness of union such as I had hardly thought possible in this world – it is quite beyond words, and as the pain of the outward horror increases, I feel your love increasing too, sustaining courage and keeping faith alive. It is strange how utterly outward barriers cease to matter at this time – I have such a sense always of your presence. My Dearest I do not know what I should have done at this time without you, or whether alone I should have had the inward courage to stand out against the world.

Now I must tell you about H.D.'s affairs. I saw her and her father together tonight, and him alone for a few minutes. He had quite decided to take her back on Saturday,[2] but I did something towards making him change his mind. His chief feeling was obviously that he didn't know of

---
1 Until 1916 Russell alternated between Trinity College, Cambridge and his flat, 34 Russell Chambers, in London. He rarely put an address on his letters to Ottoline, but his location can often be inferred from the postmark.
2 In fact, Dr Dudley returned to the US the following Thursday, 20 August.

any household where she could be. I said nothing definite, but said I thought it could be managed.¹ He has an engagement tomorrow, and will not reach Bedford Square till about 11. I will bring her about 10.30, unless you send round a note to the contrary. Probably you would rather I left you alone with her; if so, you might give me a hint and I will go to the Library. I wonder whether she will give you her tiresome side or her good side. Her father is a worthy soul, but an awful bore, and very stupid in human things. I praised her writing to him, and said she ought to see literary society; I also said I was sure she could get it. He will no doubt only be at Bedford Square a few minutes, but it would be well if you could reassure him.

I don't think she realizes *quite* what you and I are to each other, and now there is no reason why she should. It would be very unfortunate if she thought you had anything to do with my change towards her; she certainly doesn't now, and has (so far as I can see) *no* feeling of hostility or suspicion towards you. I am sorry you should have this to attend to just now, but I do think it is really important for her to be able to stay. It was my feeling that Chicago was killing her that first moved me; and I am sure that feeling was right.

At the Vienna Restaurant at dinner I found Ramsay MacDonald,² Charles Trevy,³ and Morel.⁴ They were not exciting – political considerations prevent their feeling whole-heartedly all that ought to be felt. But they are good souls, and there are not too many in the world.

I hope you managed to make your peace with Molly.⁵

I come up again on Monday. Please let me know some time about seeing you. What a blessed change it is that P. and I are friends – it makes everything so easy. I *really* love him now. Goodnight my dear dear Love.

Your
B.

---

1 At this time, Bertie and Ottoline were hoping that Helen could stay with Philip Morrell's sister, Margaret Warren.
2 James Ramsay MacDonald (1866–1937), one of the founders of the Labour Party. In 1914 he was forced to resign as party leader over his opposition to the war, but in 1924 be became Britain's first Labour Prime Minister.
3 Charles Philips Trevelyan (1870–1958), a Radical MP until 1914 when he switched to Labour. He had been a friend of Russell's since their undergraduate days at Cambridge.
4 E.D. Morel (1873–1924), author and journalist. In 1911 he had attracted world attention to Belgian atrocities in the Congo. Morel, Trevelyan, and MacDonald were among the founders of the UDC. Russell probably thought their opposition to the war less wholehearted than he wished, because at this stage they were still hoping to rally left-Liberal support to the UDC. Any hope of this evaporated the following month when the press, imaginatively supporting government policy, ran stories declaring the UDC to be a sinister German conspiracy.
5 Probably the writer, Molly MacCarthy (1882–1953). She was married to Russell's friend, Desmond MacCarthy, the literary critic. The nature of the quarrel is not clear.

Ottoline's first meeting with Helen the next day seems to have gone off fairly smoothly, though Ottoline was hardly impressed:

> She was an odd creature of about twenty-seven, rather creeping and sinuous in her movements, with a large head, a fringe cut across her forehead, and thick lips ... [S]he was languid and adhesive, sympathetic but insensitive and phlegmatic, and entirely without self-assertion.
>
> (*Memoirs*, vol. ii, p. 286)

She was even less complimentary after a longer acquaintance:

> A queer creature. So lethargic and feline. She must be a strange descendent of vampires ... She sits and looks at the fire for hours and seems to be remembering sadly what a wonderful time vampires had in old days before they strayed into this degenerate intellectual world. She seems to be trying to accustom herself to talk, and she does so by repeating after one what one has said, then she will go on and on and learn what the next person says. She is really only a vampire of ideas and sentences. Meanwhile her body is laced and anaemic. What she really needs is blood, not ideas and words.
>
> (*Memoirs*, vol. ii, p. 98)

None the less, although they avoided talking about private matters on their first meeting, Ottoline was sympathetic to Helen as an aspiring writer and offered, as she often did, to do what she could to help. Like Bertie, she thought that it would be better for Helen's literary career if she could stay in England, especially since Helen herself was still keen to do so. But the problem of where she could stay was still unsolved. Helen wanted to take a flat on her own, but her father was opposed to this idea. Ottoline was still pursuing the possibility of her staying with Philip's sister, Margaret Warren, and her husband.

Meanwhile Bertie was facing other problems, this time in his relations with the Whiteheads. Though both supported the war, Alfred was more pacific than Evelyn, who was vehemently anti-German — 'the bully must be stopped', as she put it to Bertie (Lowe, *Whitehead*, vol. ii, p. 28). Their eldest son, North, was making determined efforts to enlist. He had been turned down at his first attempt, but, to Bertie's horror, the Whiteheads used family connections to get him accepted. He was shipped to France with the Second Division of the British Expeditionary Force on 21 August. Russell had been particularly close to North and felt concern for him as he would his own son. Moreover, he had no illusions about the war: North's commission, he thought, was virtually a death sentence.

3   [To Ottoline Morrell]   **[Trinity College]**
                                                  [13 August 1914]
                                                  Thursday night

My Darling

Thank you for your little note. My feeling about you is infinitely deeper and (in a way) more calm than it ever was before – I feel it has become what it always might have been but failed to be. It makes *no* demands, and is all one with what one feels about the war and about humanity.

When I got here I found a *very* war-like letter from Mrs Whitehead, saying North wants to enlist and she thinks he is right. I can't tell you how much I mind – I feel as if my relations with the whole family could never again be quite the same. Next to you they are much the most important people in my life.

Poor old Dr. Dudley has bored me almost beyond endurance, though I think him admirable in many ways. I have had him on my hands the whole day till 10.15 – since I found Mrs Whitehead's letter he has particularly tried me. I had about two words with Helen, who seems to have been very much touched by your kindness, and to be ready to love you. I wonder what you thought of her.

Molly[1] was very nice to me as she went away. I hope you made things all right with her.

My brother[2] is coming for the week-end which is a bore. The Dudleys go tomorrow morning, which I am glad of. I want to write, but am not clear how to do it yet.[3] I feel the Whiteheads *terribly*. I feel the anguish they must be suffering about North – and for the first time since I have known them well I can't give sympathy that will be any good. It is ghastly. It is a strange division of love against love – my love for them against the feeling of humanity. I see no issue – there ought to be one – I thought one could always find an issue through love but I don't see how.

Goodnight my Dearest. One must just go on and trust that some good some day will grow out of love.

   Your
      B.

---

1 Molly MacCarthy, see previous letter.
2 John Francis Stanley ('Frank'), 2nd Earl Russell (1865–1931). In the event, he proved a great source of support for Bertie during the war.
3 Russell wrote a number of short articles and letters about the war at this time. But this remark probably refers to *War, the Offspring of Fear*, which was written at this time for the *Contemporary Review*, which rejected it. It was eventually published in November as a pamphlet by the UDC. (See *Papers*, vol. xiii, pp. 37–47.)

By now Helen realized that Bertie's feelings for her were not what she had expected. 'She had come', Ottoline wrote, 'panting with high hopes and ardour' only to find that 'Bertie's whole attention and passion were concentrated on the war, and he had no room for any thought of her' (*Memoirs*, vol. ii, p. 286). 'I broke her heart', Russell confessed in his *Autobiography*. 'If the war had not intervened, the plan which we formed in Chicago might have brought great happiness to us both. I feel still the sorrow of this tragedy' (vol. i, p. 214). Helen was indeed heartbroken but she faced the situation bravely and continued to hope that a deep friendship, if not a great love, might still be possible. There are a few sad, and in the circumstances remarkably understanding, letters from her in the Russell Archives. (Russell published one in his *Autobiography*, vol. ii, p. 47). All of them are undated, so they do not help to determine exactly what took place, and no letters from Bertie to Helen have been located.

The plan to have Helen stay with the Warrens fell through for some reason, and, at this point, events took a turn which no novelist would have dared to invent. Dr Dudley, blissfully unaware of what was going on, had the disastrous inspiration that Helen should stay with Ottoline at 44 Bedford Square. Ottoline, though reluctant, said she felt she had no choice but to agree (*Memoirs*, vol. ii, p. 287). Bertie must have viewed this arrangement with apprehension, though he gives no sign of it in the next letter. Thrusting Helen into Ottoline's care could only jeopardize his recently improved relations with Ottoline, while doing nothing at all to mitigate Helen's distress. Helen herself presumably still did not realize quite what Bertie and Ottoline were to each other; had she done so she would surely not have put herself in this unenviable situation.

[To Ottoline Morrell]   **[34 Russell Chambers]**   4
[18 August 1914]
Tuesday night

My Darling
    I have read what George gives of Bright's letter; it is *most* wonderful.[1] I should like to see the whole. Yes, I should like to write like that – if I could. It is dreadful that there is *no one* like Bright in politics now. But

---

1 'George' is George Macaulay Trevelyan (1876–1962), the historian and brother of C.P. Trevelyan. In 1913 he had published a biography of John Bright (1811–1889), the British orator and politician who had been one of the main opponents of the Crimean War. Trevelyan paints a heroic picture of Bright's lonely opposition to a popular war and credits him with having helped keep Britain out of Continental wars for the rest of the century. He quotes from several of Bright's letters which might have appealed to Russell, but the one Russell probably has in mind is Bright's long critique of the policies which led to war published in *The Times* on 3 November 1854. Trevelyan quotes it extensively, see *The Life of John Bright*, pp. 220–4, 227–9.

people will come round after a time – perhaps after a short time. I wish I could see the German White Paper.[1]

Dearest it is dreadful to see you so terribly weary – I am *very* sorry that I had to put the weight of H.D. on you, but I did not see how I could help it. I believe you have made *all* the difference to her – without your help, I don't see what future she would have had. I am sorry I was so worried while you were here today – I was obsessed by the thought of her committing suicide on the way back to America. If she stays here, I feel sure she won't. *Please* don't think anything that has happened is your fault – all would have gone well but for the war. And the war would have made the same difference however much you had withdrawn yourself.

I understand much better now how the misunderstandings between you and me about P. arose in early days. I had not given a thought to them for a long time, but today I suddenly realized how they had come about. I find it impossible to say exactly what I felt about H.D., because I felt twenty different things in the course of a day. I do not now feel that I could enter upon *any* new relation – I *may* feel differently later, but I think it very likely I shan't. And certainly I could not think of any open relation. For the present, the war makes all private things seem of very little moment, except when they can enter into connection with what one feels about it.

My Dearest Dearest I feel most absolutely united with you, even in the constriction that has come to you through feeling for H.D. I have *no* impulse now to make demands upon you of any sort – I do respect your liberty inwardly and instinctively and in my most secret thoughts. Goodnight my Dearest. I do hope you will be able to get rested soon.

    Your

      B.

Once her father had left for home, Helen duly turned up at Bedford Square accompanied by a mountain of trunks filled with 'cheap and vulgar underclothing and dresses', as Ottoline put it (Seymour, *Ottoline Morrell*, p. 198). Though Ottoline was not anxious to have 'the weight of H.D.' put upon her, she was apparently quite willing to become Helen's confidante. Ottoline was a

---

[1] Presumably *The German White Book: How Russia and Her Ruler Betrayed Germany's Confidence and Thereby Caused the European War,* a propagandistic account of the origins of the war published in Berlin on 3 August.

skilled confidante and Helen was soon divulging details of her unhappy love. The story Ottoline got from Helen was different in tone, if not in content, from the one she had had from Bertie. According to Helen, Bertie had declared himself to be much more deeply in love with her than Bertie had given Ottoline to understand. Even allowing that Helen had as much cause to exaggerate as Bertie, it was a disquieting revelation which Ottoline passed on indignantly to Bertie.

Bertie was prepared to admit that he had been 'most terribly to blame towards H.D.' (23 August) but, as Ottoline continued to receive fresh revelations from Helen, he reacted with ill-justified irritation. His attitude to Helen was not improved by the increasingly passionate letters he was receiving from Ottoline – she spoke swooningly of the 'sacred and mystical joy' of a kiss on 28 August – and her brisk reassurances that Helen would 'soon pick up' (27 August) and that the best policy was for him to be firm with her (28 August). Ottoline's own indignation reached its peak when Helen showed her some of Bertie's letters. Ottoline was horrified to discover that Bertie had used some of the same phrases to Helen that he had used to her. She thought, in fact, that Bertie's letters to Helen were more passionate than the ones that she had received, though it strains credulity to think that she was entirely accurate in this assessment. There was little Bertie could do but try to minimize the damage.

[To Ottoline Morrell]   [34 Russell Chambers]   5
   [1 September 1914]
   Tuesday night

My Darling Darling

I am thankful for the great happiness of the end of our time today – at first it seemed so very hopeless. Will you try to make up your mind that I have behaved very badly, that I am so full of shame that at moments I can hardly face you, and that I have had a lesson which will keep me from anything of the sort again. And please please don't think you were in a fool's paradise at Burnham Beeches[1] – it is quite untrue. Don't let us lose the wonderful union that came the other day in the Library.[2] What is past is past, and *that* is the truth now. I really don't think it is good for any of us that you should go on letting yourself hear her talk about me. There is nothing new, and

---

1 Between Bertie's return from America in June and the outbreak of war, he and Ottoline had gone every Tuesday to Burnham Beeches near Slough. These had been some of their happiest times together. The last such occasion was the day on which Austria declared war on Serbia. (See *Autobiography*, vol. i, p. 213.)
2 At Ottoline's home, 44 Bedford Square, the previous Thursday, when the sacred and mystical kiss had occurred.

it is merely upsetting; and I don't believe it can do her any good after this.

There is not the *faintest chance* of any revival of the feeling I had for her – it is utterly dead, and when a thing is really dead it never revives. If it were not selfish, I should wish most intensely never to see her again. I made an absolute mistake – I never was as fond of her as I thought, and towards the end I forced the note from a hope of being able not to hurt her. Will you try to believe this, to fix it in your mind? I am really not making a mistake now. All my behaviour for two years past has been due to the fact that I had an instinctive grudge against you – now I have none. And the attempt to imagine what it would be like to go away with H.D. made me realize that, apart from her, that is no longer the *sort* of thing I want. I am much more anxious to have full opportunities for work than I am to have that sort of thing. I have thought this out, and I know it was already true before the war. Only then I felt I must try to make her happy.

I couldn't understand your saying my letters to her were more passionate than any I ever wrote to you. I think you must have forgotten. I copied out for *Forstice* part of a letter I wrote you about the 23rd of March 1912[1] – I enclose it – every word of it is true now, except about fierceness – that is gone – I am altogether less fierce than I was then. You never acknowledged that letter, so I thought you felt it excessive – but it was true to what I felt. Now my love for you is more welded with love of humanity – it wouldn't let me do anything that would be against love of humanity, and as soon as that grows dim I feel less fully united with you than when it is strong.

I came to think you disliked passion, and to try and express as little of it as I could. It is only quite lately that I have felt you did not mind it. Expression is such a need with me that it was difficult keeping it back. Now I know there is no need.

Dearest, whatever I may have said and done and thought, it has been you *only* that I have truly loved ever since that first Sunday in Bedford Square. I have behaved quite horribly, but although I tried to be faithless, I have never been so in *feeling*. I am terribly afraid you will think this is only words, but it isn't. There is something

---

1 'Forstice' was a novella, *The Perplexities of John Forstice*, which Russell wrote in 1912 with some assistance from Ottoline. (It is published in *Papers*, vol. xii, pp. 128–54.) The passage in question came from a letter of 24 March 1912. It was never included in the manuscript of *Forstice*, but it can be found in *Papers*, vol. xii, p. 535. Ottoline now vowed to commit it to memory.

involuntary and coercive in my love for you, and it never grows less, and never will, because it has to do with the essential hunger of the soul. Dearest Dearest do *do* let yourself be happy in my love – it is so untrue and so unnecessary not to be. Just when we have found each other again after years of difficulty, it would be too dreadful if a ghost came between us. You *must* believe that I love you most deeply and truly and eternally. I haven't said a hundredth part of what is in my heart. Goodnight my Darling. I am not worthy of you, but I am yours utterly.

Your

B.

In the end, Ottoline grew tired of Helen's constant presence at Bedford Square. She felt, perhaps, that her duty was done now that she had helped Helen make some friends and some literary contacts. Further help no doubt seemed unnecessary when she discovered that some of the male friends were turning into lovers. At all events, her 'tolerant good nature' was 'ruffled' when she came home to find Helen 'in my grey room, in clouds of cigarette smoke, talking with some man' (*Memoirs*, vol. ii, p. 287). After a few such occurrences, Helen was packed off, about the middle of September, to stay as a paying guest with the novelist, Gilbert Cannan and his wife. Shortly after that, she took rooms of her own in Chelsea, though Ottoline still continued to invite her regularly to Bedford Square.

The new academic year at Cambridge began on 13 October. Russell was still teaching there but, with most young men rushing off to enlist, his classes were almost empty. Troops had been stationed at the university during the summer and Neville's Court, where Russell had his rooms, had become a military hospital. By the time term began, however, the wounded had been moved and Russell got his rooms back, but the place was not the same. Almost every letter he wrote from Cambridge during the war contains some despairing remark about the changes that had occurred, from the loss of promising young thinkers to the intolerably warlike spirit of the older dons who did not have to risk their own lives for the policies they enthusiastically supported. The emptiness of the classrooms was a daily reminder of the hundreds of intelligent and idealistic undergraduates who were now being maimed and killed at the front.

It was difficult, in these circumstances, to think that philosophy itself mattered very much, let alone teaching it to a generation about to be slaughtered. The philosophical plans that Russell had formulated before the war no longer commanded his attention. Instead he devoted himself to trying to uncover the truth about the policies that had led up to the war. In particular, inspired by Bright's opposition to the Crimean War, he sought to expose the treacherous diplomatic machinations of the Liberal government which had led to Britain's involvement.

An important step in this self-education, as the next letter reveals, came from reading E.D. Morel's *Morocco in Diplomacy* (London, 1912), from which he learnt for the first time of the devious path of Anglo-French diplomacy. In 1904 Britain and France had signed a treaty designed to settle their long-standing colonial differences. Publicly both countries recognized the independence of Morocco, but in the event that the Sultan lost power, secret clauses allowed Spain and France to partition the country. Germany learnt of the secret clauses in 1905 and the Kaiser, fearing German political and commercial exclusion from Morocco, went there to state Germany's interest in maintaining the *status quo*. This first Moroccan crisis was resolved in 1906, largely against German interests, by a great power conference at Algeciras.

The agreement at Algeciras enabled France to continue to enhance its position in Morocco to the point where, in 1911, French troops were sent in. This precipitated the second Moroccan crisis, which occurred when Russell was with Ottoline at Marienbad. On this occasion, the Germans sent a gunboat to Agadir, on the Atlantic coast of Morocco, to protect their interests. The British saw this as a threat not merely to their Entente with France but to their naval power in the Atlantic. Germany's main concern, however, was with the expansion of French power in Morocco and in July 1911 the two countries entered into negotiations to resolve the issue.

It was now Britain's turn to feel excluded, and on 21 July Sir Edward Grey, the British Foreign Secretary, called in the German Ambassador to tell him that the terms Germany was seeking from France were unacceptable to Britain. On the same day, to emphasize the point, Lloyd George, the Chancellor of the Exchequer, with Asquith and Grey's approval, made a striking entry into foreign policy with a very bellicose public speech at the Mansion House in London in which he declared that peace on the terms Germany was proposing would be a humiliation Britain could not accept. German public opinion was inflamed enough to demand war, but cooler heads prevailed and Germany backed down. Instead of the treaty on Morocco Germany wanted, and might have achieved from France, the partition of the country according to the Anglo-French treaty of 1904 went ahead (at which time, November 1911, the secret clauses of the 1904 treaty became public) and Germany retained only an open door for trade. The danger was that Germany, having been once outvoted at an international conference and once outwitted in bilateral negotiations, felt that her options had narrowed to either fighting or continuing to back down.

[To Ottoline Morrell] [Trinity College]
[14 October 1914]
Wednesday night

My Darling

Thank you for your dear letter. I quite understand your feeling dead – I do too, except for a deep-down feeling of clinging to you and getting strength from you. I have been so oppressed by finding nothing to do that I began to feel as if you would think me feeble. But I don't expect you to be demonstrative these days – one doesn't feel so.

Thank you for repeating Hirst's remarks.[1] I will bear them in mind. The *New Statesman* won't print my stuff on the Balkan wars, and is in fact shocked by it. I suppose I had better fall back on the *Labour Leader*.[2]

Morel on Morocco amazes me. So much happened while I was at Ipsden and while we were at Marienbad that I know less about it than about most political things.[3] Over and over again, France and Germany were on the verge of becoming really on good terms, when Grey intervened with some clever plan to make them quarrel; Lloyd George's surprise speech at the Mansion House is a case in point. The whole trouble arose because in 1904 we made a treaty with France, half public, guaranteeing the independence and integrity of Morocco, and the other half secret, arranging for its partition between France and Spain. Over and over again we lied; we helped and urged France to acquire Morocco by the shadiest methods, and Germany only stood for the *status quo*, which we were *nominally* supporting. It is obvious that Grey deliberately used Morocco as a means of breeding hatred between France and Germany. He comes out *much* worse than even I had supposed.

---

1 Francis William Hirst (1873–1953), the editor of *The Economist* and a long-time critic of Grey's foreign policy. Russell, on the advice of an American acquaintance, Elizabeth Perkins, who thought she could get him an audience with President Wilson, was thinking of going to America to urge Wilson to act as an intermediary between the warring powers. Hirst had told the Morrells that it would be a good thing if Russell went (though the anti-war movement in England could ill-afford to lose him) and offered to help with introductions to Wilson and others. In the event, Wilson refused a meeting (presumably under British diplomatic pressure) and Russell did not go.
2 The 'stuff on the Balkan Wars' was 'A True History of Europe's Last War' (*Papers*, vol. xiii, pp. 107–112), a review of the *Report of the International Commission to Inquire into the Causes and Conduct of the Balkan Wars* (1914), prepared for the Carnegie Endowment for International Peace by a commission chaired by Baron d'Estournelles de Constant, a French diplomat whom Russell had met while an attaché at the British Embassy in Paris in 1894. *The New Statesman*, under the editorship of Sidney and Beatrice Webb, rejected the piece on the incredible ground that the journal was avoiding comment on the war. The article was eventually published in March 1915 in *The Labour Leader*, the journal of the Independent Labour Party. *The Labour Leader* had previously published several anti-war pieces by Russell, but he had hoped for a wider circulation through the *New Statesman*.
3 The period from 24 July to 29 September 1911, when Russell was either staying at Ipsden in Oxfordshire close to Peppard, Ottoline's country cottage near Henley, or else was with Ottoline in Marienbad, where she was taking a cure.

Yes, the war looks very bad.[1] I really rather enjoy seeing Russia defeated,[2] because I feel more and more strongly that in the East the interests of mankind are on the side of Germany and Austria; but I don't wish to see the Germans able to bring troops back to the West. Santayana,[3] who has been here, thinks they will get Paris very soon, and will win even in the end; I don't think he can be right. I hear Wittgenstein[4] is fighting, and was in Cracow when last heard of. Littlewood[5] is joining the territorials, and I suppose will go out sooner or later. I didn't much believe what my soldier said yesterday, but I was interested to find that a collection of average Englishmen found pleasure in believing it.[6]

I hear Lucas[7] and Taylor[8] – two of our Fellows, the latter the friend of Philipovitch[9] – are engaged in inventing new sorts of aeroplanes. They have made one which will go 150 miles an hour, and is to be used to destroy Essen; but as it can't land at less than 90 miles an hour, it is certain death to go in it. Till the war came, they were innocent theorists.

---

1 Trench warfare was just beginning. With the Battle of the Marne in September the initial German push on Paris had been stopped. What this meant, however, was that first the French, and now the German, plan for winning the war had failed, and the two sides had fought each other to a stalemate on the Western Front. It seemed inevitable now that the war would be a long one.

2 Russia had invaded East Prussia early in the war, but its advance had been stopped by a massive defeat at the Battle of Tannenberg, 31 August. By mid-October Russian forces had been pushed back into Poland and the Germans seemed poised to capture Warsaw with the same ease they had captured many other towns in Western Poland. At Warsaw, however, the Russian line held.

3 George Santayana (1863–1952), the American philosopher and man of letters. He was in England when war broke out.

4 The Austrian philosopher Ludwig Wittgenstein (1889–1951), had been the most brilliant of Russell's students at Cambridge before the war. He enlisted in the Austrian army when war broke out and was assigned to a boat which travelled down the Vistula River from Cracow behind the Austrian 1st Army advancing on Lublin. Unknown to the Austrians, however, the main Russian force was to the south, round Lemberg (now Lvov). When the Russians took Lemberg, the flank of the Austrian 1st Army was exposed and it had to retreat back towards Cracow, on which the Russians were now advancing. As Russell wrote, Wittgenstein was still on his boat, behind the front line, travelling back the way he had come after a singularly futile campaign.

5 John Edensor Littlewood (1885–1977), a Cambridge pure mathematician. He never did serve in France, but he did become a lieutenant in the Royal Garrison Artillery at Woolwich Arsenal.

6 The previous day, when travelling to Cambridge, Russell had shared his carriage with a wounded soldier who told him that the French killed their prisoners and made necklaces of their ears. The other occupants were delighted at the news, but looked grave when German atrocities were mentioned.

7 Keith Lucas (1879–1916), a student at Trinity, had graduated with a first in the Natural Science Tripos of 1898. Since then he worked at Cambridge doing research on muscles and nerves. When war broke out he went to work at the royal aircraft factory at Farnborough. He was killed in a flying accident in 1916.

8 Geoffrey Ingram Taylor (1886–1975), a distinguished mathematician who had been a Fellow of Trinity College since 1910. His early work was in meteorology, but he took up aeronautics during the war and obtained his pilot's licence in 1915. During the Second World War he worked at Los Alamos on the atomic bomb.

9 Apparently a nickname for Philip Morrell, occasioned by his new passion for Russian novels.

A second American has turned up; probably that will be all my class.[1] I am glad Hirst thought it would be useful my going to America, but if it is no more use than what I can do here, it does not come to much.

Goodnight my Dearest.

Your

   B.

The stalemate developing on the Western Front that Russell had bemoaned in the previous letter offered one faint hope: that the two sides might sue for peace since a prolonged war could not be in anyone's interest. The US might play an important role as a broker in any such negotiations and Russell was more keen than ever to go on his peace mission to President Wilson. (Wilson himself in his annual speech to Congress on 8 December 1914 reaffirmed American neutrality and offered his services as a mediator. Russell welcomed the offer enthusiastically, see *Papers*, vol. xiii, pp. 53–5.) While there was a chance of peace talks, and a chance that he might get his audience with Wilson, Russell was anxious not to appear as a strident opponent of British policy. He proposed moderating his public remarks accordingly, though, as the next letter shows, he was worried lest Ottoline should think he had sold out. A crucial point in any peace settlement acceptable to the Allies would be German withdrawal from France and Belgium.

[To Ottoline Morrell]   **[Trinity College]**   7
                                                         [29 October 1914]
                                                          Thursday afternoon

My Darling

It is very sad that George[2] was so disagreeable, it is *horrid* of him. I am afraid he has lost his soul over the war. I should have expected Sir V. Chirol[3] to be disagreeable, from the way he treated MacDonald. Each fresh time people are disagreeable is a fresh trial – it is extraordinarily painful.

---

1 He had an audience of two Americans, an Italian, a Japanese and a woman – 'not a single male Englishman' he noted ruefully in a later letter.
2 George Trevelyan. Ottoline had complained that he had been rude to her about the war at dinner on the 27th. Ottoline had described him as happy and warlike.
3 Sir Valentine Chirol (1852–1929), also at Ottoline's dinner, had been director of the foreign department at *The Times* from 1899 to 1912. He wrote extensively on Indian and Middle Eastern affairs. The details of his treatment of Ramsay Macdonald are not known, but Chirol was a prominent 'hawk'.

The discussion with P[hilip] made me think a great deal. I am glad he is not going to a recruiting meeting,[1] and yet, if he did, I don't think one could say anything against him except on grounds that go against *all* war. It seems clear the Germans mean to annex Belgium if they can, which will be a great wrong, and an encouragement to the use of force; so that, although in the beginning I think we ought to have kept out, we seem bound now to undo, as far as possible, the harm we brought on the Belgians by encouraging them to resist. Do you disagree?

It seems to me now that it is quite useless to find fault with the Government until they reject some offer of peace which involves restitution to Belgium. Anything done in favour of reasonable terms of peace has more chance of success if it is dissociated from criticism of the past, which no one will listen to. For instance, if I go to America I do not wish to appear there as a critic of our Government, and I believe that Simon[2] e.g. would agree with everything I should wish to say there. You suggested my seeing him, and I think if I do go to America it would be just as well. But until now I have felt I could not bring myself to behave with apparent friendliness to any member of the Government. The whole problem is difficult. My feeling is now that one can only abstain from actually supporting the war, and that it is a waste to oppose it – the thing is to concentrate on terms of peace. I don't say this from failure of courage, but from desire to be of use. But I want to know what you think.

What I want to say in America is something like this: Modern war is very harmful to neutrals as well, and therefore it is the interest of pacific powers to prevent others from fighting. England and France, at least, would be thankful for any arbitration system which made another great war less likely. The Allies have been concluding arbitration treaties with USA[3] and would probably be willing to conclude them with each other. Germany and Austria might be compelled to conclude similar treaties as part of the terms of peace. If all the Powers guaranteed all the treaties, and undertook to oppose any Power which infringed them, no single Power would be strong enough to compel war, and a stable peace might

---

1 It is not clear what this meeting was except that it was pro-war. It was possibly a Liberal meeting in Philip's constituency of Burnley, where there was some disquiet about his opposition to the war. Philip had told Ottoline he would attend an 'ordinary' meeting if required (Ottoline to Bertie, 28 Aug.).
2 Sir John Simon (1873–1954), the Home Secretary until 1916, when he resigned over the introduction of conscription.
3 William Jennings Bryan, Woodrow Wilson's Secretary of State in the early years of the war, had negotiated a series of bilateral arbitration treaties between the USA and other nations (including Britain, France, and Russia). Under their terms, disputes were to be submitted to an international commission whose findings could be rejected by either party. Thirty such treaties were signed by the USA in 1913–1914. Germany negotiated a treaty but then refused to sign, a propaganda victory for the Allies who cited Germany's refusal as further evidence of her warlike intentions.

be secured. In that case, a great diminution of armaments would also be possible. America will have to represent the interests of neutrals in the peace negotiations, and can hold the balance in the interests of permanent peace. But unless some scheme is adopted, America will require a huge increase of armaments for the future protection of the Monroe Doctrine.[1] Thus America at this moment can fittingly champion the interests of humanity, as opposed to those of either side in the war. Liberal opinion throughout Europe, which is momentarily dumb owing to the war, would whole-heartedly support America in such action, and after the war all Europe would be glad to be saved from itself.

I am more and more convinced that stable peace requires all disinterested nations to form a police force in any quarrel. Mere humanity is not strong enough.

I should like to know what Simon and others like him think about it all.

I have to lecture in Oxford three weeks hence, and the lecture will have to be published.[2] It is terribly hard to think about philosophy. My thoughts are full of what I want to say in America, and I can't turn them on to anything else without a *great* effort. The appeal in America would be primarily to humanity, but one would have to argue that their self-interest was on the side of humanity.

Jourdain[3] yesterday showed me an American-German publication, full of German justifications of the war – it seemed to me they were worse even than our jingoes.

Don't think me an apostate – I have only been thinking how to be useful. As things stand, it seems as if one must hold one's tongue about some things for the present if one is to be useful. Do let me know what you think.

Goodnight my Darling. This is an awful time – one has to hope that it will pass. But there is no knowing what sort of world will emerge after the war. I grow less and less hopeful as to the future.

Your
B.

---

1 One of the cornerstones of American foreign policy since President Monroe promulgated it in 1823. Monroe declared that attempts by European powers to extend their colonial interests in the Americas would be regarded as hostile but that the US would not interfere with existing European colonies in the Americas nor intervene in 'wars of the European powers in matters relating to themselves'. The second part of the doctrine became inoperative when America entered World War I.
2 Russell was to give the Herbert Spencer Memorial Lecture at Oxford on 18 November. His topic was 'On Scientific Method in Philosophy' (see *Papers*, vol. viii, pp. 57–73). It was a reprise of some of the themes he had aired at greater length in his Lowell Lectures at Boston earlier in the year.
3 Philip Edward Bertrand Jourdain (1879–1919), one of Russell's first students in mathematical logic.

Ottoline agreed with Bertie's policy of moderation. Indeed, there was little need for him to explain his views on the war to her: they agreed completely about it. Ottoline's letters at this time were both longer and more affectionate than previously and filled with political information. She regularly passed on to him the opinions of the politicians she met, as well as her own views on the tactics the pacifists should adopt. She was deeply shocked by the warlike enthusiasm of some of her friends, some of whom she refused to see as a result. She was also concerned by the plight of German nationals in Britain, who had become targets for popular hostility. Many had lost their jobs and were living in poverty. By Christmas 1914 she had enlisted Bertie's help in her welfare efforts on their behalf.

To his other correspondents, especially those living abroad, Russell had to explain his views on the war at greater length. Two such were his old American friends, Helen Flexner and Lucy Donnelly. He had seen both of them on his trip to the US the previous spring. The views he expresses in the next letter to Helen Flexner about the desirability of avoiding concepts like vice and virtue arise from the emotive theory of ethics that he first publicly espoused in an article, 'The Ethics of War', he had just written for the *International Journal of Ethics* (*Papers*, vol. xiii, pp. 63–73). He had come to think that belief in objective standards of right and wrong did much to foster the sort of intolerance that leads to war. The letter to Flexner is one of the first statements of this view, which he repeated many times subsequently.

8   [To Helen Flexner]   [Trinity College]
                                          16 November 1914

My dear Helen

I very nearly wrote to you yesterday, but I put it off, and now I have your 2nd letter, of November 3. It was *really* kind of you to write it, and I was touched and grateful. The happy days I spent in your house are very vivid to me, though they seem to have happened in some previous existence, when life still held hopes and one fancied oneself part of a community, not a lost soul strayed from some other planet into an asylum of homicidal lunatics.

I do not think we could have kept out of the war at the last, but we could have prevented it by greater wisdom and justice in past years, and we could probably have saved Belgium by a more honest policy. Of course I think Germany much more to blame than England, and more of a danger to peace; and I think our victory very desirable. But even in time of war I continue to believe in truth, and I find everybody in Europe averse from truth at present, inventing lies whose purpose is to inflame hatred. It is not good to hate even the wicked, even if oneself is virtuous; and I think wickedness and virtue are barbaric notions, savouring of Yahweh and the Inquisition. People act according to their natures, just as stones or planets do. A stone which falls on your head is inconvenient, not wicked. English and German newspapers are exactly alike, barbaric, unbalanced, untruthful, brutal, full of hatred; I am sorry that is the way most men are made, but I will not wallow with them in the pig-trough. Meanwhile young men whom I love, full of innocence and intelligence, are killing each other in a frenzy of self-immolation before false Gods, yielding to the claims of their country and forgetting Europe and mankind. My heart goes out to them, whatever nation they belong to; but I can only wonder silently whether reason and mercy will ever acquire dominion over the passions we inherit from the brute. I am glad America is on our side, for, since there is war, I believe it is better we should win – certainly we have committed no crime comparable to the violation of Belgium. But I cannot join in the orgy of self-righteousness, which I find sickening.

Some few people – Shaw,[1] Romain Rolland,[2] Liebknecht,[3] the Socialists in the Russian Duma,[4] seem to me to have remained sane and just; but they are universally decried, and regarded as madmen.

There is a simple and feasible road to peace, which is that, in every dispute, neutrals should *insist* on mediation, or, failing that, on participating collectively on one side or other. In this way, one side could be made so overwhelmingly the stronger that war would not occur. I am not without hope that something of the kind may emerge gradually out the horror caused by this war.

Conrad is back safely[5] – I long to see him but have not yet had time. His view of it all will interest me profoundly. His general view of life was well adapted to meet such a tragedy.

---

1 George Bernard Shaw's *Common Sense About the War* had appeared on 14 November as a supplement to the *New Statesman*, the Webbs having apparently conceded that the war was worth the journal's attention.
2 Romain Rolland (1866–1944) the French writer then living in Switzerland. He was one of the most prominent European pacifists during the First World War. Some of his anti-war writings were collected in *Au-dessus de la mêlée* (1915).
3 Karl Liebknecht (1871–1919), German revolutionary politician, the chief spokesman for the German Social Democrats in the Reichstag. When, on 3 August, the Social Democrats split over support for the war, Liebknecht became the leader of the minority which opposed it. After the war he was murdered by the police during the Spartacist uprising.
4 On the outbreak of war, the Menshevik and Bolshevik deputies in the Duma, Russia's rather remote approximation to a parliament, had united in refusing to vote for war credits.
5 Joseph Conrad, the novelist, with whom Russell had recently struck up a deep friendship, had been trapped by the outbreak of war in Poland, where he was visiting the town in which he had grown up.

I am doing little. I have joined a body[1] founded by J.R. MacDonald, Charles Trevelyan, Norman Angell,[2] Ponsonby[3] and Morel – I don't think it will achieve anything but I agree with its aims and principles. I have written a pamphlet for them,[4] and various articles in a Socialist paper called the *Labour Leader*,[5] the only one willing to print what I want to say. I have *no* doubt whatever of the victory of the allies – the only fear, to my mind, is that they may be *too* victorious. I should regard the victory of Germany as a great disaster.

My usual work at Cambridge goes on, but does not interest me, and naturally I have few pupils.

Do write again soon. It is a solace to hear from you.

Yours affectionately
   Bertrand Russell

The war put many of Russell's old friendships under strain. If the breach with the Whiteheads was the hardest for Russell to adjust to, that with Gilbert Murray was probably the next and in this case the break was a good deal more bitter. It would have been hard to predict what Murray's attitude to the war would be. On the one hand, he enjoyed his position close to the Liberal establishment, especially to Asquith with whom he shared a background in classics. On the other, he still had radical sympathies – e.g. on women's suffrage and Irish Home Rule – as well as contacts with the ILP. It seems that it was Grey's speech in Parliament on 3 August that converted him to support of the war. Once converted, he immediately started to make himself useful to the government as a writer for the unaptly named Bureau of Information. Among other services, he signed 'The Writers' Manifesto' supporting the war which appeared in *The Times* on 18 September, and wrote another manifesto addressed to Russian intellectuals urging them to support their country's war effort. It was no doubt Murray's work for

---

1 The Union of Democratic Control.
2 Norman Angell (1874–1967), an economist and journalist and one of the leaders of British pacifism before World War I. In his most famous book, *The Great Illusion* (1910), which sold two million copies between 1910 and 1913, he argued that an integrated world market had made wars among commercial powers economically counterproductive. Angell received the Nobel Peace Prize in 1933; Russell was among those who nominated him.
3 Arthur Augustus William Henry Ponsonby (1871–1946), a prominent pacifist. Though a Liberal MP since 1908, he had been a critic of Grey's foreign policy before the war and in 1914 joined the Independent Labour Party (ILP), the only British party that continued to oppose the war. He joined the Labour Party in 1922 but resigned from it in 1940 when it joined the wartime coalition government.
4 *War, the Offspring of Fear*, *Papers*, vol. xiii, pp. 37–47.
5 See *Papers*, vol. xiii, pp. 10–27.

what Murray himself called 'The Mendacity Bureau' that explains the acerbity with which Russell turned away from him. The final straw was Murray's pamphlet, *Thoughts on the War*, published in October 1914, in which Murray not only expressed his satisfaction at German casualties but took a strongly pro-Russian line as well. For Russell, hatred of Tsarist Russia ran almost as deep as hatred of war itself. On the Western Front Russell could have some sympathy for the Allies' immediate war aims, but in the East he found it simply intolerable that supposedly Liberal England should find itself the ally of the Russian autocracy. Murray's attempts to present Russia as a suitable ally earned Russell's most ferocious contempt. Murray was 'as squashy as a slug' he told Ottoline immediately after his Herbert Spencer Lecture at Oxford on 18 November. His fury had not cooled a month later when he wrote to Lucy Donnelly.

[To Lucy Donnelly]   **34 Russell Chambers**   9
Bury Street. W.C.
14 December 1914

My dear Lucy

Your letter of December 4 arrived today, which is quick in these times, as it went to Cambridge and back. I have also your letter of 10 November to answer, and now that term is over I have more time. The pamphlet you write about is printed for the 'Union of Democratic Control' whom your papers may have mentioned – Ponsonby, N. Angell, E.D. Morel, Ramsay Macdonald and Charles Trevelyan are the chief people. I have been working with and for them from the start. They succeed much better than one would have thought – I find in Cambridge quite half the people under 30 (including those who have gone to fight) seem to be prepared to join in.[1] The newspapers do not represent public opinion, and have not mentioned the U.D.C. except to say it is financed by German money.[2] Everybody feels we must liberate Belgium and France, but very few have any desire to prolong a war of conquest or to humiliate Germany. I will send you my pamphlet if I can. But it may be impossible.[3]

I am going to do a good deal of speaking and lecturing during the Vacation, and probably afterwards too. Feeling here is much sobered lately. Everybody has close friends gone or just going – and the casualties have been very serious. Nobody (not even I) would sacrifice

---

1 Russell had been active in setting up a Cambridge chapter of the UDC.
2 An article in the *Morning Post* (10 September) had accused the UDC of being funded by Germany.
3 On account of government censorship of mail. The pamphlet was *War, The Offspring of Fear* (see Letter **8**).

Belgium, and that may involve a lot more fighting; but the feeling against war in general is continually growing. It is not impossible that some good may come of it in the end.

My pamphlet was written in the first days of the war. It was meant for a magazine article but I could not get it accepted.[1]

My Austrian,[2] at the outbreak of the war, was in the artillery at Cracow; since then, of course, I have known nothing of him. As he is a 'modern Hun' and therefore wicked, it is much to be hoped he has been killed.

Mildred,[3] I hear, is sailing for America on Wednesday. I suppose you will see her. She seems happier than she was some time ago. She enjoys the baby.

Gilbert Murray is a snivelling sentimental ass. I went to Oxford to give a lecture, and saw him there. I told them evolution was supposed to involve progress because it developed from the protozoon to the philosopher; but it was the philosopher who considered this a progress, and perhaps the impartial outsider would think differently.[4] Oxford is loathsome, even more than usual. The Oxford historians' book on the war shows absolutely no attempt to tell the truth.[5] The best of the books to my mind is the French *Yellow Book*.[6]

Yours affectionately
Bertrand Russell.

Although the war had thrown Ottoline and Bertie closer together, Ottoline was beginning, once more, to find Bertie's attentions oppressive, especially now that Helen Dudley had been driven from the field. (She had returned

---

1 See Letter **3**.
2 Ludwig Wittgenstein (see Letter **6**).
3 Mildred Minturn Scott (1875–1922), an American friend. Her unhappiness was due to marital difficulties, but the improvement Russell notes was only temporary – she eventually separated from her husband. She had recently given birth to a son of whom Russell was the godfather.
4 The Herbert Spencer Lecture, 'On Scientific Method in Philosophy', *Papers*, vol. viii, p. 62.
5 *Why We Are At War. Great Britain's Case* by members of the Oxford Faculty of Modern History (Oxford, 1914).
6 Within days of the beginning of the war each of the major warring powers published a collection of official documents proving that peace had all along been their deepest desire. These documents were colour coded: The Germans got in first with their *White Book*, the British followed with a *Blue Book*, the Russians with *Orange*, and the Belgians with *Grey*. The French were a bit behindhand and their *Yellow Book*, subtitled *How Germany Forced the War*, did not appear until 1 December.

to the USA.) Ottoline thus revived her plan of attaching Russell to some other woman, thereby leaving herself free to play her preferred role of Platonic (or nearly Platonic) muse. In theory the plan should have worked well, but in practice Ottoline rarely found herself as entirely free of jealousy as she expected and Bertie, for his part, was still apt, in any new relationship, to let his emotions run away with him. Moreover, Bertie had been burnt quite badly over Helen Dudley, and set his heart resolutely against future entanglements. He reaffirmed his intention to avoid 'philandering' in the next letter, in which he proudly recounts his success in fighting off the attentions of Titi d'Aranyi. The d'Aranyi sisters, Adila, Hortense Emilia ('Titi'), and Jelli, were the great nieces of the violin virtuoso, Joseph Joachim. (They were thus indirectly related to Bertie, since Joachim's niece married Bertie's uncle Rollo.) All three sisters were themselves violinists, Adila and Jelli of sufficient stature to have their own entries in Grove. (Ravel's *Tzigane* was written for Jelli.)

Titi d'Aranyi, however, was not Ottoline's choice of a companion for Bertie and, in declaring his victory over temptation with Titi, he had reckoned without Ottoline's legendary tenacity. Ottoline's choice was the 'Miss C.W.' mentioned later in the letter, in the innocent context of Spinoza. This was Irene Cooper-Willis, the young secretary-companion to one of Ottoline's old friends, Violet Paget, the novelist and critic who wrote under the name 'Vernon Lee'. Irene Cooper-Willis had studied mathematics at Girton College, Cambridge and in her forties became one of Britain's leading female barristers. She was young, attractive, and intelligent but apparently completely browbeaten by Paget, who was a domineering and cantakerous employer. When the pair of them turned up at Bedford Square in October, Ottoline decided that Irene needed emancipating and that Bertie was the person to do it. For three weeks she urged Bertie to take Irene out for a meal to no avail. At last she had to resort to bringing them both to Bedford Square in order to effect a meeting. The first meeting went well, and Bertie seemed interested (not surprisingly, in view of Ottoline's advance publicity). It says something for Bertie's resolution against philandering, however, that by the end of December things had only got as far as Spinoza lessons.

Ottoline's plan for Irene involved more than a romantic liaison with Bertie. In order to extricate her from Paget, Ottoline thought it would be a good idea if she became Bertie's research assistant instead. Bertie was planning a substantial book on the foreign policy of the great powers from 1870 to 1914, and the plan was for Irene to gather information for it from the newspaper files in the British Museum. Bertie and Ottoline had obviously discussed Irene's involvement, but as the next letter shows Bertie did not have to ask – Irene proposed herself.

10 [To Ottoline Morrell] [34 Russell Chambers]
26 December 1914
evening

My Darling

I *was* glad to get your two letters this morning. Owing to Xmas posts I got none yesterday or the day before – I thought it was the fault of the post, but it seemed sad not hearing. J[ulian]'s[1] card came on Xmas day – please thank her for it very much from me. Very many thanks for the Marvell[2] – yes, his diction is *wonderful*.

Your first letter does *really* make me happy – war and winter have had a good deal of the same effect on me, and I don't mind what is due to them. Yes, I feel the war has made quite a new bond between us, and one which *nothing* in the future could ever break – I *do* feel the difference in you. And in me there is a *great* difference. I have a really firm resolve to avoid philandering in future. I feel inwardly and profoundly that it is unworthy. Titi Aranyi made an amazingly fierce assault – formerly I should have drifted on and let things take their course – now I kept resolutely to treating everything as a mere joke. She and Jelli came to tea, invited themselves to stay to dinner, and only left at 10:30. I told them I should probably be too busy to see them again till the Easter Vacation. I felt a sort of terror at the approach of a flirtation – I wish it could have been avoided. Jelli is obviously the most interesting by far, but they all make me light and gay, which I am very grateful for. But it will be wiser to keep out of their way. When I danced with Titi I was quite unaware of her, thinking only of the madness of motion, but she seems to have been less impersonal. When I called the other day she monopolized me entirely. I enjoy their great vitality – it is refreshing and takes one out of the grumps. But they disconcert me by trying to make me believe in God.

Yesterday at the Whiteheads passed off peacefully – Phelan Gibbs[3] was there, rather a bore I thought. The Whiteheads are *much* milder since North came home.[4] When the Mirrlees[5] boy came home, his sister greeted him with 'I hope you've not become a pro-German like

---

1 Ottoline's daughter.
2 Ottoline had said she was sending him a 'little Marvell'. Presumably it is *The Poems and Some Satires of Andrew Marvell*, edited by Edward Wright, (London, 1904) which is in his library.
3 Harry Phelan Gibbs, an Irish painter who had lived in Paris until the war when he moved to London. Gertrude Stein was enthusiastic about his work and introduced him to the Whiteheads.
4 North was home on leave for Christmas.
5 The son of Lena and William Julius Mirrlees, who had taken the lease on the Whiteheads' old house in Cranmer Road, Cambridge when the Whiteheads moved to London in 1910. Their daughter was Hope Mirrlees, a poet and novelist.

North', but he had. I believe the soldiers will really prevent bitterness in this country – but not in Germany I'm afraid.

Tomorrow I speak at the P.S.A.[1] at Willesden. I wonder how it will go off. Miss C.W. comes on Tuesday for Spinoza and a walk – she has been away for Xmas. When I told her of the book I was planning, she offered of herself to help me, so I felt no scruple in accepting. I feel *intensely* interested, and I *feel* the book – it is very much alive in me. It will be a merciless savage attack on the whole tradition of diplomacy in all countries.

Dearest I feel *quite* happy now about you, and my work, and my morals – all three hang together. This book feels *natural* just as matter[2] did – I believe in it, and feel confident I can make it a really *important* book – it will be a vehicle for an immense volume of pent-up passion. But I think only the Labour Press will be willing to print it.

Goodbye my Darling Darling. My deepest love is with you always.
Your
B.

The Spinoza lessons led at last to other things. Irene Cooper-Willis was, with difficulty, extricated from Violet Paget's clutches and taken on as Russell's part-time research assistant. Meanwhile, Ottoline continued to press Irene's advantages as a lover as well as an assistant. By 7 January Bertie went so far as to concede that he might 'come to have a very great affection for Irene' and that an affair with her might 'give happiness and be free from the pain of passion'. But he evidently still had deep misgivings.

[To Ottoline Morrell]   **[34 Russell Chambers]**   11
                                               [8 January 1915]
                                               Friday night

My Darling

It was a strange time today – I was going through a fearful tangle of feelings. I feel you are trying to make me think you will go on giving more than will be possible, so as not to discourage me. I had a deathbed feeling – not your deathbed, but the deathbed of the glory and wonder

---

[1] Pleasant Sunday Afternoons. These were organized by the National Union Brotherhood, a working-class Christian organization advocating 'practical Christianity' in the form of democracy, socialism, and social reform. Russell spoke at several PSAs over the next year.
[2] The work on epistemology and the philosophy of physics that Russell had been working on before the war.

of your love – which I have killed by wanting it – for *all* that I have done amiss has come from that one source. A ghost-like procession of the wonderful times we have had together was passing through my mind, and I was kept silent, because I felt I could win no response by speaking of them. The recesses of your spirit seemed closed to me – I don't mean only tonight, when you were ill, but for some time past. My own judgment, as I told you when we first talked of it, is against going far with Irene. But I distrust my own judgment, and I feel you want me to go on, and instinct works the same way. Underneath all that is the terrible sadness of vanished things, the feeling that real life is over, and the rest is a dull dream, fading away into old age and death. There was a moment in the Library in August,[1] and some moments here soon after; since then, darkness has descended and ice has come between us. I still care for you, but I feel you are bored with me, and that I can no longer touch the springs of your spirit. Those things can't be cured when they have happened. Only please don't imagine that it is I who am deserting you. Our failure seems to me quite infinitely tragic, and it will leave a deep core of sorrow which time will not cure. I no longer feel it with wild passion, because I am too hopeless. But I do feel a sadness which is almost too deep for words.

    I feel all that is important in my personal life is ended, and that it only remains to slip through the days without such a realization of loss as would make life unbearable. Please forgive me for speaking the truth – I simply can't keep up pretences with you. And it is a mere pretence that Irene could take your place. But I feel you will think this is one of the things I tell myself. What keeps me silent is often the feeling that you won't believe me – I have loved you with more passion than you wanted, and the result was unavoidable. But you have made me know the depths and heights of life, and I bless you always.

    Your
    B.

Despite his misgivings, an affair with Irene did actually begin, though it is not clear exactly when. Hitherto, while she hatched the liaison, Ottoline's letters had been cool, but on Monday 11 January, when she returned from a weekend in Brighton, a different person emerged. The transformation

---

1 See Letter **5**.

was astonishingly abrupt even for this pair of complicated lovers. Once again, the presence of another woman made Bertie seem much more desirable to Ottoline. Long, passionate letters urging meetings arrived from her. Since her affair with Bertie began they had operated under the restriction, imposed by Alys's brother, Logan Pearsall Smith, that they should not spend a night together. Now, for the first time, Ottoline lamented this condition, blaming it for all their difficulties. It is not clear that they ever broke Logan's prohibition. (Although, by the following weekend, they were both writing of two wonderful days together, this need not be taken to imply a wonderful intervening night.) Then there followed a meeting on Tuesday the 19th the 'flame and wonder' of which (as Bertie puts it in the next letter) would be with him for a long time. Bertie was completely unable to resist: on Ottoline's letter arranging the Tuesday meeting he wrote 'This Tuesday evening was the gate of heaven'. A meeting with Irene the next morning seemed flat and dull in comparison and Bertie was led to reconsider whether he was willing to forego the pains of passion now they seemed to be available again.

[To Ottoline Morrell]   **[34 Russell Chambers]**   12
                                                  [20 January 1915]

My own Darling

Your *wonderful* letter came while Irene was here and I had to wait till she was gone before reading it. I will answer it later – this must be business. Irene's passion develops, but I have not enough to give her – I did not think so at the beginning of the morning but I do now. She dreads scandal on account of her people, and can't tolerate secrecy (which I too would not undertake for her). So she feels she must give me up. I feel convinced she would be seriously unhappy if she became involved in a scandal – not *wholly* on her people's account. I see no issue – but what is more important, I don't wish to see any, though I have not the heart to say so to her. She is too law-abiding, too destitute of recklessness, quite without love of danger. It is only while we were discussing that I realize how deep this goes, and how great a division it would make. She is very unhappy in the thought of having to give me up. I am in 20 minds, but on the whole I feel her too tame – nothing fires my imagination. The one thing I *really* mind is losing her help over work. I should like to keep that, even at the cost of leaving matters undecided for a while. I care far more about things to do with work than about her. She means (I think) to talk to you, and will give the impression that I care greatly for her; the new feeling, that I am telling you, only came up towards the end of the morning, and had not yet pushed its way to the surface, so she saw nothing of it. She is not going away for the weekend, so I said I could see her Sunday morning 11 till lunch. The only time I hurt her was by not seeming keen on seeing her Sunday. I don't want to hurt her.

I feel the cruelty of this letter towards her. But I don't want you to make too light of her family difficulties, from a feeling that it is your duty. I have a real and great affection for her, but I do like people to be willing to shoot Niagara. This is quite impersonal – I have no great *wish* that she should do it.

I must fly. Darling I will write of love later. The flame and wonder of last night is around me and within me. Goodbye.
   Your
      B.

Irene, for her part, did not seem too upset at losing her chance to shoot Niagara with Bertie. She told Desmond MacCarthy, with whom she subsequently had an affair, that though 'there were things in [Russell] which I positively hated', she had felt a 'violent attraction to him . . . And sometimes when I was with him I forgot everything and only knew that I was with him and was happy – but that did not happen often.' The affair with MacCarthy also soon came to an end – the result, she decided in the course of a long analysis, of 'an utter, fundamental indifference in me to sex' (Cecil, *Clever Hearts*, pp. 164, 166). In this, perhaps, she was more fortunate than Helen Dudley, who, to everyone's alarm, turned up in Britain again, having spent only Christmas in the US instead of returning there permanently as Bertie and Ottoline had supposed. In the next letter, Bertie tried to appear indifferent to news of her return. In the event, however, though she appeared occasionally at Bedford Square, she seems to have made little attempt to revive her relationship with Bertie, who saw little of her.

A more serious disruption heralded in the next letter was less easily anticipated. In December Ottoline had read a collection of short stories, *The Prussian Officer* (1914), by D.H. Lawrence, then at the beginning of his literary fame. She was attracted especially by his descriptions of the North Nottinghamshire and Derbyshire countryside in which she, like he, had grown up. In January she had invited him for dinner at Bedford Square, by all accounts a rather awkward affair though Lawrence had none the less invited her to stay with him at his cottage at Greatham in Sussex. In Sussex Lawrence was more relaxed and Ottoline became as fascinated by the man as by his books. Meanwhile, she had lent *The Prussian Officer* to Bertie who became equally enthusiastic to meet Lawrence.

[To Ottoline Morrell] **[Trinity College]** 13
[22 January 1915]
Friday night

My Darling Love

I was *very* glad to get your dear letter tonight – it was an unexpected joy. I am *so* glad my letter told something of what I felt.[1] I find every moment the memory of Tuesday evening grows more wonderful – it colours every moment, and fills all my thoughts with an unearthly joy. And now I think of next Tuesday – but I dare not think much of it so far ahead. We will settle all about it tomorrow. I will come up in the afternoon, and be ready for you when you come about six. I *long* for you Dearest.

Sunday I should be free from six o'clock onward, but Sunday *morning* is no good. Irene still wants to come. She is willing to go on and be friends, but she wants Sunday to be like the last few times I have been with her, and begin a strict régime after that. I am very glad she is willing to go on with the work. It is a pity to be afraid of life as she is, and governed by bogies. She has the defect of most women, of having no inner purpose, nothing she wants independently of other people. That makes her passive and submissive. She would never in any case love very passionately, because she would be afraid of the wildness of passion – if she saw it growing on her, she would discipline it. I know there is much to be said for being like that, but it is not interesting.

Fancy Helen being back! What a bore. I thought she was gone for good.

I am glad you liked Lawrence. One feels from his writing that he must be wonderful – a man with a real fire of imagination. I should like to know him.

My Darling, I can't tell you how wonderful the thought of next Tuesday is to me. It fills me almost with awe. My Life, my Soul, I *long* for you – my whole being is *filled* with love –

Your
B.

Ottoline took Russell to see Lawrence at Greatham on 8 February. Lawrence had told her that he was 'still a bit scared of Mr Russell' (Lawrence, *Letters*, vol. ii, p. 274), but the meeting was a success and Russell, at least, was wildly impressed. According to Ottoline, as they drove away Russell said:

---

[1] A very eloquent declaration of love written on the same day as Letter **12**.

'He is amazing; he sees through and through one.' 'Yes. But do you think he really sees correctly?' I asked. 'Absolutely. He is infallible,' was Bertie's reply. 'He is like Ezekiel or some other Old Testament prophet, prophesying. Of course, the blood of his nonconformist preaching ancestors is strong in him, but he sees everything and is always right.'

(*Memoirs*, vol. i, p. 273)

For once, it was Ottoline who, wisely, had her doubts. What drew the two men together was a common sense of bitter rebellion against wartime Britain and a feeling that each had what the other lacked: Lawrence supplying passion to Russell's intellect and vice-versa. Lawrence had only recently started the attempt to formulate what he called his 'philosophy', a project on which he set great store. No doubt he hoped Russell might be helpful in these unaccustomed labours. Years afterwards, Russell attempted to explain Lawrence's attraction for him:

I liked Lawrence's fire, I liked the energy and passion of his feelings, I liked his belief that something very fundamental was needed to put the world right. I agreed with him in thinking that politics could not be divorced from individual psychology. I felt him to be a man of a certain imaginative genius and, at first, when I felt inclined to disagree with him, I thought that perhaps his insight into human nature was deeper than mine.

(*Portraits from Memory*, pp. 106–7)

Before the year was out, however, Russell would think that each differed from the other more than either differed from the Kaiser (*ibid.*, p. 106). Some intimation of these later difficulties is already present in the next letter.

Different problems were looming in Russell's relations with Trinity College. In 1910 he had been appointed to a five-year lectureship (without a college fellowship attached) and the question of what to do when it came to an end had now to be considered. It was unusual that someone of Russell's eminence, living and teaching in college, was not a fellow and had, as a result, no say in the college government. On 12 February 1915, therefore, the college council voted to offer Russell a fellowship when his lectureship expired. This should not have posed problems, but Russell was ambivalent about staying at Cambridge. Even before the war he had considered leaving when his lectureship expired. Now there seemed even less reason to stay, especially since he wished to be free to devote himself to politics. The proposal from Trinity, therefore, placed him in a dilemma from which he sought to extricate himself by indicating he would accept the fellowship while asking for a year's leave of absence to pursue his campaign against the war.

[To Ottoline Morrell]   [34 Russell Chambers]   14
                        [13 February 1915]
                        Saturday morning

My Darling Darling

Your letter from Oxford has just come. I am sorry I wrote to Bedford Square yesterday but I hope this will reach you tonight. I hate to think of your being imprisoned at Oxford – it is so wretched. I have had a long long letter from Lawrence[1] – saying it is no good to do *anything* till we get Socialism – and thinking (as the young do) that because *he* sees the desirability of Socialism it can be got by a few years' strenuous work. I feel his optimism difficult to cope with – I can't share it and don't want to discourage it. He is extraordinarily young. I will send you the letter when I have answered it.

I don't want to reprint my article on Religion in the *Hibbert* – I don't think it is good enough. But I will put in 'History'.[2]

I read the article on Cramb[3] with great interest – it quite makes one feel his quality. The article on 'national moods' seemed to me excellent too – and I thought the writer was well aware that it applied to England, and meant the reader to come to that conclusion.

I don't believe Mrs Bob[4] would be shocked by trousers! Who were the young ladies and how did you pick them up?

I have to make up my mind at once about the College offer of a Research fellowship. I feel practically decided to accept, but to demand a year's leave of absence first. Do you think that the right decision?

I am finishing my lecture on Matter – it is nearly done.[5] I am too busy to write an interesting letter![6]

---

[1] See Lawrence, *Letters*, vol. ii, pp. 282–6. Unfortunately, Russell's letters to Lawrence are lost.
[2] Russell was selecting essays to include in his collection *Mysticism and Logic* (1917). 'The Essence of Religion', originally published in *The Hibbert Journal* (1912), was the only part he had published of 'Prisons', a book on religion that he had written in conjunction with Ottoline. Wittgenstein had criticized it severely. Russell himself never reprinted the essay because he thought it was too religious, but in old age he allowed Robert Egner and Lester Denonn to include it in their collection *The Basic Writings of Bertrand Russell* (1961). 'On History' was an earlier essay from *The Independent Review* (1904). Both can be found in *Papers*, vol. xii.
[3] John Adam Cramb (1862–1913) professor of modern history at London who wrote novels under the name of J.A. Revermort. Cramb had become infatuated with Ottoline in 1903 and they had an apparently platonic relationship lasting about a year. His novel, *Cuthbert Learmont* (1910) is based on it. His passion for Ottoline, like his novel, seems absurdly out of touch with reality, but Cramb was very widely read and an excellent teacher who passed his passion for French literature and medieval romance on to Ottoline. The article on him which Ottoline had sent cannot be identified; nor the article on 'national moods' which accompanied it.
[4] Elizabeth Trevelyan, the wife of Russell's old friend Robert Trevelyan. She had been a dinner guest at Bedford Square, when Vernon Lee had turned up accompanied by two young ladies in trousers.
[5] He had to lecture on 'The Ultimate Constituents of Matter' at Manchester University in two days' time. See *Papers*, vol. viii, pp. 74–86.
[6] Or apparently to sign this one.

The success of his meeting with Lawrence encouraged Russell to invite him to Cambridge. Lawrence, with characteristic directness, expressed his misgivings beforehand:

> I don't want to be horribly impressed and intimidated, but am afraid I may be. I only care about the revolution we shall have. But immediately I only want us to be friends. But you are so shy and then I feel so clumsy, so clownish. Don't make me see too many people at once or I lose my wits.
>
> (2 March 1915; *Letters*, vol. ii, p. 300)

In the event, the visit, which took place on the weekend of 6–7 March, was a notorious failure. Lawrence told David Garnett it had sent him 'mad with misery and hostility and rage' (*Letters*, vol. ii, p. 321). And to Russell he complained of Cambridge's 'smell of rottenness, marsh-stagnancy' (19 March; *ibid.*, p. 309). However, at this time, Russell's feelings about Cambridge were so ambivalent and his admiration of Lawrence so extreme, that, as he said afterwards, 'For a time I thought he might be right' (*Portraits from Memory*, p. 106). Their friendship was not adversely affected and at the beginning of April Russell went on his own to stay with the Lawrences at Greatham. Lawrence reported enthusiastically back to Ottoline: 'We have had a good time with Russell – really been people living together. He is very natural to me – sort of kinship, so we are free together' (2 April; *Letters*, vol. ii, p. 312).

15 **[To Ottoline Morrell]** **[Trinity College]**
[8 March 1915]
Monday morning

My Darling Love

Lawrence is gone, disgusted with Cambridge, but not with me I think. I felt that we got on *very* well with each other, and made real progress towards intimacy. His intuitive perceptiveness is *wonderful* – it leaves me gasping in admiration.

Keynes came to dinner, and we had an interesting but rather dreadful evening. Keynes was hard, intellectual, insincere – using intellect to hide the torment and discord in his soul.[1] We pressed him hard about his purpose in life – he spoke as though he only wanted a succession of agreeable moments, which of course is not really true. Lawrence likes him but can't get on with him; I get on with him,

---

1 Though Keynes, like most of those in the Bloomsbury Group, was opposed to the war, his work in the Treasury meant that he spent much of his time trying to finance it. The tension this created weighed heavily upon him and it was probably this that Russell had in mind when he spoke of the 'torment and discord' in Keynes's soul.

but dislike him. Lawrence has the same feeling against sodomy as I have; you had nearly made me believe there is no great harm in it, but I have reverted; and all the examples I know confirm me in thinking it sterilizing.[1]

Lawrence is wonderfully lovable. The mainspring of his life is love – the universal mystical love – which inspires even his most vehement and passionate hate. It is odd that his *thinking* is coloured by Self – he imagines men more like him than they are. I think his thinking is quite honest, but there are painful things it hasn't realized.

I am *longing* for Wednesday. I suppose you won't come to the meeting in Little Russell Street at 8 tomorrow,[2] or be free after it? I am coming up in the afternoon, seeing Irene 5:30 to 6:30 (she dines with Vernon) – otherwise free except for the meeting. Dearest, Dearest, I love you with all my soul.

Your
B.

During the summer term Russell spent as little time at Cambridge as possible. He had no lectures that term and there were, in any case, few students to teach: only five or six hundred in the whole university. Russell felt the absence of the others deeply. What they were going through was hard to ignore when there was a major military hospital in the town and trains full of wounded arrived each night under cover of darkness. The university itself had been rapidly militarized. The chemical laboratories were working on gas weapons; the physics laboratories on ordnance. But perhaps most odious to Russell, because he had to confront it so frequently, was the childish jingoism of the older dons. Henry Jackson, the Vice-Master of Trinity, was especially warlike, eagerly taken in by every report of German villainy and fondly recounting tales of happy heroism by the British troops. 'The front', he reported cheerily, 'was like a first-rate club, as you met all your friends there' (Parry, *Henry Jackson*, p. 96).

Trinity College had not actually offered Russell a fellowship in February; it had merely announced its intention to do so when his lectureship came to an end. Russell's request for leave of absence to continue his political work thus re-opened the entire negotiation – and in a very much more politicized

---

1 In his long letter to Russell on 12 February, Lawrence, having disposed of economic issues, went on to rant against sodomy and masturbation. Keynes's bisexuality deeply offended Lawrence (see his letter to David Garnett, *Letters*, vol. ii, pp. 320–1).
2 A UDC meeting.

atmosphere than had existed in the college a few months earlier. On 21 May the college council decided that it would 'consider favourably' an application from Russell for leave only if he undertook to devote it to mathematics and philosophy. Since this was the purpose of the fellowship, the college could claim justification in not allowing Russell to spend his time on other pursuits, but it would hardly have acted in the same way had Russell wanted leave to devote himself to patriotic propaganda. The fact is that Trinity was becoming increasingly hostile to Russell because of his attitude to the war.

Instead of giving the required undertaking, Russell proposed, as he explains in the next letter, that the college not offer him a fellowship but merely extend his lectureship for a further five years and grant him leave of absence for its first two terms. In the letter he summarizes the advantages to the college of this course of action. (One was financial: a fellow received his stipend during a leave; lecturers were not paid while on leave.) The college council agreed to this new proposal on 28 May. That Russell continued at Trinity as a lecturer and not as a fellow had serious consequences for his dealings with the college the following year, by which time feelings against him were running even higher.

Russell had felt more at home at Trinity than anywhere else, and he had got used to living there on the assumption that any views, however unpopular, could be expressed and discussed on their merits. The hatred he experienced as a pacifist during the war hurt him deeply. Not only was he disillusioned by the intolerance of the college, but he felt himself shut out from the only group of people to which he felt he had truly belonged. None of this, however, caused him to consider, even for a moment, moderating his opposition to the war.

16   [To Ottoline Morrell]   34 Russell Chambers
                                                     Wednesday night
                                                     [26 May 1915]

My Darling

Here I am just returned from dining with the Whiteheads. The time went off fairly peacefully. She has now grown more or less sane, but he is utterly wild and mad in his determination to crush Germany, and his belief in the quite special wickedness of Germany.

It is such a comfort to be away from Cambridge. I suffer there from the close contact with people who think me wicked. They are much more fierce this term than they were before. I think I have managed to come to an agreement with them about my future. They *had* proposed to make me a research fellow instead of a lecturer, and I found they would be greatly relieved if they could withdraw that offer and merely continue my lectureship. This avoids an announcement in the *Times*, which they consider would be damaging to the College, and keeps me (as I have been hitherto) without a vote in College affairs, which it is feared I might use to further the advancement of learning. It appears the offer of a research fellowship (which they made in February) is considered a great honour – I was not aware of it at the time. I have written to them to say I shall be quite satisfied if they will renew my lectureship and give me two terms' leave of absence. By this I lose £140, but gain in freedom. They are sure to jump at it. I have been made aware of a mass of hostile feeling which I had hardly realized. I am particularly sorry that McTaggart[1] is so hostile – he has been their ringleader.

I am only just realizing how Cambridge oppressed me. I feel far more alive here, and far better able to face whatever horrors the time may bring. Cambridge has ceased to be a home and a refuge to me since the War began. I find it unspeakably painful being thought a traitor. Every casual meeting in the Court makes me quiver with sensitive apprehension. One ought to be more hardened.

My Dearest, forgive me that I have been so horrid lately. But really I have had rather a bad time, and I have been haunted by horrors, and I didn't want to speak all that was in my mind until it had subsided, because it was excessive and mad. So I got stiff and dull. But I shall be all right again now till some new unbearable thing happens. Goodnight my loved one. My heart yearns to you.

Your
B.

In mid-May the Morrells moved into Garsington Manor, the Tudor house five miles south of Oxford that has become inextricably linked with them. They had bought the house in 1913, together with 360 acres of farmland, two farms and a handful of cottages, but could not move in immediately since the sitting tenant had a lease that ran until 1915. The tenant, however, did not stay for the full term of her lease, and the Morrells took possession in 1914. The house and garden were woefully neglected and the winter of 1914–1915 was taken up with extensive renovations. Ottoline was clearly in love with the house, and had been since she had first seen it in 1903. Bertie viewed the move with concern. It was much further from his usual haunts than 44 Bedford Square. But, more important than geography, Ottoline planned to

---

[1] J.M.E. McTaggart (1866–1932), the idealist philosopher and formerly one of Russell's friends at Trinity.

turn Garsington into a haven for writers and artists, large numbers of whom could be expected to be in residence at any given time. Evidently Bertie could expect to have little time alone with her there.

Bertie got to see Garsington on 12 June, when he was a houseguest there along with the Lawrences. The decorations were still not complete and Ottoline put her guests to work painting the Red Room. Bertie was assigned to gild the ceiling beams while Lawrence painted a thin gold line round the wall panels and Frieda sat on a table swinging her legs and mocking the whole operation. Frieda, characteristically, managed to quarrel with everyone. Apart from offending Ottoline, she took a dislike to Bertie, and tried to turn Lawrence against him 'because Bertie didn't flatter her', according to Ottoline. Finally, she quarrelled bitterly with Lawrence, who appeared on the morning of their last day 'looking whipped, forlorn and crestfallen'. Frieda departed for London in a huff while Lawrence hesitated in the hall as to whether he should stay or follow her – predictably, he followed. She was, Ottoline declared, the sort of woman, 'that Strindberg might have married' (*Memoirs*, vol. ii, pp. 36–7).

[To Ottoline Morrell]   **[34 Russell Chambers]**
[17 June 1915]
Thursday

17   My Darling Love

In spite of Mrs Lawrence, it was really a *very* happy time to me – and our moment in the evening was *wonderful*. I like the atmosphere of your house and garden *immensely*. It did me all the good in the world being out of doors all day – I feel a new person in nerves and body. I was all full of crossness before I came, and now I feel quite set up, as if I had had a long holiday.

I am sorry Lawrence wouldn't stay this morning. I did *long* to stay, but I don't think it would have been a good plan. Irene was agreeable but not exciting. Tomorrow I have to see Mildred,[1] whom so far I have avoided since she came home from America. Goldie says he will leave the UDC if it goes in for opposing conscription![2] Doesn't that seem extraordinary?

---

1 Mildred Minturn Scott (see Letter **9**).
2 Conscription was not introduced until 1916, but the heavy losses in the war had already made it inevitable. On 6 June the General Council of the UDC had rejected a motion, supported by Russell, to oppose the introduction of conscription. This decision contributed to Russell's disillusion with the UDC as a focus for opposition to the war, though he never broke with the group. 'Goldie' was Goldsworthy Lowes Dickinson, an old Cambridge friend.

I can't tell you how I love to hear you reading poetry. I have never known a voice like yours – so poignant and vibrating – it moves me profoundly.

Goodnight my dearest dearest. I love you with all my being.
Your
   B.

After Frieda's visit, Ottoline was no doubt pleased to have Garsington to herself. Bertie, however, had plans to spend the following weekend with the Lawrences at Greatham. He can hardly have relished the prospect, but without Ottoline it turned out well. Russell's admiration had even survived reading Lawrence's 'philosophy': 'I can't make head or tail of Lawrence's philosophy', he'd told Ottoline on 11 June. 'I dread talking to him about it. It is not sympathetic to me.' Now, amazingly, they got on so well that they hatched plans for a series of lectures together. 'We think to have a lecture hall in London in the autumn', Lawrence told Ottoline on 20 June, 'and give lectures: he on Ethics, I on Immortality.' After this they were to form a religious circle devoted to 'Knowledge of the Infinite' at Garsington, over which Ottoline was to preside – she was instructed to keep her strength up for it. Russell, it seems, had come on well as a philosopher under Lawrence's guidance. Though hitherto he had been too temporal and immediate, he was now 'coming to have a real, actual, logical belief in Eternity and upon this he can work' (*Letters*, vol. ii, pp. 358–9). Russell was more circumspect when he reported the same events to Ottoline the next day.

[To Ottoline Morrell] In the train 18
[21 June 1915]
Monday morning

My Darling
   The visit to the Lawrences is safely over. I am glad I went, it was really not trying. I mind her much more when you are about. Lawrence wrote you a long letter yesterday, but she possessed herself of it and tore it up. Then he wrote another which I hope will reach you. He was *very* angry. She appeared on the little wall by the flower-bed, jeering. He said 'Come off that, lass, or I'll hit thee in the mouth. You've gone too far this time'.
   He has a very profound and wise admiration for you. He keeps saying you are a priestess, a Cassandra, and that your tragedy is to

have never found the God Apollo.[1] He is quite right. He *feels* all your quality as no one else seems to. It makes me love him.

I don't think, though, that he knows that kindness is as deep as anything in you.

We talked of a plan of lecturing in the autumn on his religion, politics in the light of religion, and so on. I believe something might be made of it. I could make a splendid course on political ideas: morality, the State, property, marriage, war, taking them to their roots in human nature, and showing how each is a prison for the infinite in us. And leading on to the hope of a happier world.

Goodbye my Darling. Lawrence is *splendid*. I like his philosophy *very much* now that I have read more. It is only the beginning that is poor. My deep love, Darling.

    Your
       B.

Though Russell seemed cooler about a collaborative lecture series than Lawrence, his attitude to Lawrence's 'philosophy' had undergone a surprising change. The philosophical manuscript Lawrence was writing is (perhaps mercifully) lost, so it is hard even to conjecture what Russell liked in it. Lawrence's remarks about it in his letters to Russell and others suggest little that would be remotely congenial to Russell. Ottoline, however, who also read it, liked it very much, and perhaps her opinion, together with the sheer vehemence of Lawrence's conviction, helped sway Russell. Lawrence's intransigent radicalism suited Russell's frame of mind far better than the timid compromises of the UDC and, spurred by Lawrence's enthusiasm, he quickly began to put together the social and political doctrine necessary for his own lectures. As he did so, his enthusiasm for the project grew.

The war had disenchanted Russell with liberalism and he had considered joining the Independent Labour Party, the only party in Britain that had refused to support the war. But, he was not prepared to embrace state socialism. Instead he began to look favourably on French syndicalism, which sought to put the means of production into the control of the trades unions through militant industrial action, and on guild socialism, its more moderate British version. Neither the syndicalists nor the guild socialists saw much to be gained from parliament, and both sought a marked reduction in state power.

---

[1] A rather ambiguous compliment. Cassandra was given her gift of prophecy by Apollo but, when she spurned his advances, he ordained that no one would believe her predictions even though they were infallibly correct. Both Russell and Lawrence seem to have hankered after the role of Apollo.

In these respects Russell found their views an improvement on those of both parliamentary and revolutionary state socialists. He started to read the writings of the French syndicalists with enthusiasm, and in his hands Lawrence's dreams of an apocalyptic socialist revolution began to take a more concrete form.

The increasing radicalism of Russell's politics was encouraged by his enforced isolation at Cambridge. Hearing of Russell's troubles with Trinity, Lawrence was delighted and urged him to have done with the College completely and become an outlaw, and this, in effect, was what he eventually did in both his public and his private life. His anxieties of the previous year about respectability receded as it became clear that those who opposed the war had little political influence whether they were respectable or not. Moreover, his very full schedule of speaking engagements made it clear that he had an audience outside academia. As his enthusiasm for his lectures grew, he began to relish the prospect of making a fresh start, even if it meant becoming an outlaw.

[To Ottoline Morrell] [34 Russell Chambers] 19
 [28 June 1915]
 Monday

My Darling Love

As you will see by the enclosed, Irene is ill so she has herself put off tomorrow. So that solves itself. I am free the whole day, in case you happen to have any free time earlier as well. Next day, Wednesday, I am engaged in the morning (I am going to see my pupil who lost his leg[1]) and to dinner, but am free for lunch and tea. Thursday I am free all day, except evening (I have a meeting at Hampstead).[2]

It was a joy to have a glimpse of you yesterday,[3] but we were too large a party for good talk, especially with Clive[4] talking nonsense. I like Cannan much better than I used to.[5] He is full of affection and kindliness. Mrs C. is a bore, but I think she has quite a nice nature. I lunched with Mildred today – she has begun to bore me and disgust me. I will see as little of her as possible.

---

1 Wallace Armstrong. He had been in the Royal Army Medical Corps and been invalided home early in the war. Back at Cambridge he became a pacifist and studied logic with Russell.
2 He spoke on 'How to secure a lasting peace' to the Hampstead UDC.
3 At Gilbert Cannan's house, where Russell had spent the weekend.
4 Presumably Clive Bell (1881–1964), the Bloomsbury art and literary critic.
5 Gilbert Cannan (1884–1955) was a friend of Lawrence's. He was a prolific writer, though he never fulfilled Henry James's hopes for him as one of the rising generation of English novelists. He had worked for a while as J.M. Barrie's secretary and caused a scandal by running off with Barrie's wife, Mary, whom he married in 1910. In 1915 they were living in a converted windmill near Cholesbury, Herts. By the end of the war his mental condition was deteriorating and he spent the last decades of his life in an asylum. In his last three novels – *Pugs and Peacocks* (1921), *Sembal* (1922), *The House of Prophecy* (1924) – Russell appears as the character Melian Stokes.

The thought of my lectures pleases me more and more. We must try to found a new school of philosophic radicalism, like the school that grew up during the Napoleonic wars.[1] The problem is to combine the big organizations that are technically unavoidable now-a-days with self-direction in the life of every man and woman. There must, for instance, be railways, but those who work on them need not be their slaves. I believe the State ought to cease altogether, and a man ought to belong to different groups for different purposes, each group chosen by himself, not determined by geography like the State.[2] But that is a distant speculation. I can imagine a country which would be happy in spite of industrialism. If one could give people hope, they would have the energy to do things.

Dearest, I feel such a profound sense of union with you these days – when I am most alive I am most one with you. I feel and hope that at last what I felt I ought to get from you is coming to fruition. I feel free, liberated at last from the old shackles – pedantry and nonconformity – and from respectability and bigwiggery. It is good to throw away one's reputation and start again at the beginning.

Goodnight my Darling.
Your
B.

In this mood Russell quickly drew up a long syllabus for his lectures which he sent to Lawrence. Lawrence hated it and returned it to Russell with angry comments scribbled all over it. '[M]ake them more profound, more philosophical' Lawrence insisted in his covering letter (*Letters*, vol. ii, p. 361. The syllabus and Lawrence's comments are published in H.T. Moore's edition of Lawrence's letters to Russell, pp. 79–96.). In fact, the two men were diverging very rapidly in their political views. Russell advocated syndicalism as a more democratic alternative to state socialism, but democracy was just what Lawrence could not stand. 'You must drop all your democracy,' Lawrence wrote on 14 July. 'There must be an aristocracy of people who have wisdom, and there must be a Ruler: a Kaiser: no Presidents and democracies' (*Letters*, vol. ii, p. 364). As Russell wrote years later, 'He had developed the whole philosophy of fascism before the politicians had thought of it' (*Portraits from Memory*, p. 107). This, however, is only hinted at in Lawrence's comments on

---

1 The utilitarian school in Britain centred around Jeremy Bentham and James Mill. They set the course for the development of liberal radicalism in the first half of the nineteenth century.
2 Russell developed these ideas further in *Political Ideals* (1917) and *Roads to Freedom* (1918).

the syllabus. In fact, Lawrence's incipient fascism seems to have developed shortly afterwards, the strange result of reading John Burnet's *Early Greek Philosophy* – ironically, a book which Russell had lent him. The full extent of their intellectual differences could thus, for a time, be overlooked and Russell continued to tolerate Lawrence's peremptory tone.

[To Ottoline Morrell] **[34 Russell Chambers]** 20
[8 July 1915]
Thursday evening

My Darling

Desmond[1] came to my tea party and helped me to entertain Jelli and Titi. Then he came to dinner and we had a nice talk. He always cheers one up. Lawrence, as was to be foreseen, is disgusted with my lecture syllabus – it is not mystical and Blake-ish enough for him. He says one ought to live from the 'impulse towards the truth' which he says is fundamental in all of us. It seems to me, in him, merely an impulse to mistake his imaginations for the truth. He talks of a desire for one-ness with others which he believes to be the same as the 'impulse to truth'. I don't believe these things exist in most people. But I find those who have a strong imagination generally read their own natures into other people, instead of getting at other people by impartial observation. Lawrence is just as furious a critic as Wittgenstein, but I thought W. right and I think L. wrong. He is coming to see me Saturday. I dread it. I don't know whether I shall still be able to feel any faith in my own ideas after arguing with him, although my reason is all against him. He is lacking in humour; he takes my irony seriously, and protests against it.

Today I had tea with Margaret,[2] and we went a walk on the Heath. I did enjoy seeing her. She is really fine – noble and courageous.

Don't bother to try to get my rooms[3] ready by Tuesday, as I can't come till Wednesday morning.

This morning I read a paper to a Pacifist Conference.[4] They were an awful crew. Pacifists are really no good.

What is wrong with mere opposition to War is that it is negative. One must find other outlets for people's wildness, and not try to produce people who have no wildness.

It is all very puzzling.

---

1 Desmond MacCarthy.
2 Probably Margaret LLewelyn Davies (1861-1944), the sister of Russell's Cambridge friend, Crompton Llewelyn Davies. Russell had worked with her for women's suffrage before the war.
3 At Garsington.
4 'The Philosophy of Pacifism' (*Papers*, vol. xiii, pp. 147–55) read at a two-day conference on the pacifist philosophy of life held at Caxton Hall.

I am depressed, partly by Lawrence's criticisms. I feel a worm, a useless creature. Sometimes I enumerate my capacities, and wonder why I am not more use in the world. I suppose scepticism is my real trouble. It is always only by an act of will that I keep it under, and it weakens me.

Goodnight my Darling. I long to be with you and in the country.
Your
   B.

Just after the outbreak of war, T.S. Eliot, who had attended Russell's classes at Harvard earlier in the year, had arrived in Britain to study for a year at Oxford with the Idealist philosopher Harold Joachim in preparation for his Harvard doctorate. 1915 was an important year in his life. It saw the beginning of his career as a poet with the publication of 'Prufrock' in the Chicago magazine *Poetry*. In the same year he met and quickly married Vivien Haigh-Wood. She was vivacious, witty, fond of dancing and the theatre. But her apparently carefree manner which so appealed to Eliot masked a personality liable to mood swings from exuberant high-spirits to deep depression and anxiety attacks. She was excessively sensitive, and emotional upsets brought on a variety of increasingly severe physical and mental symptoms. Neither she nor Eliot had told their parents of their marriage and Eliot, faced with a summer trip home, was anxious about his parents' reaction to Vivien. Russell quickly took stock of the situation when Eliot brought her to meet him on 9 July.

The next day, Russell went with trepidation to visit Lawrence in London. Lawrence told Ottoline afterwards that he had 'rather quarrelled with Russell's lectures' but not with Russell: 'We have almost sworn Blutbruderschaft' (*Letters*, vol. ii, p. 363). In spite of this development (or perhaps because of it) Russell came away depressed. Still, the purported collaboration on the lectures limped on.

21   **[To Ottoline Morrell]**   **[34 Russell Chambers]**
                                                              [13 July 1915]
                                                                      Tuesday

My Darling

I was very glad to hear from you this morning – I had not been surprised at not hearing sooner. I am sorry I can't stay for the week-end, but I have to speak[1] at a P.S.A. at Ilford, and I have grouped

---

1 On 'Principles of Peace' on Sunday 18 July.

various other things about that. My gums are gone wrong again, and I shall probably have to go often to the dentist.¹ It is a nuisance – but it brings back all the mental symptoms I used to have, hating everybody, and feeling ill-used. It doesn't get the better of me because I know it is physical, but it interferes with work. I expect it was gums that made me like the baboon.²

Yes, the day Lawrence was with me was horrid. I got filled with despair, and just counting the moments till it was ended. Partly that was due [to] liver, but not wholly. Lawrence is very like Shelley – just as fine, but with a similar impatience of fact. The revolution he hopes for is just like Shelley's prophecy of banded anarchs fleeing while the people celebrate a feast of love.³ His psychology of people is amazingly good up to a point, but at a certain point he gets misled by love of violent colouring.

Friday evening I dined with my Harvard pupil Eliot and his bride. I expected her to be terrible, from his mysteriousness; but she was not so bad. She is light, a little vulgar, adventurous, full of life – an artist I think he said, but I should have thought her an actress. He is exquisite and listless; she says she married him to stimulate him, but finds she can't do it. Obviously he married in order to be stimulated. I think she will soon be tired of him. She refuses to go to America to see his people, for fear of submarines. He is ashamed of his marriage, and very grateful if one is kind to her. He is the Miss Sands⁴ type of American.

Last night C. Delisle Burns⁵ and his wife asked me to speak to about 20 people about the ideas in my lecture-syllabus. I did so, but I felt sceptical as to the importance of my ideas. Perhaps there is something in them, but I don't know.

---

1 In 1914 Russell had suffered from pyorrhoea which had been treated by an American dentist during his trip to the US. In his *Autobiography* (vol. i, p. 206) he blamed the bad breath which resulted for some of his difficulties with Ottoline.
2 In an earlier letter he had told Ottoline of a visit to the zoo where he had been delighted by a baboon which snarled at its audience with 'inconceivable hatred and disgust. Swift would have loved it.'
3 In Shelley's poem *Hellas* 'banded anarchs' flee when the spirit of God unfurls the flag of freedom in the great morning of the world. Lawrence had been reading H.N. Brailsford's *Shelley, Godwin, and their Circle* (1913).
4 Ethel Sands, a wealthy and highly cultivated American expatriate. At her manor house in Newington she entertained a circle of Americans living in Britain, including Henry James, Edith Wharton, and Russell's brother-in-law Logan Pearsall Smith. Ottoline had got to know Henry James through her, and the leisurely, luxurious life at Newington inspired some of Ottoline's hopes for Garsington.
5 Cecil Delisle Burns (1879–1942), a political philosopher then working as a university extension lecturer. After the war he did research for the Ministry of Labour and the Labour Party. In 1915 he was the British editor of the journal *Ethics*.

I get to Oxford[1] 11:15 tomorrow morning. I have no luggage and a bicycle. Next week, if the dentist is kind, I shall be able to stay longer. I have no more P.S.A.'s. Goodbye my Darling.
    Your
        B.

T.S. Eliot had sailed for America on 24 July, while Vivien stayed behind as planned. Eliot had asked Russell to see her in his absence, since her mental condition was already giving cause for concern and Eliot, at least, seemed to think her in need of constant company. Russell did have lunch with her one Sunday in August, but no other meetings are recorded. The trip was a difficult one for Eliot. His parents were expecting that he would return to complete his degree at Harvard and take up a career in America as a philosophy professor. Eliot, however, was ambivalent about a career in philosophy. More importantly, he wanted to live permanently in England – he planned to write his thesis there and return briefly to Harvard in 1916 for his *viva*. Of all the reasons he had for living in Britain, Vivien was the one he used to best effect with his parents. In fact, in a note written after her death, he said 'I believe that I came to persuade myself I was in love with her simply because I wanted to burn my boats and commit myself to staying in England' (Eliot, *Letters*, vol. i, p. xvii). It was Vivien, in fact, who, by falling ill while he was away, precipitated his early return to England at the end of August.

With this, indeed, he did burn his boats – though his father lived until 1929, Eliot never saw him again. (The 1916 trip for his doctoral *viva* was called off due to the war and Harvard awarded the degree without an examination.) It seems that many of the changes in Eliot's life at this time were due to a desire to escape his family. Yet, ironically, in breaking free from his parents, he found himself under an even more stringent burden of proving himself to them – to show that his decisions had been good ones; that his marriage was viable; that he could make a successful career for himself (even if it was not the one his parents envisaged for him); and that he could earn enough to support himself and Vivien. Moreover, he had to do all this as, by his own admission (*Letters*, vol. i, p. xvii), a 'very immature ... very timid, very inexperienced' young man in a new country, dislocated by war, where he had few contacts. Above all, it had to be done in a loveless marriage to a seriously disturbed woman.

It is not very surprising that, having cast off one father, Eliot should have sought another in Russell. Nor is it surprising that Russell, whose desire for children of his own was 'almost insupportable' (*Autobiography*, vol. ii, p. 150),

---

[1] The station for Garsington, five miles away.

should have accepted the role with enthusiasm. Russell was as yet indifferent to Eliot's poetry (though, in fairness, he had probably not yet read much of it) and did not regard him as a struggling genius. (Russell's preconception of genius was rather narrow and very firm, and embraced a quite different type of person to Eliot.) But he had recognized something of Eliot's ability when they had first met at Harvard, and Russell (like Ottoline) enjoyed helping the young and talented. Accordingly, he took Eliot's problems in hand and started to solve some of them in eminently practical ways.

To make ends meet Eliot had taken a job as a schoolteacher at High Wycombe. When this proved insufficient Russell gave him £3,000 in debentures in an engineering company. (The company was making munitions and Russell felt obliged to disinvest. Eliot returned the debentures in 1927.) He also employed Vivien as a typist and lent the Eliots the spare bedroom in his flat in Russell Chambers, since Eliot needed a London base to launch his literary career. In addition, he introduced Eliot to Sidney Waterlow, an editor of the *International Journal of Ethics*, and to Philip Jourdain, the British editor of *The Monist*, in the hope that they would be able to give him paid reviewing work. Eliot reviewed for both journals, and Waterlow put him in touch with the *New Statesman*, the *Manchester Guardian*, and the *Westminster Gazette*, for which he also wrote.

The reviewing work, besides the money it brought in, was also useful in convincing Eliot's parents that their son was beginning a promising career. To this end, also, Russell wrote to Eliot's mother, reassuring her about her son's philosophical ability and his prospects for a university post after the war. He even put in a good word for Vivien, on which topic Eliot's family was much in need of reassurance. He credited her with the fact that Eliot was 'no longer attracted by the people who call themselves "vorticists" . . . in that I think her influence is wholly to be applauded' (letter of 3 October 1915).

But Eliot's most intractable problems were marital rather than financial. On his return to England he found Vivien's illness was quite serious. She had a perplexing mixture of physical and mental symptoms – stomach cramps, headaches, and faintness being the most easily identifiable. They went to Eastbourne together for what Russell described as a 'pseudo-honeymoon', but Vivien's condition only deteriorated. From Eastbourne in early September she wrote Russell a letter (now lost) which suggested to him that she was close to suicide.

A bond had been formed between Russell and Vivien from the time of their first meeting two months earlier when she had taken him into her confidence about her marriage. Ottoline, who had been kept informed of the Eliots' marital troubles, was worried. In September, she wrote to warn Bertie of 'what might happen if [Vivien] became in love with you which is evidently quite likely'. She worried about the damage a scandal would do to Russell's public work and about the consequences for the Eliots' marriage: 'Don't think

I want to interfere or stop you but I feel *very* strongly that in getting her confidence you are rather separating her from Eliot – and besides running an awful risk for your reputation . . . and the big things you *can* do are more important' (Seymour, *Ottoline Morrell*, p. 245). It was wise advice which Bertie tried to shrug off in the next letter.

22 [To Ottoline Morrell]

[34 Russell Chambers]
[10 September 1915]
Friday

My Darling

I will come tomorrow by my usual train, and get to Garsington about 12. Today I am seeing Irene and dining with the Lawrences. I have just found your letter about the Eliots – really there is no occasion for your fears. He is not that sort of man, and I will be much more careful than you seem to expect. And I feel sure I can make things come right. We can talk about it when I come. I would not for the world have any scandal, and as for the Eliots it is the purest philanthropy. I am sorry you feel worried – there is *really* no need – I am fond of him, and really anxious to be of use to him. The trouble between them was already at its very worst before I came into the matter at all – it is already better, and when I saw him he was very full of gratitude. I must have given you quite a wrong impression when I wrote.

I had a long talk with Elizabeth.[1] She is full of doubts and hesitations, which I urged her to overcome. I don't know what she will do.

Dearest *please* don't be worried about my doings – it is *really* nothing to worry about it [*sic*]. Darling I am *longing* to be back with you – all my soul is yours my Dearest Dearest

Your
B.

The ill-fated collaboration with Lawrence came to a decisive end on 14 September, though not directly over the lectures themselves. With Katherine Mansfield and Middleton Murry, Lawrence was planning a little magazine, *The Signature* (three issues actually appeared), and had asked Russell to

---

1 The pen name of Mary Annette von Arnim (1866–1941), an English novelist best known for *Elizabeth and her German Garden* (1898), a sometimes satirical account of her trying life in Prussia with her husband Count von Arnim. Her doubts and hesitations concerned whether to marry Russell's brother. Unwisely, she overcame them. After divorcing him, she wrote an entirely savage novel, *Vera*, about her even more trying life as Countess Russell.

contribute. Russell sent him 'The Danger to Civilization' (*Papers*, vol. xiii, pp. 329–38), a general essay on the damage war does to science, art, and a humane way of life. Lawrence hated it:

> You simply don't speak the truth ... [I]t isn't in the least true that you, your basic self, want ultimate peace. You are satisfying in an indirect, false way your lust to jab and strike. Either satisfy it in a direct and honorable way, saying 'I hate you all, liars and swine, and am out to set upon you', or stick to mathematics, where you can be true. But to come as the angel of peace – no, I prefer Tirpitz a thousand times, in that rôle ... The enemy of all mankind, you are, full of the lust of enmity. It is *not* the hatred of falsehood which inspires you. It is the hatred of people, of flesh and blood. It is a perverted, mental blood-lust. Why don't you own it?
>
> (14 September; *Letters*, vol. ii, p. 392)

Ironically, when Russell had come out 'in a direct and honorable way', in a savage attack in *The Labour Leader* on Lord Northcliffe, the press baron and chief government propagandist, Lawrence had immediately taken fright: 'you do say rash things ... Let me beg you not to get into trouble now' (*Letters*, vol. ii, p. 357).

Russell's reaction to the diatribe of 14 September was extraordinary, as he later recognized:

> I find it difficult now to understand the devasting effect that this letter had upon me. I was inclined to believe that he had some insight denied to me, and when he said my pacifism was rooted in blood-lust I supposed he must be right. For twenty-four hours I thought that I was not fit to live and contemplated committing suicide. But at the end of that time, a healthier reaction set in.
>
> (*Portraits from Memory*, pp. 109–10)

Lawrence's ill-temper was not the only thing to depress Russell at this time. Ottoline was drifting away, this time irrevocably. A remark of hers in mid-July, which both agreed was trivial, none the less cast a pall over their correspondence for two full weeks. In August and September, even their correspondence began to dry up. At first, Ottoline would excuse the long gaps between her letters by the demands of guests at Garsington, while Bertie kept up a regular flow of letters. But by September even Bertie was writing less frequently, though he was still trying to keep the relationship going. A meeting in November seems to have led to a quarrel, but also to a reconciliation. He wrote to her later in the day from High Wycombe where he was staying with the Eliots who had borrowed a cottage there. Meanwhile, Lawrence was staying at Garsington – a good reason for Bertie to stay away.

23 [To Ottoline Morrell]

[Sydney Cottage,
Conegra Road,
High Wycombe,
Bucks.][1]
[10 November 1915]
Wednesday

My Darling Love

I feel so *much* happier since our talk, in spite of being sad that I made you unhappy. I am sure it is a *very* superficial thing in you that I was finding fault with, not at all a thing hard to get rid of. It will be some time before I can make myself believe in my instincts that you do not hate me – *please* don't be *froissée* if I am a little shy for some time.

I wonder very much how Lawrence's visit is going off, and what mood he is in.

Eliot had a half holiday yesterday and got home at 3.30. It is quite funny how I have come to love him, as if he were my son. He is becoming much more of a man. He has a profound and quite unselfish devotion to his wife, and she is really very fond of him, but has impulses of cruelty to him from time to time. It is a Dostojewsky type of cruelty, not a straightforward every-day kind. I am every day getting things more right between them, but I can't let them alone at present, and of course I myself get very much interested. She is a person who lives on a knife-edge and will end as a criminal or a saint – I don't know which yet. She has a perfect capacity for both.

I have been busy with writing and with proofs of my Murray article.[2] Unless Lawrence stays on, I will come home Friday morning (arriving Wheatley 1.30).[3] I am longing to be back – the situation here is anxious and painful, although it is too interesting to be left alone, apart from kindness.

Goodbye my Darling. I feel as if I had found you again after a long long time of having lost you.

Your
    B.

---

1 The letter is written on Trinity College letterhead.
2 *The Policy of the Entente, 1904–1914*, published by the National Labour Press in December 1915. It was a reply to Gilbert Murray's propaganda pamphlet *The Foreign Policy of Sir Edward Grey, 1906–1915*, which was being distributed covertly by the Foreign Office. The pamphlet is all that Russell completed of the book on foreign policy on which he had started work with Irene Cooper-Willis earlier in the year. The day-to-day exigencies of opposing the war left him insufficient time to complete the larger work.
3 'Home', interestingly enough, was the set of rooms Ottoline had prepared for him in the Bailiff's House on the Garsington estate.

With Lawrence gone Russell continued with the lectures alone. They were delivered between 18 January and 7 March 1916 at the Caxton Hall in London under the title 'Principles of Social Reconstruction'. In them Russell developed an account of social and political organization based on a theory of human nature which saw impulse as the chief determinant of human action and divided impulses into those which are possessive, which aim at acquiring or retaining something that cannot be shared, and those which are creative, which aim at producing something which can be shared. Sound political and social organization should foster the latter and diminish the former. After setting up this framework, successive lectures deal with social institutions: the state, war, property, education, marriage, and religion.

The lectures were a new type of writing for Russell and they caused him some great anxiety as the time for their delivery drew near – partly because the distinction between creative and possessive impulses became clear to him only late in the process. Once they were written, however, he planned to take Vivien Eliot away for a holiday in Devon so that Tom could work on his thesis. Ottoline was worried at this news, and even tried to lure him back by telling him she would be coming to London while he would be away. Bertie tried, perhaps halfheartedly, to extricate himself from the holiday, but to no avail. Vivien and Bertie left on 3 January, with Bertie returning on the 12th after Tom had arrived to stay with her (at Bertie's expense). At some point in 1916, Bertie and Vivien, who had become increasingly close, began an affair. Quite possibly it started while they were in Devon. If they did become lovers while on holiday, Tom seems to have had no suspicion of it, he was effusive in his thanks to Bertie: 'no one could have been so wise and understanding with her as you' (14 January), 'I believe we shall owe her life to you, even' (11 January) (Eliot, *Letters*, vol. i, pp. 129, 127).

[To Ottoline Morrell] **[London]** **24**
[3 January 1916]
Monday morning

My Darling
    I made a valiant attempt to get out of going away with Mrs E., but to no purpose. The whole thing rather amused me, because it was so unlike the way things are conventionally supposed to happen. First I talked to him, and said I felt the responsibility for her health, and wished he were going as he knew better what to do. He was willing to take my place, but reluctant on account of his work. (He has to take a Ph.D. degree at Harvard, and his only time for preparation is during the school holidays.) However, he would have gone; but when I said the same things to her, she wouldn't hear of it, again on account of his work. So I had to let the matter be.

It would hardly be possible to go on such a journey less willingly, though a month ago I should have enjoyed going. What I meant to do for those two is done, except to some slight extent as regards money (I must go on giving her my typing) – he is extraordinarily good and unselfish, and she is quickly becoming unselfish to him.

I have practically finished re-writing my lectures. I have a free mind about them now. I feel as if I would not undertake another serious piece of work for a long time. These lectures nearly drove me into insanity. I am afraid of sinking gradually into a condition of melancholia, not from outward reasons, but from fatigue. I have practised concentration so long that I can work when I am very tired, and probably it is bad for me. I do think if I *could* do nothing for a year, it would be a very good thing. But I wonder if I am capable of it. Perhaps I ought to see Vittoz?[1] Almost the whole of what is tiresome in me is the result of the effort of not yielding to fatigue.

This is a very self-centred letter, but as I have finished my lectures it is a moment for decisions, and I don't want to sink again into the condition of mind that I have been in ever since I began writing them. It is dreadful to feel oneself hateful to everybody. But the effort of creative work grows more and more terrible every year – I feel as if no one could imagine the exasperated exhaustion it produces. Because my lectures are done (I worked at them all day yesterday) I feel just as if my sight had been restored after blindness – the outer world is there again, and other people are not a mere blur through a fog. I cannot tell you what an utter hell it has been. I want to wipe out the last 6 months and begin again where we were before – but I suppose that is impossible.

I shall be back at latest this day week, very likely sooner. If you write, address Post Office Torquay for the present. I shall go to the Post Office by myself in the morning.

    Your

      B.

Russell's lectures were a great success. A large crowd turned out to hear him, including most of the Bloomsbury group. 'It is splendid the way he sticks at nothing', Lytton Strachey wrote to Ottoline on 16 February, 'Governments,

---

[1] Ottoline's Swiss psychiatrist. He taught techniques for clearing the mind of unpleasant thoughts – a skill in which Bertie was clearly deficient. Though he did not go, Russell seems to have been quite serious in his suggestion.

religions, laws, property, even Good Form itself – down they go like ninepins – it is a charming sight! . . . I don't believe there's anyone quite so formidable to be found just now upon this earth' (Holroyd, *Strachey*, vol. ii, p. 173). The success cheered Russell up a good deal.

[To Ottoline Morrell] **[28 January 1916]**[1]
Friday morning

My Darling
Thank you very much for your letter. I was interested in the Lawrences' letter.[2] If I were you, I should not dream of going to Cornwall. It would tire you dreadfully, and would be sure to cause trouble with Frieda. Is Lawrence right in his advice to you? about letting go of your will and resting, I mean. I always think people who advise letting go of will don't realize how hard it is to recover it. Lawrence has a prejudice against will – no doubt he is right in a way, but in the world as it is, I don't see how one can accomplish anything, or make anybody happy, without it.

Yesterday Bob[3] came in the morning to talk again about points of style in my lectures, and to bring me Havelock Ellis on the *Psychology of Sex*.[4] It is very interesting, and full of things that every one ought to know. I think a good deal of it would be useful to you for Julian's education. It has been forbidden by the police, because it is not amusing or lascivious.

Irene came to lunch – she is in the middle of one of her quarrels with Vernon. Vernon has behaved abominably, but of course it is partly Irene's fault for being so yielding. In the evening I had Mrs Hamilton[5] to dine with me at Frascati's, and, as I had expected, I grew quite intimate with her in the course of dinner. She talked about her marriage and her ambitions and such matters. I like her very much, but there is always just that quality that makes her novels bad – something that makes her not *exciting*.

---

1 It is not known where this letter was written.
2 The Lawrences were now living in Cornwall, where they soon got into trouble with the authorities who feared (absurdly enough) that they were signalling to German submarines. Ottoline, despite vituperative letters from Frieda, had intended to visit them, but was prevented by ill-health. Lawrence had suggested, delightfully, that she 'must lie and lapse all unloosed' in order to get well (*Letters*, vol. ii, p. 512).
3 Trevelyan.
4 Havelock Ellis's *Studies in the Psychology of Sex* was published in six volumes between 1897 and 1910 (a seventh volume appeared in 1928). The first volume published (actually vol. 2, on homosexuality) was immediately suppressed in England. Ellis, who disliked controversy, then had the whole series published in America. No British edition was published in his lifetime.
5 Mary Agnes Hamilton (1882–1966), a novelist and biographer then working for *The Economist*. She had studied at Newnham College, Cambridge and later became a Labour MP. She was helping to promote Russell's lectures.

The Labour Congress has let itself be bamboozled.¹ It is dreadful the way uneducated people are at the mercy of scoundrels. However, Labour will be all right after the war.

I am *very* sorry your eyes ache so much. I *do* wish you could come up for one of my lectures.² It would make me so happy.

It is no wonder you are sad, from being inactive. If you were in London you would find a lot to do. There are, for instance, the conscientious objectors to be helped, especially with advice. If P[hilip] were out of Parliament, you would be in some ways freer politically, wouldn't you?³

Isn't it really remarkable how well our Cambridge friends come out at this time? It does show that what the Society⁴ gives is something real. When one thinks how *very* few in the whole country have done as well, it is really notable. I feel that those who are standing out now are gradually being brought together and becoming an intellectual force which must have great effects in the long run. Sooner or later you will have to come back to London, if you are to take your part in a work in which you might do great things. But there is no hurry about it.

I haven't been so care-free since the war began. I am *so* happy that things are right between you and me; and life is very easy when one has just finished a piece of work and not yet started on another.

Goodbye my Darling. My love is with you always.

Your

B.

Once his lectures were finished, Russell got away for a walking holiday in Sussex with a French student, Jean Nicod, who was studying logic at Cambridge, where he was already doing original work. He had escaped the war because he had tuberculosis, the disease which killed him in 1924 at the age of 31. Russell described him as 'one of the most delightful people I have ever known, at once very gentle and immensely clever' (*Autobiography*, vol. ii, p. 96).

---

1 The Labour Party conference being held at Bristol had voted against conscription and the Military Service Bill which was then being drafted, but had also decided against agitating for the repeal of the bill once it became law. The next day the party also voted to continue participation in Asquith's wartime coalition government.
2 Ottoline had suggested doing so.
3 Philip Morrell had been in Burnley talking to his constituents, who were now very unhappy with his attitude to the war.
4 The Cambridge Conversazione Society, better known as 'the Apostles'. Many members were now opposed to the war.

While Russell had been preoccupied with his lectures, the pacifists faced their worst crisis of the war. The Military Service Bill was passed at the end of January. At Asquith's urging, the government had added a clause exempting those who had 'a conscientious objection to bearing arms'. The validity of claims for exemption was to be decided by local tribunals. The conscience clause was no doubt intended as a genuinely humanitarian measure, but in practice the tribunals, which had been set up as recruiting bodies before conscription was introduced, robbed it of most of its value by seeking any excuse to reject a claim. Success before a tribunal typically depended upon being properly coached beforehand and being well represented by people prepared to speak for you. This required a great deal of the organizations trying to help COs which had to supply quasi-legal as well as moral support to many men who found themselves in a difficult and often very dangerous situation.

Their efforts were made more difficult by a peculiarity of the Military Service Act which, instead of a selective draft, had actually conscripted all single men between the ages of 18 and 41, though, of course, not everyone entered service at the same time since the armed forces could not deal with such an influx. This meant that all claims for exemption had to be made at once, placing an enormous strain on the pacifist organizations.

The main organization helping COs was the No Conscription Fellowship (NCF). It had been formed in November 1914 by Fenner Brockway and Clifford Allen, two members of the Independent Labour Party, and consisted entirely of men of military age, most of them radical socialists and pacifists. With the introduction of conscription its members were liable to be called before tribunals, conscripted, arrested, and otherwise harassed. As a result non-members came to be responsible for the day-to-day running of the NCF, since only these 'associate members' were not liable to conscription. Chief among them was Catherine Marshall (1880–1960), who had come to the NCF from the National Union of Women's Suffrage Societies where she had been one of its leading strategists. In the face of continual harassment by the authorities, she built the NCF into a well-organized and highly effective pressure group. In the face of the Military Service Act, Marshall set about recruiting other 'associates' to help run the NCF against the time when Allen and the other leaders would be in jail.

Russell was, at first, reluctant to commit himself, no doubt because he was still not entirely free of the profound depression, personal and political, that had settled on him at the end of the previous year. In the end, however, Marshall's entreaties were impossible to resist, and he agreed to join (temporarily) with the radical journalist, H.N. Brailsford and J.S. Middleton (the assistant secretary of the Labour Party) to form the Associates' Political Committee which was to make propaganda on behalf of conscientious objectors. Joining the committee was a decisive event in Russell's life. By the end of the year it had changed him from a dissident academic into one of the leaders of an organization that the government regarded as subversive.

Russell became, in effect, Marshall's personal assistant. She was not an easy person to work for. She found it difficult to delegate work or allow others to take initiative and was harshly critical of their efforts when they did so. Russell often found himself acting as a buffer between Marshall and other workers at the NCF offices whom she had upset. She was very effective, but not easy to like. One of the pacifists said later: 'She was the only person military enough to lead us.'

26 [To Ottoline Morrell]   **Anchor Hotel,
                                              Chichester
                                              [29 March 1916]**
                                              Wednesday evening

My Darling

I wrote you a horrid letter this morning and I am ashamed of it. But now I have to say that Miss Marshall who has been running the N.C.F. lately has written to me every day beseeching help and at last I can resist no longer so I return Saturday morning early. I don't know where I shall live in London.[1] Letters to my flat will find me. I have promised *all* my time till April 25 so I suppose I shan't have one spare moment. I am quite rested and shall be happier helping the objectors. They seem to be in great need because their organization gets broken up, since it consisted of men liable to conscription.

Tomorrow we sleep at Station Hotel, Rowlands Castle. Next night, P.O. Petersfield. Then London – somewhere. Don't write to Petersfield – I have to start so early that I shouldn't get it.

The Eliots' affairs are arranging themselves without my help, which is a great comfort. He will probably not go to America.[2] She is probably not really ill – she wasn't before – but her nerves are all to pieces. It is the worry of his going that upset her. She was afraid he would be sunk by a submarine.

I am *delighted* to be going to be busy – I shall probably be *very* busy.
Dearest, my deepest love is with you always always.
Your
    B.

---

1 He had sublet his flat in Russell Chambers. He ended up staying with his brother or with Clive Bell until his own flat was free again in May.
2 To be examined on his doctoral thesis. In fact he planned to sail on 1 April, but the boat was delayed for five days and he cancelled.

The Military Service Act permitted both absolute and conditional exemptions. In practice, it was rare for COs to obtain absolute exemptions and most were exempted only from combatant service. This meant that they were either assigned to the non-combatant corps (where they often ended up driving ambulances at the front) or were assigned to work of national importance. Many COs, however, objected to any work that would benefit the war effort. The Act did not address their claims and their harsh treatment soon became a major issue for the pacifists. On 8 and 9 April the NCF held an large emergency convention in London which voted unanimously against the non-combatant corps and almost unanimously against the idea of civilian service.

The convention marked a turning point in Russell's involvement with the NCF. He was swept up in the enthusiasm it generated and abandoned his original plan to work for the NCF only until 25 April. It was work to which he was entirely unaccustomed, and plagued by all kinds of difficulties, but he took to it with enthusiasm. The NCF not only provided him with a focus for his opposition to the war, it transformed his personal life as well, providing new friends and political allies who differed in class, education, occupation, and age from those he had previously associated with. The young people with whom he worked day by day in the NCF provided the sort of revitalization that he had sought in vain through 1915.

[To Ottoline Morrell]   46 Gordon Square,   27
Bloomsbury[1]
[9 April 1916]
Sunday night

My Darling

Here I am, back again after two delirious days and nights of conference of the N.C.F. The whole Committee slept at an hotel in the City so as to be together and near the meeting.

It has been a *wonderful* two days – the most inspiring and happy thing that I have known since the war began – it gives one hope and faith again.

Most of the time was business: about 1,000 delegates from branches all over the country, and about another 1,000 London members. It was a joy to see such crowds of young men, and no khaki. We met yesterday in Devonshire House, The Friends' Meeting House in Bishopsgate, today in a queer place in North London – great and successful efforts were made to prevent the *Express* and the Anti-German Union from

---

[1] Clive Bell's address.

finding out where we were,[1] and the proceedings passed off without any interruption.

Yesterday we had a public speech-making meeting as well – Snowden,[2] Dr. Clifford,[3] Mrs Swanwick,[4] Lansbury[5] and others spoke – I missed most of that, because news came of a young man who had been arrested and would be let out on bail, so Dr. Salter[6] (of Bermondsey) and I went off to Lambeth in a taxi, fetched him out of his prison cell, and brought him back to the meeting, where he received a great ovation. (He said he was reading one of my pamphlets when they arrested him!)

The spirit of the young men was magnificent. They would not listen to even the faintest hint of compromise. They were keen, intelligent, eloquent, full of life – vigorous, courageous men, full of real religion, not hysterical at all – not *seeking* martyrdom, but accepting it with great willingness. I am convinced that at least half will not budge an inch for any power on earth. The whole assembly was full of fun, and never missed a chance of laughter.

It was the very last moment. Most of them will be arrested within the next few days, and taken to camp. What will happen there, no one knows. I don't think they will be shot, though they certainly can be, at any rate if they are taken to France.[7]

They got through immense masses of business, all of it important, with extraordinary speed – one saw how business was done in the

---

1 Prior to the conference the *Daily Express* had published the address at which it was to be held, in the hope that demonstrators would turn up to disrupt the meeting. Then it erroneously announced that the NCF had changed the venue – sending its demonstrators to the wrong address. None the less, on Saturday night an angry crowd gathered in Devonshire Place – though Russell did not seem to have been aware of it. The Anti-German Union, later called the British Empire Union, was an extreme right-wing group devoted to agitation and propaganda against pacifism and all things German. They were involved in breaking up meetings, making threatening phone calls and other forms of intimidation. The police rarely stopped them.
2 Philip Snowden (1864–1937), ILP MP for Blackburn. Though known before the war as 'the English Robespierre', he was far from a radical either as a pacifist or a socialist. He became Chancellor of the Exchequer in the Labour governments of 1924 and 1929–1931.
3 Dr John Clifford, a leading Baptist. He supported the war but opposed conscription.
4 Helena Swanwick (1864–1939) a feminist, socialist, and pacifist who had been active in the UDC and now was chair of the Women's International League.
5 George Lansbury (1859–1940), the Christian pacifist and Labour leader.
6 Alfred Salter, a Quaker and member of the ILP.
7 COs who refused non-combatant service became liable to imprisonment often under very harsh conditions. On their release they were often conscripted again and returned to jail if they still refused to serve. Others were involuntarily inducted into the armed forces, where they faced the tougher penalties of a court martial. Some of these were shipped to France under military discipline where the penalty for refusing to obey orders was death by firing squad.

French Revolution. Allen[1] wields the sort of power over them that leaders had then. He is a man of genius – not at all simple, with a curious combination of gifts. At the opening of the Conference, when he first rose, they wanted to cheer him till they were hoarse, but he rang his bell and held out his hand for quiet: they stopped at once, and he began 'Will you turn to p. 1 of The Agenda' – it is something like the way Parnell treated the Irish Members.[2] I have never seen any one comparable to him as a Chairman.

All the intervals were filled up with Committee meetings, so we were all kept pretty busy. I said a few words of sympathy, and they gave me a great cheer.

I really believe they will defeat the Government and wreck Conscription, when it is found they won't yield.

I can't describe to you how happy I am having these men to work with and for – it is *real* happiness all day long – and I feel they can't be defeated, whatever may be done to them. I think of you constantly and wish you were with them – you would love them and feel refreshed by them. They are so splendid.

If I can get away, I should very much like to come for Saturday to Monday the end of this week – but I may be prevented at the last moment, if anything important turns up. Shall I bring Eliot (not Mrs)? I saw them both a moment the other day – she is all right again. I find he has an *intense* desire to see you again – he is rather lonely, and very lovable – I am sure you would like him.[3] I would *much* rather come without him, but he seemed so *very* anxious to come. Now that he has not gone to America he has nothing to do till School Term begins again.

Goodnight my Darling. I love you always, and feel very much with you in spirit in all this.
    Your
      B.

The Conscientious Objectors are holding open-air meetings in Burnley, and the sympathy of the crowd is with them. Some one proposed that P[hilip] should be asked to go down and speak to them. I was *very* sorry he couldn't get in the other night to speak in the House.[4] I *loved* seeing him for a moment in the middle of business.

---

1 Clifford Allen.
2 Charles Stewart Parnell (1846–1891), the Irish nationalist leader. His authority over the Irish members of the House of Commons was unquestioned until his career was ended by scandal.
3 She found him 'dull, dull, dull' (Morrell, *Memoirs*, vol. ii, p. 101).
4 He had tried to ask a question in Parliament, but was not called.

Clifford Allen (1889–1939), later Lord Allen of Hurtwood, whose handling of the NCF's convention gained Russell's admiration, was the undisputed leader of the organization. Educated at Cambridge where he had come under the influence of G.L. Dickinson, he had been manager of a Labour paper, *The Daily Citizen*. The war brought him to prominence among anti-war socialists. He was an astute politician but at the same time possessed such an unassailable moral authority that admirers thought him a saint – a somewhat mind-boggling combination nowadays. He needed both qualities to form the unruly collection of religious pacifists, class-war socialists, and disgruntled liberals who made up the NCF into an effective organization. Russell became deeply attached to him during the war. Allen, like Russell, was a guild socialist, radically critical of capitalism but suspicious of state power. But what most attracted Russell were his personal qualities – his gentleness, moral integrity and, above all, the iron will with which he resisted the years of imprisonment, forced labour, solitary confinement, and punishment regimes by which the military authorities destroyed his health but failed utterly to break his spirit or exact from him the slightest compromise. Allen was rarely far from Russell's thoughts for the rest of the war but, because Allen was so often in jail, there are few wartime letters from Russell to him (and those mostly concern details of NCF business).

Russell made his case against Military Service Act more formally in the following angry letter to Gilbert Murray. Murray had been lecturing in Sweden, ostensibly on classical history, though he was covertly acting for the Foreign Office to try to undermine Swedish sympathy for Germany. Though Murray supported the war, he was not enthusiastic about conscription and appeared himself before tribunals on behalf of COs. None the less, he was surprised to find the idea of non-combatant service so roundly rejected by the NCF and felt it undercut the efforts he was then making to get better treatment for COs. He wrote to Russell asking if there was any way the Military Service Act might be amended to allow a CO to demonstrate that his objection was conscientious and that he was willing to make some sacrifice comparable to that of the men who were conscripted.

28 **[To Gilbert Murray]**   **46, Gordon Square**
                                                                                            17 April 1916

My dear Gilbert,

Your second letter shows the effects of your absence in Sweden, otherwise the decision of the N.C.F. Convention would not have taken you by surprise. It expressed what has been throughout the attitude of about three quarters of the Conscientious Objectors, and indeed to my mind the unavoidable attitude for those among them who are capable of logical thought. Harvey[1] and a few other elderly Quakers, against the corporate opinion of the Friends, particularly of the Young Friends (who are the ones directly concerned), have arrogated to themselves the right to say what conscientious objectors ought to do, and have concealed from the authorities the fact that they disagreed with those for whom they professed to speak. The result has been the production of schemes which never could have been accepted, and which no one in touch with C.O.'s would have ever regarded as affording a possible solution of the problem.

I will try to explain the situation to you.

If you had read the reports of the Tribunals, you would have seen that the Tribunals regarded every form of National Service that is open to a working man as proof positive that the man was not a genuine conscientious objector. A Post Office sorter was condemned because he had sometimes sorted letters for soldiers at the front. A bricklayer was condemned because he had laid some bricks in a building which, when completed, was going to be a munition factory. Examples might be multiplied endlessly. When it was a question whether a plea of conscience should be allowed, the Tribunals saw the logic of the situation quite clearly. But as soon as a man's conscience has been recognized, a complete blindness to logic on the part of the authorities replaced their previous perspicacity.

Most of the C.O.'s hold that under all circumstances it is wrong to take human life. Others, among whom I should be, are not prepared to lay down this proposition universally: They might concede that the Greeks were right to resist the Persians, and that the Franks were right to resist the Moors; they would also concede the hypothetical extreme cases with which opponents are fond of confronting them.[2] But they would say that killing is very seldom justifiable – so seldom, in the modern world, that the exceptions are of hardly any practical importance. They consider wars between civilized States a folly and a crime on both sides, and they do not shrink from the consequences of this opinion. When an opinion is held passionately and vitally, its

---

[1] Thomas Edmund Harvey (1875–1955), Liberal MP for West Leeds. Harvey and another Quaker MP, Arnold Rowntree, had helped draft that part of the Military Service Act which specified the obligation of alternative service. This helps explain Murray's surprise over the opposition to alternative service by many younger Quakers, especially those on the Friends' Service Committee.

[2] It was common at the tribunals to ask the CO what he would do if, e.g., a German soldier were about to rape his sister (a question to which Lytton Strachey famously replied: 'I should attempt to interpose my body between them'). Willingness to use force in such circumstances was taken as grounds against an exemption.

consequences are apt to be seen very clearly and felt very strongly. For this reason, they are led on by their respect for human life to conclusions which are not at once obvious corollaries to those who disagree with the premise.

We, who believe that it is wrong to fight, are bound not only to abstain from fighting ourselves, but to abstain from abetting others in fighting. What would you and the police think of a man who had a conscientious objection to being a burglar, but was willing to undertake 'non-combatant service' by standing in the street and giving warning of the approach of the constable? And as regards 'work of national importance', there are two arguments which I see no way of answering. The first is, that by leaving one's present occupation for some other which the Government judges to be indispensable for the prosecution of the war – such as, say, agriculture – one is liberating others for the trenches, thus both causing others to fight and sheltering behind those who have no conscientious scruples. The second is, that if the Government at this moment demands a change of occupation, the obvious motive is to organize the national resources better for the prosecution of the war, which, to one who objects to all war, appears utterly inconsistent with his principles. For this reason, all schemes such as those you mention seem to many of us to embody a compromise which we could not accept without fundamental treachery to all that we believe.

The question of 'national service' has been endlessly debated among conscientious objectors. Many of them, including Chappelow,[1] have always held that there was no objection to national service, provided it was not directly concerned with the war. The N.C.F., unlike you and the Tribunals, makes no attempt to judge the individual conscience, and has never made any recommendation to its members as to what they should do in this matter. The vote at the Convention was a vote as to what the Fellowship collectively could accept; but the vote was not intended to bind the separate members in any way, though undoubtedly it expressed what most of them felt to be the right course for themselves as individuals, as well as for the Fellowship.

You ask whether I have 'any positive proposal to make by which the Act could be administered or modified' and whether I can suggest

---

1 Eric Chappelow, a poet, whose original exemption had been rescinded on appeal by the military, and who was now held at Kingston barracks. The previous day Chappelow had sent to Russell's friend, the lawyer C.P. Sanger, a horrifying description of the physical and psychological abuse to which he was subjected. Russell took up his case with various influential people (including Murray, who promised to do what he could). But nothing could get him released. He ended up in Wandsworth prison.

any plan by which a conscientious objector can '(a) prove that his objection is a matter of conscience, and (b) show that he is willing to make some sacrifice approximately comparable to that which his fellows are making.' I must reply to this purely as an individual, and you must understand that I cannot speak for the N.C.F.

My first proposal is that an inquiry should be held immediately into the action of the Tribunals, and that meanwhile proceedings against those who claim to be C.O.'s should be suspended. The decisions of the Tribunals were biased, variable in principle, and often illegal. Very many men who are quite obviously sincere have failed entirely to convince the Tribunals. I think if this inquiry were conceded, and those who have claimed to be C.O.'s were set at liberty meanwhile, there would be time to consider further schemes. Otherwise, nothing can be satisfactory, since nothing will relieve those who have been unjustly condemned.

As to proving that the objection is a matter of conscience, what has been and is being endured by C.O.'s is abundant proof. After the ordeal they have been through, a simple affirmation would be sufficient.

As to 'equality of sacrifice', I am astonished that you can mention such a thing in this connection. The sacrifice of the C.O.'s is immensely greater than that of men at the front. So far as I can see, the risk they run of being shot by the military authorities in France is as great as the risk the ordinary soldier runs of being shot by the Germans. They are being informed in barracks, with what truth I cannot judge, that they are to be sent to France; and the law certainly gives the military authorities power to shoot them for disobedience at the Front. At Guildford, in civil trial of Alfred Paice, Major W. MacLaughlin, chief Recruiting Officer, being asked 'supposing he refused to put on the uniform of the King and goes on disobeying orders, what will the consequences be?', replied 'He may be shot in the end.' Like ordinary deserters, they would merely appear in casualty lists; the public would not know the manner of their death, and you would not believe it. Those who escape this fate will have long terms of hard labour or solitary confinement in military prisons. And every imaginative person knows that obloquy and the active contempt of those among whom one is compelled to live is far harder to bear than the prospect of death.

Almost all the C.O.'s have a much greater sense of public duty than the average man. They are intensely desirous of serving the community. But for the moment they see no better way of serving it than by suffering for their faith. Many of them are somewhat impatient of any talk about persecution; it is sympathisers not subject to the Act who feel the persecution intolerable. Do you consider that Lloyd George during the Boer war ought to have abandoned politics for mangold wurzels?[1]

Of course we are opposed to the Act: you cannot expect men who disapprove of war to be in favour of Conscription. But it is not our primary object to defeat the Act by agitation: our primary object is to take no part ourselves in what we regard as a crime. Of course we wish, like the rest of mankind, to bring others to our way of thinking; but our action is not due to this wish. Our action would be the same if we knew that we should all be shot and public opinion would be unaffected by our death.

Yours,
B. Russell.

P.S. You say in your pamphlet on the foreign policy of Sir E. Grey that in England those who oppose wars are 'unpopular, but nothing more' – or words to that effect.[2] I hope you will delete this passage in your next edition.

On 11 May Russell took the COs' case to Asquith, the Prime Minister, as part of a deputation consisting of Catherine Marshall, Philip Morrell, and Philip Snowden. They hoped to get the government to reform the operation of the tribunals, to admit absolute exemptions, and to have all COs dealt with under civil rather than military law. The government conceded much of this in the so-called 'Home Office Scheme' which came into force in July. A more urgent issue dominated the meeting, however, for on 8 May the first COs had arrived in France where they could be shot for desertion if they continued to refuse orders. Here, too, the meeting was a success. Asquith was genuinely concerned and, although he did not offer the group any firm assurances at the time, his private secretary wrote to Marshall the next day to inform her that General Haig, commander of the British forces in France, had received an order that no COs were to be shot for refusing to obey orders. None the less, thirty-four of them were condemned to death, though in each case the sentence was commuted to ten years' penal servitude.

---

1 David Lloyd George, in 1916 the minister responsible for munitions, had been a pacifist and had opposed the Boer War, for which he was almost lynched by an angry mob in Birmingham in 1901.
2 The remark occurs in the first paragraph of Murray's *The Foreign Policy of Sir Edward Grey.*

[To Ottoline Morrell]　　　　　　　　　　[Trinity College?]　　**29**
　　　　　　　　　　　　　　　　　　　　[12 May 1916]
　　　　　　　　　　　　　　　　　　　　Friday

My Darling

You will have heard from P[hilip] about the P.M. I was immensely encouraged by the occasion; the old man knew so much about the question that one could not doubt the genuineness of his interest. He was very sympathetic and talked almost as if he were one of us – how weak he is to yield as he does on every occasion. I thought he was prepared to exert himself to prevent C.O.'s being shot, and he seemed to realize they would be if they were sent to France. I rather liked him. I said practically nothing, because he was so satisfactory that I thought anything I might say would only put his back up.[1] P. was *admirable*.

Yes, there is the beginning of a reaction against brutality. The case of Skeffington has shocked people.[2] And the Press is getting much better about C.O.'s. That is largely Miss Marshall's doing; she is very good with the Press.

I am *intensely* disliked by the older dons, and still more by their wives, who think I should not mind if they were raped. It is the young who like me.

I *long* to stump the country on a stop-the-war campaign. The time has come. By June 10 I shall be free;[3] I don't think then there will be anything to do for the C.O.'s. We must get Snowden into it. The *Labour Leader* accounts of May Day in Scotland are *most* encouraging.[4]

A man in Wales got a long term of imprisonment for distributing a leaflet about Everitt [*sic*.], which I wrote. Why do they let me alone?

Goodbye till Monday – I shall be in London tomorrow and Sunday. Much love, my Darling. I do feel hope in the air.

　　Your
　　　　B.

---

1 Philip Morrell had invited Russell to join the delegation to 'supply any ginger that may be lacking' in the others.
2 Francis Sheehy Skeffington was an Irish journalist and pacifist. He was not involved in the Dublin Easter uprising, but was arrested on 25 April during the course of its suppression and shot the next morning without trial, along with two other radical journalists. His execution provoked a wave of revulsion in Britain and a subsequent inquiry conveniently found that the officer who ordered it was insane.
3 The end of term at Cambridge.
4 That day the *Labour Leader* (the journal of the ILP) reported that the May Day celebrations in Scotland had taken the form of large demonstrations for peace which had provoked very little opposition.

The reference in the previous letter to the 'leaflet about Everitt' marks the beginning of Russell's first legal battle with the wartime government. In April the NCF had issued an anonymous leaflet written by Russell about the case of Ernest Everett, a pacifist schoolteacher, who had refused non-combatant service and been sentenced to two years' hard labour. On 4 May, two Welsh members of the NCF were fined £10 and jailed for one month for distributing the leaflet; shortly afterwards three other members were arrested for the same offence. Russell tried to force the authorities to act by writing to *The Times* (17 May) admitting his authorship of the offending leaflet. But they held back, reluctant to give him any fresh publicity, until they were prompted by the Foreign Office which had reasons of its own for wanting Russell charged (see Letter **33**). On 30 May he was summonsed for 'impeding recruiting and discipline', a somewhat bizarre charge, as Russell pointed out in court, since the leaflet merely chronicled Everett's case and noted the savagery of his sentence – an unlikely way of encouraging others to follow his example.

30   **[To Ottoline Morrell]**   **[Trinity College?]**
1 June 1916
Thursday

My Darling
    Thank you very much for your letter which came this morning. I wrote you a hurried line yesterday to catch the post – now I will tell all there is.
    On Monday night, two detectives called at my flat just after I had started to come back here – the door was opened to them by Clifford Allen,[1] who told them I was here. On Tuesday morning they came here and served a summons on me, for impeding recruiting and discipline by the Everett leaflet. They had that and my letter to the *Times* with them, and asked if I acknowledged authorship. They were quite pleasant and polite. Yesterday I saw the solicitor, George Baker, who always acts for the N.C.F.: it appears that I have an appeal to Quarter Sessions, which can't come in till September, so as I shall certainly appeal nothing can happen to me till then. We decided (as I wished) that I should defend myself in the first Court, and employ a barrister at the Appeal Court. My own view is that the leaflet is not illegal, but they *must* convict me because of the obscure men whom they have already convicted for the same leaflet. I think it is a gross violation of the law to convict on it; but of course I am not anxious to secure

---
1 Russell and Allen were sharing Russell's flat.

an acquittal. It is delightful to have brought it on in just this way – a way which no one can regard as wanton or groundlessly provocative, because there were the poor men to champion. I fully expect them to inflict only a fine. I wonder if they will call Lord Derby.[1] I should enjoy cross-examining him.

After seeing the lawyer, I met Allen and the rest of them, and they did the obvious things in the way of publicity. The lawyer had nothing much to say. He obviously felt certain of an adverse verdict, but whether fine or imprisonment he didn't say. I think his professional instinct is worried by these cases in which people don't wish to get off. All the same, if I could get off by the sheer merits of the case it would of course be a good thing, as it would involve the liberation of the others who have been prosecuted. But I think there is no real chance of that.

My brother and Elizabeth[2] were coming to me tomorrow but I have to see the lawyer then; so I went to their house to put them off – found Elizabeth, who is desperate, and *begged* me to come to Telegraph House[3] for a few days. So I am afraid I *must* go for WhitSunday. After that, I must have 10 days' real holiday before I go to South Wales, which will probably be June 24.[4] But I have stipulated for one day a week with no meetings, so I shall be able to come to Garsington for a night sometimes. I *do* want to see you. I suppose there is no chance of your being in town? If not, would it suit if I came Wednesday for the night? I would arrive 12.10 and leave Thursday 10.50. I feel I shall make a fiasco of my case – it is such an opportunity that I feel nervous. But I am loving it really. Ever since I got in with the N.C.F. life has been full of happiness.

I was going to Crompton[5] for the week-end but have had to put it off and stay in town. I am there tomorrow till Monday.

Goodbye my Darling. Your letters make me *very* happy.

Your

B.

---

1 Lord Derby was Director-General of Recruiting. Presumably he might have been called to testify that recruiting had actually been impeded, though in the event Russell did not get the chance to cross-examine him.
2 They had married in February.
3 Frank Russell's home on the South Downs. The precise cause of Elizabeth's desperation is not recorded, though earlier she had complained to Bertie that Frank slept with seven dogs on his bed and read Kipling aloud – either of which might seem sufficient (*Autobiography*, vol. ii, p. 54).
4 Russell's hope 'to stump the country on a stop-the-war campaign' (Letter **29**) had come to fruition with a speaking tour of South Wales. The tour ran from 1 to 24 July.
5 Crompton LLewelyn Davies (1868-1935), one of Russell's oldest friends from his student days in Cambridge.

Russell was tried on 5 June, found guilty and fined £100 plus £10 costs or sixty-one days in jail. His appeal (which was heard on 29 June, not in September as he had expected) was dismissed and he refused to pay the fine. There was little danger of his going to jail, however, since the bailiffs seized his furniture and books and put them up for auction to pay the fine. But his library was saved by a group of friends, organized by Philip Morrell, who covered the fine and costs with a bid for the first lot. Despite his misgivings, Russell made a good show at his trial, which was attended by Ottoline and several other friends, including Evelyn Whitehead. (An account of the proceedings can be found in *Papers,* vol.xiii, pp. 380–407. Russell gives his own account of the case in 'For Conscience Sake', below pp. 203-208, which also includes the text of the offending leaflet on Everett.)

31 [To Ottoline Morrell] [Trinity College]
[8 June 1916]
Thursday afternoon

My Darling

I was very glad of your letter which came this morning. I am *so* glad you thought I did well. The excitement has produced its reaction, and I feel incredibly tired. But I am going to have a holiday so it doesn't matter. Saturday I shall be in London for lunch, then I go to Cardiff for N.C.F. Committee Sunday – from there I shall come back to Garsington as early Monday as it can be managed. My last days here are terribly busy – meetings and lectures all day long. I shall be glad to get away.

This morning I had a visit from a Girtonian named Miss Wrinch,[1] whom I had never seen before. She wants to learn logic, but Girton doesn't want her to, and threatens to deprive her of her scholarship if she does. She has just finished her mathematical tripos, and is just the sort of person who ought to do it – she is very keen, but has not a penny beyond her scholarship, and is at the mercy of Miss Jex-Blake,[2] a Churchy old fool. It makes me mad. If she could get £80 a year, she would ignore the College. But she doesn't see how to. If I had it, I would take her on as my Secretary. But I don't see how I can manage it.[3]

Ogden tried to report in the *Magazine* Snowden's remarks in the House about C.O.'s taken to France – but the Censor forbade any

---

1 Dorothy Wrinch (1894–1976), she became a Fellow of Girton and had a distinguished scientific career in Britain and America.
2 Katharine Jex-Blake (1860–1951), Mistress of Girton College.
3 In the end Russell tutored her privately in logic each week, in return for which she did odd jobs for him.

mention of it.[1] Ogden doesn't dare to say one word about my case beyond what has already appeared in patriotic papers.[2]

I don't have the *option* of 6l days – if I don't pay, I am sold up, and if my goods don't realize £110, then I get 61 days, but not otherwise. It is doubtful if the appeal comes in quite soon or in three months. I don't want to be in prison just now. P. will get a full report of my speech in the course of nature – you can get it from him.

If you are going to be in London Monday and Tuesday, I could see you there, which would be *delightful*. After that I must seize the moment for a holiday, as I start in South Wales June 24.

The Skeffington business is *horrible*. They ought to Court-Martial the people who put a madman in a position of authority.

Goodbye my Darling. I love you with all my soul, and feel very near you in spirit.

Your
B.

Russell's speaking tour of South Wales was delayed slightly by the appeal of his conviction and did not start until 1 July. It was Russell's first experience of stump oratory and, despite some initial misgivings, it went off well. Russell was evidently surprised by the support he got from the Welsh workers. Plainclothes policemen attended his meetings and duly took down what he said.

[To Ottoline Morrell]   **[Grand Hotel]**
Port Talbot
[4 July 1916]
Tuesday morning

My Darling

I have just got back here and found your letter, which was a great joy to get. It is the first letter of any sort or kind that has reached me since I left London – I did not know what address to give Mrs. Saich.[3]

---

1 In question period on 9 May, Snowden had asked the Prime Minister whether COs taken to France would be shot.
2 *The Cambridge Magazine* reported Russell's conviction on 10 June in the form of a long, unattributed press report. Ogden did, however, append the following comment: 'It is not part of our programme to incur the displeasure of the powers that be, and since we understand that it is now illegal to give publicity either to the treatment of objectors or even to the behaviour of Tribunals, the Editorial Committee has no option but to omit from this issue some four pages in which these matters were to have been dealt with.' He also pointed out that Russell's defence speech could be found in *The Labour Leader*. Ogden, in fact, was having trouble with his printer and publisher who were refusing to publish anything not cleared by the censor.
3 Russell's housekeeper in London.

The state of feeling here is quite astonishing. This town subsists on one enormous steel works, the largest in South Wales; the men are starred,[1] and earning very good wages; they are not suffering from the war in any way. Yet they seem all to be against it. On Sunday afternoon I had an open-air meeting on a green: there were two Chapels on the green, and their congregations came out just before I began. They stayed to listen. A crowd of about 400 came – not like open-air meetings in the South, when people stay a few minutes out of curiosity, and then go away – they all stayed the whole time, listened with the closest attention, and seemed unanimously sympathetic. The man who has been organizing for me here works 12 hours every day except Sunday in the steel works. Their energy is wonderful.

Sunday evening I spoke at Briton Ferry – a really *wonderful* meeting – the hall was packed, they were *all* at the highest point of enthusiasm – they inspired me, and I spoke as I have never spoken before. We put a resolution in favour of immediate peace negotiations, which was carried unanimously. (I did not notice any abstentions, though presumably the two plain-clothes men who had come to take notes must have abstained.) Those who had not already signed the peace petition signed it in large numbers.[2] One needs no prudent reticences – no humbug of any sort – one can just speak out one's whole mind. I thought the great offensive would have excited them, but it hasn't.[3]

Yesterday evening I spoke at Ystradgynlais, a mining town of 16,000 inhabitants. The meeting was smaller, and my impression was that a good many people at it were undecided in their minds – that sort of meeting is really more useful than an enthusiastic one. The audience were almost all miners. They seemed intelligent and thoughtful.

I enclose a little leaflet which is distributed at my meetings.[4] If you don't burn it at once, you are liable to imprisonment.

My next address is
        c/o Mrs Morrison,
        322 Whitchurch Rd. Cardiff.

---

1 Men in starred occupations (i.e. those considered essential to the war effort) were exempt from conscription.
2 This was a petition calling for peace negotiations organized by the Peace Negotiations Committee. Various organizations were involved in it, including the NCF. Russell was among its sponsors. The petition was eventually presented to the Prime Minister in August 1917 with 221,000 signatures.
3 The allied offensive on the Somme started on 1 July after five days' preliminary bombardment. The British suffered 60,000 casualties (20,000 killed) on the first day – the heaviest loss in one day suffered by any army in World War I. General Haig had managed to persuade himself that the war could be won at the Somme and clung to this delusion until mid-November, a million casualties later, when the offensive finally petered out in the mud having achieved absolutely nothing of importance.
4 Probably the leaflet *Why Not Peace Negotiations?* (see *Papers*, vol. xiii, p. 418).

I speak in Cardiff on the 6th. I don't know where I shall stay, but she is organizing my meetings in that neighbourhood.

Tell P. from me to hang on, to fight tooth and nail, to insist on meeting his whole Association, to address them in a long and eloquent speech.[1] It won't be long before they forgive him, and he must manage somehow to pull through the time till then.

It is *awful* having Lloyd George and Lord Derby at the War Office.[2] The worst feature of Asquith's statement is that it involves distinguishing between religious and socialist C.O.'s.[3] Those who are not vouched for by Ministers of Religion are to be punished worse than ever.

After I had left the Committee on Saturday they abandoned the idea of a Convention, which was obviously rather impracticable.[4] They seem to have not arrived at any definite solution, but I don't think they will break up. I heard what had occurred from Davies, the Welsh member of the National Committee, who took the chair for me Sunday night.

Many thanks for the three silly books which arrived all right.[5]

Yes I should like some Congreve etc. very much. At least I should like Vanbrugh[6] – I have read Congreve not long ago. I have leisure in the mornings as a rule – except for journeys. Then I collect my thoughts for the evening. I am not unhappy at all, quite the contrary. But I shall be very grateful for letters, and for everything you can tell me. I am afraid there is very little hope of the war ending this year. I feel little doubt that I shall spend the winter in prison, but I don't think I should mind much, because I should not feel it was a waste of time.[7]

---

1 Philip Morrell was still in trouble with his riding association over his opposition to the war.
2 On 5 June, Lord Kitchener, the British war minister, had been killed when the ship on which he was sailing to Russia hit a mine – he was the only prominent military leader to be killed in action in the entire war. His death could not have come at a better time, since he was widely held to be responsible for the failures of the British war effort and ambitious politicians were anxious to take over from him. On 6 July Lloyd George became Secretary of State for War and Lord Derby, formerly the minister in charge of recruiting, his Under-Secretary.
3 On 29 June, Asquith announced details of the Home Office Scheme to Parliament: COs sentenced by court martial would have their cases reviewed by the Central Tribunal, they would be released if the tribunal found their objection genuine, otherwise they would be returned to detention barracks to complete their sentence. Asquith's statement ended with a strong restatement of the distinction between genuine and spurious conscientious objection – a distinction widely assumed to be co-extensive with the distinction between religious and non-religious objection. Asquith assured Parliament that fraudulent objectors would be treated with 'the utmost rigour'.
4 Presumably because most of those who might convene were now in jail.
5 It is not clear which books Ottoline sent. Her letters to Bertie while he was in Wales seem to be lost.
6 William Congreve (1670–1729) and John Vanbrugh (1664–1726), two Restoration dramatists.
7 There was clearly some danger of this. The Director of Public Prosecutions decided in the end that a prosecution would do Russell's cause more good than harm. Instead he proposed a press ban on reporting Russell's speeches.

Is there any hope of Casement's sentence being commuted?[1]

Do write as much and as fully as you can. I shall be *very* grateful for letters all this time. My love is with you every moment, my Dearest.

Your
   B.

Stump oratory, though exhilarating, was also a strain; it was not the sort of activity one could keep up for long periods. Moreover, it made little use of Russell's intellectual talents and he began to consider what he would do after the war. There were, in any case, external reasons for him to reconsider his academic career. In January he had received an invitation from Harvard inviting him to return as a lecturer for six months starting in February 1917. One of the offer's chief attractions for Russell was that he was asked to teach a course on politics as well as ones on philosophy and logic. He accepted and arranged leave of absence from Trinity, while Harvard arranged other speaking engagements for him across America. However, as he told Harvard, there was a possibility the British government would not allow him to leave the country. To improve his chances it was decided that Harvard would approach the British embassy in Washington for permission on his behalf. On receipt of this request the British ambassador cabled the Foreign Office for advice. The issue was delicate. American opinion was important to Britain, and British hopes of bringing America into the war might be harmed if Russell stumped the country talking peace. On the other hand, if they prevented Russell from taking up an academic position at Harvard by bureaucratic *fiat* it might undermine their pretensions to the benign liberalism with which they hoped to keep America's sympathy. The Foreign Office therefore, on 29 May, asked the Home Office whether it planned proceedings against Russell which would 'pave the way for refusing to issue a passport' (minutes in PRO). This, rather than Russell's letter to *The Times*, seems to have spurred the Home Office into action, for the next day it summonsed Russell under the Defence of the Realm Act (DORA) over the Everett leaflet. Once Russell had been convicted the Foreign Office could refuse him a passport on apparently principled grounds. This they did, two days after Russell's conviction – and three

---

[1] Sir Roger Casement (1864–1916) had made his reputation as a British consul in Africa where he had exposed atrocities committed by Belgian colonists in the Congo. Ill health forced him to retire to Ireland in 1912. Early in the war he travelled to Germany to seek German support for an Irish uprising against British rule. The Germans refused, but the Irish decided to go ahead anyway during Easter 1916. Casement, who thought German help was essential, travelled back to Ireland to try to stop the uprising. He was caught, convicted of treason and sentenced to death. Despite pleas for the sentence to be commuted, he was executed on 3 August.

weeks before his appeal. The British ambassador in Washington duly informed Harvard. Russell received the news on 7 July.

Meanwhile, Russell's conviction under DORA got him into trouble at Trinity, where a motion removing him from his lectureship was passed unanimously by the college council on 11 July 1916. In this, council was helped by not having given Russell a fellowship the previous year – fellows were far harder to remove than lecturers. As it was, the council's vote occasioned a bitter split within the college: twenty-two Fellows signed a memorial to the council objecting to the decision. Writing to Ottoline, the day before the Council's vote, Russell had no illusions about the likely outcome and turned his thoughts enthusiastically to a philosopher's life outside the established academic system.

[To Ottoline Morrell]   **[Central Hotel]**   33
[Merthyr Tydfil]
[10 July 1916]
Monday evening

My Darling

Your letter to Pontypridd reached me today – I was very glad to have it. I missed the *Times* leader on the C.O.'s but saw various letters about it next day[1] – not one from P. – I suppose his was not put in. It seems clear things will be better for many of them henceforth, but the thing still needs urging. We have been so many times flattered with false hopes.

I am sure I shall *love* Shelley's letters.[2] I have read both the Stendhal novels and loved them.[3]

Many thanks for sending me *The Manchester Guardian* leader – I am glad to have it. I am very glad my brother did so well.[4] He was stirred up by the case of Norman,[5] whom he knows well.

---

1 *The Times* ran a lead article, 'A Policy for Conscientious Objectors', on 6 July urging a relatively moderate position. Most of the letters which followed also urged that genuine conscientious objection should be recognized.
2 A new two-volume edition of Shelley's *Letters*, edited by Roger Inkpen, had been published in 1915.
3 Presumably *Le Rouge et le Noir* (1830) and *La Chartreuse de Parme* (1839).
4 On 4 July in the House of Lords, Frank Russell had cunningly proposed 'That in the opinion of this House it is undesirable to subject military prisoners to punishments not authorized by law'. Had they rejected the motion the Lords would have explicitly approved illegal punishments; in passing it they implicitly criticized the government's treatment of COs. The *Manchester Guardian* reported the debate on 5 July.
5 Clarence Henry Norman, one of the leaders of the NCF and the first to be arrested. He was an abrasive personality with a will of iron which he pitted against Lt. Col Brooke, the commandant of Wandsworth Detention Barracks. Brooke treated him with great savagery, confining him for long periods in a straight-jacket and force-feeding him even when he was not on hunger strike. But it was an unequal battle, and Brooke was relieved of his command when the NCF brought his brutality to the attention of the Prime Minister.

I am afraid I must have written rather a worried letter. I had the feeling of a mouse walking into a trap – but I don't really mind – I can be just as useful in prison as out of it. I should rather enjoy the leisure to think things out in prison – and I should be immensely glad to have had the experience.

Today I had lunch and a country walk with the Rev. Morgan Jones,[1] a prominent pacifist here and a real saint. Then I went to a neighbouring town for a meeting – it was to have been in the school, but that was refused at the last moment, so we had it in the open air. A Unitarian Minister spoke who has a son a C.O. It is wonderful what the C.O.'s have done for the cause of peace – the heroism is no longer all on the side of war.

I ought to have gone into more hostile districts. Here it is merely a pic-nic and I feel I should be better employed in town. After the 23rd I shall be back in town – by then most of our National Committee will be gone.

I am *longing* to know how Allen's visit went off.[2] I am so terribly afraid it will have been a failure.

Speaking is a great nervous strain – I feel very slack all the rest of the time. But I sleep well and my mind is at peace so I don't get *really* tired. I never have any fundamental worries now-a-days.

I realize that as soon as the worst of the stress is over I shall want some more intellectual occupation. But I see room for endless work on political theory. And it will have the advantage that it will involve seeing all sorts of people and getting to know all sorts of human facts – it won't leave half of me unsatisfied as abstract work does. The only doubt is whether I shan't some day be suddenly overwhelmed by the passion for the things that are eternal and perfect, like mathematics. Even the most abstract political theory is terribly mundane and temporary. But that must be left to the future.

It is very sad seeing you so seldom. I feel as if we should lose intimacy and get out of the way of speaking of personal things – it would be a great loss if that happened. I know extraordinarily little of your inner life now-a-days, and I wish I knew more, but I don't know how to elicit it. My own existence has become so objective that I

---

[1] Another leader of the NCF. With ten other members he had recently been convicted for publishing a pamphlet calling for the repeal of the Military Service Act. It was not in itself illegal to call for the Act's repeal, but to do so was considered to be impeding recruitment, which was illegal.

[2] Clifford Allen had been visiting Garsington, largely at Russell's insistence. It was not a great success. 'He was good-looking in an etherial, Shelley-like style, but rather surburban', Ottoline commented haughtily (*Memoirs*, vol. ii, p. 147).

hardly have an inner life any more for the present – but I should have if I had leisure.

I shall be very poor, having lost America and probably Trinity. I shall have to find some other way of making money. I think if Trinity turns me out I shall advertize academic lectures in London on philosophical subjects. It would be delightful if they succeeded, as they wouldn't interfere with political work. I have often dreamt of having an independent school like Abelard.[1] It might lead to great things. I feel I am only on the threshold of life – the rest has been preparation – I mean as far as work is concerned. Quite lately I have somehow found myself. I have poise and sanity. I no longer have the feeling of powers unrealized within me, which used to be a perpetual torture. I don't care what the authorities do to me, they can't stop me long. Before, I have felt either wicked or passively resigned – now I feel fully active and contented with my activity. I have no inward discords any more – and nothing ever really troubles me.

My Dearest I am *full* of love to you – visions are always in my mind of happy days after the war, when we shall get back to poetry and beauty and summer moods, and the vision of things outside this earth. But the war keeps one tied to earth. And sometimes I wonder if we have both grown so impersonal that it has become difficult to give oneself to personal love – it always was difficult for you. It is a great loss if it is so – I hope it isn't. *Do* write a full letter when you *can*, and tell me something of your inward life.

Goodnight my Darling Ottoline.
Your
   B.

Address   Thursday night, Royal Hotel, Cardiff.
             Friday and Saturday nights, Russell Chambers.

Russell's plans for a life as an independent teacher developed quickly thanks largely to Clifford Allen. Soon after Russell had been thrown out of Trinity, Allen proposed that he prepare another series of lectures, more popular in tone than 'Principles of Social Reconstruction', to be delivered in different cities. Before Allen's arrest on 31 July, he had arranged for talks to be given in Manchester, Glasgow, Leicester, Bristol, Birmingham, Edinburgh and

---

1 Peter Abelard (1079–1144), another logician who was constantly in trouble with the authorities.

Newcastle. Russell, just back from Wales, took up his pen again. Though 'terrified at the prospect of plunging into writing' (to Ottoline, 30 July) and 'most frightfully tired' (17 August), he soon found that he could 'write faster than any typist can keep up with me' (16 Sept.). The first lecture was given in Manchester on 16 October. The title for the lectures was 'The World As It Can Be Made'; they were published (in America only) as *Political Ideals* (1917). At the beginning of September he reported on his work and on his personal life to Ottoline.

34 [To Ottoline Morrell]   57 Gordon Sq.[1]
1 September 1916

My Darling

I got a letter from you at Telegraph House just as I was starting yesterday, and another (a *very* dear letter) this morning here. You have not done any mischief at all[2] – there had to be a readjustment, and I have only been doing what I felt necessary in any case on account of my work. Yesterday I came up by way of Chichester, and had a talk with Eliot there (I didn't see Mrs E. who was ill); it was rather gloomy, but I got quite clear as to what must be done, so I shan't worry any more. It is fixed that I go to Bosham[3] Monday to Friday; then I don't expect to see her during the winter – seeing her is worrying, and takes up my time and money and her health. I shall go on doing what I have done in the way of money during the winter, but beyond that I have said I can't foresee what will be possible. I can't now decide anything beyond this winter.

The whole matter has left me very dry and unemotional, not expansive but only wanting to work. It really was not anything except the need of economizing time and money that decided me. I found that although I *can* make money quite easily, I shall have more influence and do better work if I don't have to think about money. And for the moment I have so much to do that all personal things seem like an interruption.

---

1 After he had been dismissed from Trinity, Russell had no permanent address, having sublet his flat as an economy measure. His brother came to his rescue by offering accommodation in his London house, 57 Gordon Square.
2 Ottoline's letter is lost and it is not known what mischief she feared having caused. Presumably it concerned Vivien Eliot.
3 A fishing village near Portsmouth where the Eliots had spent the summer. The summer had gone well, except that Vivien's health had once more given way towards the end of their stay. Tom had to return to London at the beginning of September, but Vivien was to stay on a few extra days to try and restore her health. It seems Russell was to join her, though in the end he was unable to.

Yesterday when I got home I was interviewed by the correspondent of the *New York Evening Post*,[1] and wrote a million letters. Today I go to Suffolk to see Norman and the other C.O.'s who are working there under the Home Office scheme. Tomorrow and Sunday I have to make a memorandum for the N.C.F. and see a Serbian Professor of Philosophy whose book I reviewed in *Mind* some years ago.[2] At Telegraph House I did a lot of writing at my lectures.

The effect of so much work is that I feel simply a machine, incapable of feeling – all poetry and all sense of beauty goes out of me, and I can't imagine doing anything for pleasure except rest. I shall have to go on in this way till Xmas time. I rather hate it. It seems to kill out so much. But I don't see how I can help it.

I think Rumania's intervention may help to shorten the war.[3] There seems no doubt now that the Allies will win.

After this next week, I shall like to come to Garsington. Matters with Mrs E. will be decided then. I never contemplated risking my reputation with her, and I never risked it so far as I can judge.

I *am* glad you are going on with your writing. I long to see it. I am glad Keynes got nice and that you liked the Murrys.[4]

The N.C.F. work does not have the joy in it that it had, because all the vigorous and delightful people who used to be on the Committee are in gaol. I miss Allen terribly.

I do hope I shall be able to come to Garsington 10 days from today. There is no fire or enthusiasm left in me, only grim will. One must exist till the war stops, and then begin to live again.

Goodbye my Darling.
Your
    B.

---

1 The interview appeared on 11 October (it is reprinted in *Papers*, vol. xiii, pp. 500–3). Russell was identified in it only as 'Mathematicus', though the disguise was very thin.
2 Branislav Petronievics (1875–1954). Russell had reviewed the first volume of his *Principien der Metaphysik* very critically in *Mind* (1905). Petronievics had written a pained letter to Russell's friend, Louis Couturat, protesting that he had been completely misunderstood. Central to their disagreement was Petronievics' belief that the number of points in space was not only finite but computable. Petronievics had been in the great retreat of the Serbian army when the Central Powers invaded Serbia. Russell was anxious to hear of his war experiences, but Petronievics wished only to convince him of the number of points in space. Russell gave an amusing account of their meeting in *Portraits from Memory*, p. 25.
3 Romania had entered the war on the Allied side on 27 August. By the beginning of October her army was routed and Bucharest fell in early December.
4 'The Murrys' were Katherine Mansfield (1888–1923), the New Zealand short-story writer, and John Middleton Murry (1889–1957), the writer and critic. They were not yet married. Keynes regularly spent weekends at Garsington through the summer of 1916, but without Ottoline's letter we do not know why he got nice.

In the previous letter Russell mentioned his intention to visit COs at an alternative service camp in Haverhill, Suffolk. News of this had reached the Home Office, which administered the alternative service scheme, where it caused some small panic. Fearing a disturbance among the COs, MI5 was asked to use its wartime powers to ban Russell from all 'prohibited areas', which included the coast and certain sensitive military and industrial areas. The official purpose of these bans was to frustrate spies and saboteurs. The government would be hard pressed to make a case for including Russell in either category, and the Home Secretary quickly got cold feet and asked MI5 to rescind the order and impose one which would prevent Russell from addressing COs. The Home Office was anxious to avoid another court case, since they had not come out of the last one particularly well. 'He would make a clever defence and would publish it as a pamphlet', warned Edward Troup, Permanent Under-Secretary (Clark, *Life*, p. 297). MI5, however, had little to fear from the courts, since it acted through a War Office Order, and upheld the banning order, claiming that it was essential to prevent Russell from airing his 'vicious tenets among dockers, miners and transport workers' (Col. Kell of MI5, quoted in Vellacott, *Russell and the Pacifists*, p. 93). The order was served on Russell just before his trip to Haverhill. Apart from preventing him speaking to the COs, it caused problems for the lecture tour he was planning for later in the year. Russell lost no time in organizing his defence.

35 **[To Ottoline Morrell]** **57 Gordon Square**
1 September 1916

I had a queer adventure today. About 12 o'clock, two men in plain clothes from Scotland Yard appeared on behalf of the War Office, and served a notice on me ordering me not to go into any prohibited area. I was just going to Suffolk, but I had to give it up. I have also had to give up going to Sussex on Monday. I shall also have to give up lecturing at Glasgow, Edinburgh and Newcastle as I had intended to do. I have no notion why they served the notice on me, or whether there is any hope of getting it rescinded.[1] I spent the rest of the day seeing the Press. Massingham[2] promised a leader; the *Daily News* and the *Manchester Guardian* were sympathetic; the *Chronicle* fairly hopeful; and the average newspapers willing to take it as news.[3] I am much more

---

1 Russell attempted to get it rescinded through negotiations with General George Cockerill at the War Office. Cockerill offered to rescind it if Russell would give an 'honourable undertaking' to 'abandon political propaganda'. Russell, understandably, refused to give any such undertaking. (See his accounts of the negotiations, *Papers*, vol. xiii, pp. 456–62.)
2 Henry Massingham (1860–1924), editor of the *Nation*.
3 A number of papers carried the story briefly on 2 Sept. The *Daily News* included some of Russell's comments on the decision.

angry than over anything yet. It is a power conferred on them for dealing with spies, and they choose to suppose that I want to give military information to the Germans. It makes my blood boil. Fortunately Oxfordshire is not a prohibited area. Probably all my letters will be read by the Censor, so prudence in writing is desirable. I think it is utterly outrageous to put such an indignity upon me. But I had an amusing afternoon seeing journalists, from the *Times* to the *Daily Sketch*.
    B.

On 31 July Russell had gone to the Lavender Hill Police Station in London to give moral support to Clifford Allen who was surrendering to the authorities there. When Russell arrived, Allen and a small group of supporters from the NCF were already there. Among them was a twenty-year-old actress, Lady Constance Malleson, who used the stage name Colette O'Niel. (The unusual spelling was the result of a spelling mistake.) She was the youngest daughter of the fifth Earl of Annesley and his second wife, Priscilla Armitage Moore, an ill-sorted couple by Colette's own account: 'He was thirty-five years older than she – and they had not a taste in common' (Malleson, *After Ten Years*, p. 13). Colette had been educated at boarding school, finished in Paris, and presented at court, but there her deference to convention ended. She had agreed to be a debutante on condition that she be allowed to go to drama school. There she became, first, an agnostic, then a member of the ILP, and finally a pacifist. When Russell met her she was working for the NCF, keeping their meticulous records on individual COs. Her acting career started well and continued for many years after the war, though during the war she had difficulty getting parts – probably for political reasons.

    In her memoir, *After Ten Years* (1931), she described her first impression of Russell:

> A small man, with a fine brow, aristocratic features, silver-grey hair, and a passionate expression. He was conventionally dressed in dark clothes and he wore a high, stiff collar. He sat very still, his hands inert upon his knees. He seemed detached in mind and body – but all the furies of hell raged in his eyes.
>
> (p. 104)

Russell for his part saw that she was 'young and very beautiful' and learnt from Allen that 'she was generous with her time, free in her opinions, and wholehearted in her pacifism'. 'On these data,' he said, 'I naturally took steps to get to know her better' (*Autobiography*, vol. ii, p. 25).

His chance came on 13 September, when they were seated next to each other at dinner at a restaurant in Soho. Afterwards Russell and Gilbert Cannan walked with her to her flat where Cannan was staying, and she found herself 'hoping Russell would not come in' because 'Cannan had a way of preventing any real talk – and one did not want any but very real talk with Russell'. Russell did not go in, but 'walked off, a curiously lonely figure, in the direction of Gordon Square' (*After Ten Years*, p. 106). Their third meeting was on 23 September at a two-day NCF convention, where Russell was one of the main speakers and received a huge ovation. Afterwards they dined together and Russell once more walked her home. This time they were alone and she invited him in. He stayed till the early hours and they became lovers, though they did not sleep together that night because, as Russell put it, 'there was too much to say'. 'We scarcely knew each other,' Russell wrote in his *Autobiography*, 'and yet in that moment there began for both of us a relation profoundly serious and profoundly important, sometimes happy, sometimes painful, but never trivial' (vol. ii, p. 26). Lack of knowledge was the theme of his first letter, written hurriedly next morning amidst the affairs of the convention – he was not even sure whether to use her stage name.

36   [To Colette O'Niel]   **57 Gordon Square**
                                       [24 September 1916]

I don't know what you would like me to call you, so for the moment I won't call you anything. I want to get to know you. I know so little about you as yet. I want to talk about a thousand things – but when? I *seized* yesterday evening because moments are few and precious. Think that a Zepp was being brought down in flames while we were talking last night![1] Think of the hatred and despair and brutal triumph that was going on at the very moment – how strange contrasts are.

The Committee waits for me and I must fly. You *were* so kind and dear last night. I wonder if you know what a joy it is to find you emerged young into the life you want – not battered and weary with struggle as we older people are. I get so oppressed often with the waste. I wonder what your thoughts are – let me see you again when it is possible.

B.R.

The Russell Archives contains over 800 letters from Bertie to Colette, but for her letters to him we have to rely mainly on a typescript prepared and edited

---

1 Zeppelins were raiding London and two were shot down in the early hours of Sunday morning.

by her friend, Phyllis Urch. The typescript is invaluable for its annotations and commentary. Unfortunately, however, it is incomplete: several letters are merely summarized and others are missing entirely. Moreover, having had the typescript prepared, Colette destroyed the original letters. (A few originals escaped this process and are in the Russell Archives.) Internal evidence, moreover, makes it clear that even some of the transcribed letters are incomplete. Even in the typescript Colette marked a number of passages for deletion, apparently on the advice of a libel lawyer to protect people who were then still living. (She also changed several names for the same purpose.) It is quite likely that the letters have been altered in other ways as well. As a result, it is difficult to be sure that one has an accurate picture of her relationship with Bertie. In subsequent commentary, Colette's letters are always cited from the typescript; quotations from the editorial material are always ascribed to Urch (although the information in many cases must have come directly from Colette).

Colette was already married to the actor and playwright Miles Malleson. But this was not an impediment to an affair with Bertie, since she and Miles had married on the understanding that each would be free to have other partners, and both of them had already done so. None the less, meetings were often difficult to arrange. Colette was not acting, but her full-time day job at the NCF and Bertie's almost continuous round of meetings and committees made it difficult for them to be together. There was also the constant fear that he would be arrested and jailed. The war gave a desperate edge to their love, as Russell recalled in his *Autobiography*:

> The harshness and horror of the war overcame me, but I clung to Colette. In a world of hate, she preserved love, love in every sense of the word from the most ordinary to the most profound, and she had a quality of rock-like immovability, which in those days was invaluable.
>
> (vol. ii, p. 26)

Unlike the days when he could rush from Cambridge to London for a meeting with Ottoline, his war work gave him no regular schedule around which to fit his personal life.

The demands of the NCF in fact contrived to separate them almost immediately. A serious dissension had broken out occasioned, ironically, by one of the organization's successes. Despite the new rules for the humane treatment of COs many were treated with great brutality. When such cases came to its notice, the NCF mounted a formidable political campaign to end the abuse. Catherine Marshall had a genius for such work, but crucial to its success was her good working relationship with General Childs, director of personal service at the War Office. Russell was not directly involved in lobbying the government – he was so hated by the authorities his presence would have been counter-productive – but he was closely involved behind the scenes, as he was in all aspects of the NCF's work.

Some NCF members, however, objected to political lobbying on the grounds that any dealings with the government would compromise the NCF, and that, since the point of pacifism was to refuse to take part in the war and to suffer the consequences, any attempt to soften the consequences would lessen the value of the refusal. This issue took over where the earlier dissension between absolutists and alternativists left off. Those who opposed the lobbying were not an easy lot to deal with. Anyone who followed their conscience against the armed might of the state was unlikely to succumb to pressure in an NCF committee. Although in April Russell had been joyfully persuaded that a majority of NCF members were absolutists, six months later it was clear that most were alternativists and even of the absolutists only a small proportion opposed the NCF's political activity. Yet that group was so firmly persuaded of the correctness of its position, so unwilling to compromise and so powerful within the NCF, that the issue threatened to tear the organization apart. The issue came to a head when four extremist committee members were released from prison, furiously indignant at the NCF's efforts on their behalf.

Poor Catherine Marshall, who had worked to the point of collapse on behalf of ill-treated COs, now found herself attacked by the very people she had sought to help. Exhausted and depressed, she was in danger of breaking down completely, and Russell thought it necessary to take her away to recover and prepare for the battle that now had to be faced in the NCF's National Committee, even though this meant putting off a meeting with Colette.

37 [To Colette O'Niel]

57 Gordon Square
[3 October 1916]
Tuesday

My dearest Love,

I *was* glad to get your dear letter this morning – and I *love* your picture, which has come. It is wonderfully good. Thank you with all my heart. I knew *at once* before I touched the parcel what it must be – but I hardly dared to open it for fear it shouldn't be. I kissed the picture when I got to it beneath all its wrappings. I am very sorry you were so dreadfully tired. I hope you are rested and had a lot of sleep. I was fearfully tired too – but when I saw Miss Marshall in the evening I found her in a *desperate* state – really terrified, and wanting to cling to any one who would save her.[1] So I shall have to take her away tomorrow, and miss our evening. It is very disappointing, but her need

---

1 She had written to him that day: 'I am drowning in a sea of loneliness . . . I want some help very badly'. Her letter was headed 'S.O.S.'

is absolute. Poor woman – she gets terribly little affection – I don't know how one manages to live with so little. I give her a great deal of respect but only a very pale affection. I think Allen gives her more – she misses him dreadfully. I know her mood well – it comes of fatigue, and is almost unbearable.[1]

I am out tonight till 10, but free every other evening except tomorrow. When shall we see each other?

I am still rather tired. Miss M's crisis took it out of me.

My Colette, my lovely love, I think of you every moment – it is such a joy to think you are in the world. That somewhere you are filling the air with joy and beauty and freedom – that some place is vivid and wonderful because you are in it.

Goodbye my heart.

B.

On 13–15 October the NCF's National Committee met to settle the question of political lobbying. It was a difficult meeting for there was a real danger the NCF would break up over the issue. Russell was trusted by both sides and was, perhaps, the only person not in jail with the stature and vision to bring them together. He was remarkably successful as a conciliator, and by the end of the month Marshall could report that things were much more harmonious.

Immediately after the meeting, Russell went to Manchester to deliver the first of his 'Political Ideals' lectures. Until 20 November he travelled regularly to Manchester to lecture. He was permitted to speak at Manchester, and also at Birmingham, where the series ran from early November to early December. However, he was banned at the last minute from Glasgow. In place of the banned meeting another was quickly organized to protest the ban. Over 1,000 people attended to hear the miners' leader Bob Smillie speak – and announce at the end that the speech he had just read was the one that Russell had been prevented from giving. The authorities were evidently annoyed and reacted by attempting to intimidate the audience at Russell's other lectures. At his third lecture in Manchester a strong force of military and police turned up to check the papers of everyone who appeared to be of military age: five were arrested. Smillie might have been arrested, but was not since the government was anxious not to upset the Scottish mine workers.

---

1 Russell's help was effective. Afterwards Marshall wrote to Clifford Allen: 'Had wonderful weekend with Mephy [short for 'Mephistopheles', Russell's nickname in the NCF] a month ago – his prescription for fatigue and bad attack of missing you. Sunshine, moonlight, wood fires; walks, talks, reading aloud . . . ; poetry, philosophy, fun' (Vellacott, *Russell and the Pacifists*, p. 143).

Russell's frequent returns to London between lectures allowed him to continue his work in the NCF offices and to keep in touch with Colette. But the pace at which he was conducting his own war was exhausting him. The trouble with his gums that had bothered him in 1914 before he went to America returned. He was as much in need of rest and personal support and, indeed, affection as Catherine Marshall. Rest was out of the question and personal support was scant, though he got some from his brother. Frank was not a pacifist, but he stood firmly behind his brother in all Bertie's conflicts with the authorities. Affection came from Colette. The trouble was that with Colette he wanted to be at his energetic best and now he found this was beyond him. But even making allowances for this, it was clear, after Bertie cancelled a number of meetings and Colette wrote worrying that she might not see him for months, that something was wrong. They arranged a meeting for Friday 20 October, but it was not a success. The following note was written later the same day in the large handwriting which appeared whenever he was distraught. Its wording suggests that he had been impotent, but later references to the meeting make this unlikely. The problem appears deeper, as if for some reason his affection had been frozen.

38 [To Colette O'Niel] [57 Gordon Sq.?]
 [20 October 1916]

One line my Beloved to tell you my love is yours absolutely – equally when I *can* show it and when I *can't*. It is with you always surrounding you like the wind. Believe me – and be happy.

It seems clear that, despite his protestations, Bertie was not as much in love with Colette as she was with him. It would be understandable, after the agonies of his grand passion with Ottoline, if he were both more cautious in allowing himself to be swept away a second time, and yet at the same time feel a bit disappointed in any love less dramatic and compelling.

> I did not know [he wrote] in the first days how serious was my love for Colette. I had got used to thinking that all my serious feelings were given to Ottoline. Colette was so much younger, so much less of a personage, so much more capable of frivolous pleasures, that I could not believe in my own feelings, and half supposed that I was having a light affair with her.
>
> (*Autobiography*, vol. ii, p. 27)

Bertie had established a pattern of being fascinated by mysterious, suffering women. He had told Colette that he had never loved anyone who was happy, which was true and rather ominous. Several times in his early letters to her, he worried whether there was anything his love could give her. She seemed perhaps too self-contained, too free of troubles that he might help her solve. It was not, of course, that he wanted her miserable, but rather that he took the lack of misery to be an indication of a lack of depth. Those who saw things deeply would, he thought, inevitably see them tragically. Colette was adventurous, independent, resourceful, full of youthful high-spirits, but she was not the soulful, tragic type to which Russell, hitherto, had responded most deeply.

In old age Colette said that when she first met Bertie '[h]e seemed humble, simple, a "real human being"' and this prevented her from 'feeling as shy with him as I did with other – far less distinguished – personages'. 'Not until several months after our first meeting did I begin to understand that he was the most complicated of men, a mass of contradictions, ... often torn between reason and emotion' ('Fifty Years', p. 17). The day after the disastrous meeting, as he travelled back to Manchester for an NCF convention, he tried to explain himself to her. It was evidently not an easy task.

[To Colette O'Niel]   **In the train**   39
[21 October 1916]
Saturday

I have meant every time to tell you many things about my life, and every time the moment has conquered me. I am strangely unhappy, because the pattern of my life is complicated and yours is simple, because I am old and you are young, because with me passion can seldom break through to freedom, out of the net of circumstance in which I am enmeshed; because my nature is hopelessly complicated, a mass of contradictory impulses; and out of all this, to my intense sorrow, pain to you must grow.

The centre of me is always and eternally a terrible pain – a curious wild pain – a searching for something beyond what the world contains, something transfigured and infinite. The beatific vision – God. I do not find it, I do not think it is to be found – but the love of it is my life – it is like passionate love for a ghost. At times it fills me with rage, at times with wild despair – it is the source of gentleness and cruelty and work, it fills every passion that I have. It is the actual spring of life within me.

I can't explain it or make it seem anything but foolishness – but whether foolish or not, it is the source of whatever is any good in me. I have known others who had it – Conrad[1] especially – and I half

---

[1] Joseph Conrad, the novelist.

think Gertler[1] – but it is rare. It sets one oddly apart and gives a sense of great isolation – it makes people's gospels often seem thin.

At most times, now, I am not conscious of it – only when I am strongly stirred, either happily or unhappily. Being busy kills it, and so does affection which is not passionate. I seek escape from it, though I don't believe I ought to – but I must if I am to live any sort of ordered life. In that moment with you by the river I felt it most intensely – I wonder if you can understand it?

Well, now I come to outward circumstances. I began telling you about my friends the Eliots. I have a very great affection for them both – my relation to her especially is very intimate. If you met her you would be utterly unable to understand what I see in her – you would think her a common little thing, quite insignificant. But when I first knew her, which was 14 months ago, after her marriage, I found her so bruised and hurt by various people[2] that I couldn't bear it, and I felt only a great deal of affection would cure her. The result is a responsibility.

I thought lately that I had come to an end, as there had been a long disagreement. But I find her mood quite changed, and all that I had tried to do for her has at last succeeded. I can explain the whole thing better when I see you. The root of the matter is that she had become filled with fear through having been hurt, and out of defiance had become harsh to everyone including her husband, who is my friend, whom I love, and who is dependent on her for his happiness. If I fail her, she will punish him, and be morally ruined. During the disagreement, I thought this had happened, but it turns out that it hasn't. I am really vitally needed there, and one can't ignore that.

Then there is the slavery of work. The sort of work I try to do is not a question of hours, but of getting ideas, which only come to one if one keeps one's thoughts on the subject – and that means that I have to keep on thrusting you out of my thoughts when I am away from you. Although liberty is one's creed, there is no inward liberty when one has responsibilities – they are and must be a slavery. I rebel against them often, but I can't escape them.

The final result of all this is that I don't very often have leisure and buoyancy of spirit together – as soon as I am at all tired I get oppressed, and often I can't shake myself free. I feel that life and the world look

---

1 Mark Gertler (1891–1939), the painter and member of the Bloomsbury group.
2 In a draft of a letter which he did not send to Ottoline, he had said she had been badly hurt in two love affairs before she met Eliot (see Clark, *Life*, p. 311).

much simpler to you than they do to me – I don't disagree in theory, but my *feeling* is different. If you are able to find any happiness in what must be rather intermittent, I know the times will come again and again when I shall be all life and fire and passion – but perhaps you will grow too frozen between whiles to be able to respond? And perhaps you will feel there is so much unhappiness in such a thing that it isn't worth having?

It was quite terrible to see you so unhappy yesterday my dearest dear. It made me feel such a criminal. Can you learn to trust my love when it gives no sign? It is only because my spirit is in prison at times – and then, if you can bear the times between, it will come out of its prison again, singing with the joy of freedom, turning to you with a fuller joy each time, learning gradually to speak to you through the prison bars. But I cannot give you a *simple* happiness. I can give you moments of heaven with long intervals of pain between – if you think them worth while.

'Windows always open to the world' I told you once – but through one's windows one sees not only the joy and beauty of the world, but also its pain and cruelty and ugliness – and the one is as well worth seeing as the other – and one must look into hell before one has any right to speak of heaven. But it makes one a little grim.

My dear one, my lovely one, my Beloved, don't, don't be unhappy. It is so dreadful to think that I am spoiling the beautiful joy of you which is like a sunny April morning. We must talk more and get to know each other better. And when we have a background of many happy times together, momentary absences won't be so hard. I am glad of the leisure of the train – it has made it possible to write things out. Goodnight my dear dear love – I would not mar your life. I would rather you should forget me than that. I love you, my Colette.

    B.

Whatever the problem had been, it surely was not the Eliots, though quite what Colette could have made of them and their troubles from Bertie's letter is hard to imagine. But maybe, as he promised, he explained it better in person than in a letter, for, once he was back in London, their meetings continued accompanied by many short, cheerful letters.

At about this time they decided to go away for a three-day 'honeymoon'. They chose a remote pub, The Cat and Fiddle, on the moors near Buxton. Colette feared Bertie was going to cry off at the last moment. But things went as planned and Colette left for Buxton early on 13 November, leaving a note for Bertie at Gordon Square on her way to the station. Bertie went that day to Manchester to give a lecture and joined her at The Cat and Fiddle the next day. Three days was all they could manage, after that Bertie had to lecture in Birmingham, while Colette returned to London. Their time in Derbyshire was ecstatically happy, though Bertie managed to strike an ominous note in the next letter, written on the train to Manchester, when he compared his response to Colette with Ottoline's to him. Colette, however, could hardly have realized all that this implied.

40   [To Colette O'Niel]   In the train
[13 November 1916]
Monday

It was quite wonderful of you my dearest Darling to find time to write this morning before such an early start. I had only just finished dressing when you were starting. It is a *heavenly* day – I do hope it will be the same tomorrow. My dear one your little letter is such a happiness. There are many ways of love that are hard to understand. It is stronger than one's self – and it is hard not to struggle against it with one's will. At the end last night I quite understood the mood you had been in. I feel oddly ashamed with you of being so old – so settled and poised. I wish I were not. But it is no use struggling against the inevitable effect of the years one has lived. If my love were more fierce it would satisfy you more. But all fierceness is gone out of me. I love you with an infinite gentleness, the sort of way the sun loves the frozen earth in spring, but I cannot be fierce any more. There is too much of all the world's suffering in everything I feel deeply. I can't separate you or my love of you from the world. The separate hope, the private heaven are things grown impossible to me. This has only happened rather lately – since the war. The last time I cared seriously, I was fierce, and she was as I am now.

    There is a development one must go through. I feel you are going through it. At first one's ego is hard and entire with firm boundaries and strong exclusions. Then some deep feeling breaks down one's defences, leaving one exposed and vulnerable. At last, if one has enough courage, one ceases to need defences or to mind exposure to the world – one's separate self seems no longer important. That happens when one has achieved a security independent of happiness.

    Dearest, Beloved, I love you absolutely. I long to give you all happiness.

    Tomorrow my Beloved
        B.

Russell's hectic round of lectures and committees came to an end early in December. Exhausting as they had been, they had served Russell as a distraction from the horror of the war and from the turmoil of his personal life. The Battle of the Somme ground to its pointless end at about the same time, the attacking army bogged down in mud and the German line as impregnable as it had been when the battle began. The British High Command said everything had gone according to plan and declared a victory. The German High Command no doubt did the same. At something of a loose end, Russell was left to brood. Writing in his *Autobiography* of that winter he said:

> The War had brought me to the verge of utter cynicism, and I was having the greatest difficulty in believing that anything at all was worth doing. Sometimes I would have fits of such despair as to spend a number of successive days sitting completely idle in my chair.
>
> (vol. ii, p. 27)

He was to spend Christmas at Garsington, where a large Bloomsbury-dominated gathering was planned. It was still Ottoline to whom he could reveal himself most fully. There was, of course, ample reason for him to minimize his affair with Colette when telling Ottoline of it, but this should not obscure the large measure of truth in his explanation to Ottoline of what his relationship with Colette lacked. There was a loneliness that Colette did not relieve, and some deep seriousness, which he called 'religion', which he found in Ottoline but could not find in Colette.

[To Ottoline Morrell] [57 Gordon Square?] 41
[3 December 1916]
Sunday

My Darling
 The date of C.A's Court Martial[1] is still undecided, but I have got permission to go to it. It keeps me dangling – it wants two permissions – the one I haven't got yet is a mere formality but keeps me occupied. I shan't be able to come to Garsington till Saturday owing to that and my last Birmingham lecture. Then, *if* you can let me, I should like to stay a longish time – would a fortnight be too long?
 A terrible longing for you has been growing and growing in me for a long time. It is not passion any more – the war has all but killed that – it is the hunger for companionship. Those days at Harrogate,[2]

---
1 Clifford Allen had been released from prison on 25 November and taken back to his unit at Newhaven. The next day he again refused an order and was rearrested. He was being held at Newhaven pending a court martial.
2 In Yorkshire, where Ottoline had been in October for yet another cure – this time for flu.

and the days together since, it was so wonderful to feel real companionship – most of one's life is very lonely, and one's relations to people have some insincerity because one conceals the loneliness they don't relieve.

I have been in the absolute abyss over the war – quite impersonal, and not the sort of thing to try to shirk. I like Katharine Mansfield – she talked of her brother whom she lost in the war and loved very much.[1] In a gay boyish mood I got intimate with Constance Malleson, but she doesn't suit serious moods. P. will have told you about my schemes.[2]

What holds me to you for ever and ever is religion. Everybody else hurts me by lack of reverence.

I hope your cold is better – write *here*.

Your

B.

Russell had met Katherine Mansfield in July 1915 along with Middleton Murry and their friend S.S. Koteliansky. His initial impression was not favourable: 'I thought Murry *beastly* and the whole atmosphere of the three dead and putrefying' (to Ottoline, July 1915). He does not seem to have changed his opinion of Murry, but a year later he was friendly enough with Mansfield to exchange manuscripts with her. That their paths crossed was only to be expected: apart from links through Bloomsbury, Mansfield was a cousin of Frank Russell's wife, Elizabeth. More surprising was the intimacy of the friendship that developed between them in November 1916. Russell's letters to her are lost, but hers to him are extraordinarily intimate (see Mansfield, *Selected Letters*, pp. 53–4). Rediscovering them among his papers in 1949 surprised even Russell: 'They read', he wrote, 'as if we were having an affair, or about to have one, but it was not so. My feelings for her were ambivalent; I admired her passionately, but was repelled by her dark hatreds' (Clark, *Life*, p. 309).

If Russell was looking for a mysterious, suffering woman he had found one in Mansfield. Troubled, turbulent, and given to wild fabrications, at twenty-four she was already dying of (as yet undiagnosed) tuberculosis. She had at the same time an intelligent mind, a brilliant gift as a writer, and an undeniable sex appeal. Russell preferred her talk to her writing, 'but when she

---

[1] Leslie Beauchamp, Mansfield's brother, had been killed in October 1915 when a faulty grenade blew up in his hand.

[2] This was probably a reference to Russell's plans to smuggle a letter to Woodrow Wilson urging him to mediate a peace agreement with America as guarantor.

spoke about people she was envious, dark, and full of alarming penetration in discovering what they least wished known' (*Autobiography*, vol. ii, p. 27). But on the war they saw eye to eye. In 1919, when Mansfield was reviewing Virginia Woolf's *Night and Day*, she complained that Woolf wrote as if the war had never happened. 'I feel in the *profoundest* sense', she told Murry, 'that nothing can ever be the same – that, as artists, we are traitors if we feel otherwise' (Alpers, *Mansfield*, p. 258). Significantly, while Russell drew away from her because of her lack of concern for other people's feelings, she drew away from him because of an outburst of savage cynicism in one of his wartime essays (Alpers, p. 235). In this instance, it seems that it was she who felt hurt by lack of reverence.

If Katherine Mansfield was too dark, Bertie was still worried that Colette might be too light. Their affair was certainly at a low ebb that winter, with Colette clearly less anxious to see him and he, as usual, torn in many different directions. He tried to hint at the problems to her.

[To Colette O'Niel] [London] 42
[4 December 1916]
Monday afternoon

My Beloved,
   Your little letter came this morning and was a comfort to me. Dearest, I love you far more deeply and irrevocably than ever before. In all that I do or think, in all that I hope and all that I suffer, I am with you in spirit. I have faith in you – chiefly because your courage is infinite and inexhaustible. I want a kind of union with you which goes deeper than happiness – a comradeship in all great things – in suffering as well as in joy, in absence as much as when we are together, in slow labour as well as in desperate ventures and great enterprises.

   I was very unhappy when you said the 'Cat and Fiddle' might as well have been a dream. I do not feel that at all. The thought of it is *always* with me – it makes me always feel a very profound union with you, which nothing can take away. It was the perfection of personal union. But on the basis of that I want something more – something to include that, but to be also an *impersonal* union – that we should be as much one in what concerns the world as in what concerns each other. And that means letting in pain, because the world at this time is one great cry of pain.

   There have been moments when I have doubted whether you really wanted that – whether you were willing to admit pain and doubt to a sufficient share in your inner life. You said once that it was not in your nature to live 'nobly' – I don't know quite what you meant, but I had a chill fear in my heart when you said it; and something of the same fear came to me *à propos* of my letter to Wilson,[1] though in that case I think it was irrational. You remember our talk in Richmond Park, about how one can't live by shibboleths but only by active love. Active love, and a kind of tenderness – a realization that it is hard to see into another soul, that when one most thinks one understands one is really furthest from understanding – and out of this, a kind of reverence towards all. This all sounds stupid I am afraid, but it lies so deep in me that I want to call it forth in you, and I know it is in your nature.

But then I have another feeling. I do love your joy – it is quite dreadful to me to see you unhappy. I would rather vanish out of your life than take away your instinctive joy of life – and selfishly too, I love it, because I catch it from you, and feel gay and jolly and young – but then when I am away from you that fades away, and the burden of the world comes over me again. And so a lot of complicated contradictory feelings grow up in me.

Dearest loved one, I don't know whether I shall be able to bear such a long long time of absence as we spoke of – it seems awful in prospect. I hope something will happen to shorten it. My heart, my soul, my life, I love you absolutely and utterly.
    B.

Bertie's holiday at Garsington was to start after his last lecture in Birmingham on 8 December, though it was promptly interrupted by Clifford Allen's court martial on the 12th at which Russell was a witness. Despite these and other NCF activities, Russell clearly felt a lull in his anti-war work. Despair over the course of the war and the futility of all efforts to bring it to an end led him to think once more of philosophy. Despite all his other work, he had continued to teach logic after his dismissal from Trinity, seeing his students whenever he could away from Cambridge. Some of them had been invited to Garsington for this purpose. But he also had plans to take up once more his work on the philosophy of physics while at Garsington. Even after making all due allowance for his phenomenal capacity for work, one begins to wonder whether he was serious in planning a major piece of philosophical research in between teaching logic during his Christmas holiday after such a frantically busy year.

---

1 See Letter **41**. It is hard to understand why his letter to Woodrow Wilson should have occasioned such feelings.

[To Ottoline Morrell]   **[57 Gordon Square?]**   43
                                                       [5 December 1916]
                                                                       Tuesday

My Darling

    I *was* glad of your letter this morning. I am sorry you have been depressed. I hope your 'cold' has not really been influenza again.

    I will tell my pupils to come to Wheatley 4.30. I shall be coming from Birmingham and shall arrive Oxford 11.2 – so we can have a little talk before they descend on us? I am sure Armstrong and Nicod won't mind sharing a room.

    I sit here waiting for a telegram to go to Newhaven[1] – hardly daring to stir out of the house. But I think now it won't be till Thursday, if then. Perhaps Birmingham will make me miss it altogether, or it may be next week. It is hateful not knowing. Miss Marshall has just come from there and I shall dine with her tonight and hear the latest.

    The crisis is very exciting. I *can't* believe Lloyd George's resignation means that he is defeated – it would be too good to be true.[2] But still, a little trickle of hope will filter in, however hard I try to keep it out for fear of disappointment.

    I have been very busy writing,[3] seeing absolutely no one, reading *Karamazoff*[4] in the intervals. It is a wonderful book. I don't know whether I am reading it with less sympathy than before, but it no longer strikes me as mad. I believe when I read it before (alone at Ipsden, after Marienbad[5]) I was more in the mood in which it was written. So I hated it and understood it. Now I don't hate it in the least. But I think I was right before.

    I want to get to know Katharine Mansfield really well.[6] She interests me mentally very much indeed – I think she has a very good mind, and I like her boundless curiosity. I do not feel sure that she has much heart.

---

1 For Clifford Allen's court martial.
2 It was. Lloyd George had resigned from the Cabinet that day. He had been scheming since the beginning of the month to wrest control of the war from Asquith. When Asquith refused his demands he resigned, as did Asquith himself hoping to be able to form a government without Lloyd George. In this Asquith miscalculated, and later the same day Lloyd George came back as Prime Minister.
3 It is not clear what Russell was writing at this time. From what he says later in the letter, it could well have been on philosophy.
4 Russell had read much of Dostoyevsky in September 1911, including *The Brothers Karamazov*. He told Ottoline (19 Sept. 1911): 'I feel the madness of his people, and they make more impression than I quite like.'
5 He had visited Ottoline at Marienbad in August 1911.
6 Mansfield was among the guests at Garsington that Christmas.

I have been in an unusual mood – I suppose from war-depression – not wanting to see people, taking great pleasure in reading, anxious to use my mind in unemotional ways. I think of writing on the philosophy of physics at Garsington.

Birrell's news is most terribly interesting.[1] I long to know more. Are you persuaded it is true?

I am full of life intellectually – not very full in feeling – I have lots of dim ideas ready to grow as soon as I have leisure. I must have time for writing and reading and just meditating.

I am *longing* for talks with you. I feel as if there were a great deal to talk about – but it may be too dim for talk yet. I remember how I used to worry you by being silent for long times, while I was trying to hear some faint inner voice which would only speak in your presence.

Sometimes I think I have grown smug – there is not a spark of madness left in me – I never feel the sort of vague despair that used to drive me on. When the war stops I shall grow fat! I believe it is the war that has made me sane.

Goodbye my Darling. I long to be with you.

Your
   B.

Russell's holiday was even more fragmented than he had expected. Less than a week after Clifford Allen's court martial he was away again, for unknown reasons. But now, for a brief moment, the political situation looked as if it might change completely, for on 18 December the British government received a peace note from Germany. No specific terms were attached, and the Germans were still hoping to retain some of the territory they had conquered, while the Allies continued to insist that they retire to their pre-war borders. The chief obstacle to peace, however, was that the politicians of all the warring nations had spoken so frequently about decisive victory that they had to continue to act as if they believed in it. Lloyd George had justified his virtual *coup* against Asquith earlier in the month by the need to conduct the war more effectively. This was no time to have peace breaking out. Not surprisingly, therefore, he took the opportunity to denounce the peace note

---

1 Ottoline's letter is lost and with it Birrell's news. It was, however, more likely news from Augustine Birrell, the critic and Liberal politician, who was an old friend of Ottoline's, than from his son, Francis, who was closer to the younger Bloomsberries.

roundly in Parliament the next day. Meanwhile, Russell allowed himself to become briefly optimistic: a negotiated peace now was so obviously in the interests of all the warring countries that it was hard to believe it would be rejected.

[To Ottoline Morrell] [London?] 44
[18 December 1916]
Monday

My Darling

I can't well come today. Whitehead is reading at the Aristotelian tonight[1] and I ought to be there — and tomorrow I have an important Committee. But I will come Wednesday morning unless you write to the contrary — *arriving Wheatley 1.30*.

I am *very* sorry about Brett[2] — but I got discouraged not finding her and I thought she would write — but when she did her invitations didn't arrive till after the time she suggested. I will try to see her today or tomorrow.

You are right, it is not a question of vitality — I want to know what it was that was said.[3]

Germany's peace proposals have filled my mind entirely. In spite of all the devilishness of the papers they have altered the situation entirely. They bring peace much nearer. I believe now that we shall have peace within a year. Bonar Law's speech confirms one in thinking that.[4] Philosophy is gone out of my head — it was only despair that made me turn to philosophy, and now one has no reason for despair. Miss Doty's articles in the *Nation* are extraordinarily interesting — they make one see why the Germans want peace.[5]

---

1 A paper called 'The Organization of Thought' published in the *Proceedings of the Aristotelian Society* (1917).
2 Dorothy Brett (1883–1977), the Bloomsbury painter. Like Dora Carrington, with whom she trained at the Slade, she was always known by her surname. In 1924 she followed the Lawrences to Taos in New Mexico, where she stayed for the rest of her life. Brett was lonely, largely on account of her deafness, and Ottoline, anxious to help her, was trying to get Bertie to befriend her.
3 Ottoline's letter is lost and it is impossible to know what Bertie was referring to here.
4 Andrew Bonar Law (1858–1923), Leader of the House of Commons, Chancellor of the Exchequer, and a member of the War Cabinet. His speech in Parliament on 15 Dec., was somewhat indirect evidence for Russell's view that peace negotiations might be started. Bonar Law down-played, but did not explicitly deny, rumours that the British Ambassador in Athens had been in contact with the Greek court. Greece was officially neutral, but the court was known to have close links to Germany. If peace negotiations were to start it would be through such deniable 'back channels'.
5 Four articles by Madeleine Doty, an American tourist in Germany, printed in the *Nation* (25 Nov., 2 Dec., 16 Dec., 23 Dec.): they give a vivid picture of the grim life of wartime Germany.

I am having a fit of unutterable weariness – I want to lie in the sun and do nothing and not think or feel – but there is no sun and one has to keep on thinking and feeling.

I *am* glad you thought my letter to Wilson good – Philip helped me with it a great deal – he was *most* useful. It is probably arriving today.[1]

I live in two layers now-a-days – one superficial, in which I have plenty of life and good spirits, and another underneath, where I feel lost and worn out and isolated and rather hopeless – that is the deeper feeling, but I keep on fighting it off with an effort of will. Nothing can be done for it while the war lasts.

I am glad you are all getting better. I am afraid you have been terribly worn out.

Your

B.

The Allies' peremptory dismissal of Germany's peace note threw Russell into perhaps the blackest despair of his entire life. He gave vent to his feelings in a New Year's letter to Catherine Marshall, who was on holiday at her parents' home in Keswick. She seems to have asked him to recommend some French prose – it is hard to think what else Voltaire's satirical novella and Stendhal's great historical novel set in Napoleonic Italy had in common with the two more recent history books on Russell's list. The historian Albert Vandal's *L'Avenèment de Bonaparte* (2 vols, 1903) is a minutely detailed and very sympathetic study of Napoleon's rise to power from June 1799 to September 1800. Eugène Melchior de Vogüé, known as 'the Chateaubriand of the Third Republic', was a conservative French writer and Russophile. His *Trois drames de l'histoire de Russie* (1911) reprinted three studies published thirty years before in the *Revue de deux mondes*: 'Le Fils de Pierre le Grand', 'Mazeppa', 'Un changement de règne – La Morte de Catherine II et l'avenèment de Paul I'.

---

1 Russell had written an open letter to Woodrow Wilson on 4 December, urging him to broker a peace. (The letter is printed below pp. 198–201.) Wilson on 18 December issued his own peace note, inviting the warring nations to state their terms. Russell's letter was smuggled to America by Helen Dudley's sister, Katherine, who was returning from a visit to Helen who was still in England. She delivered it to a pacifist conference in New York on 22 December and it was widely reported in the American press. Dudley's identity was never revealed, but the British government soon identified her and resolved that if Helen should ever return home 'she should be carefully serched' (Clark, *Life*, p. 316).

[To Catherine Marshall] **[57 Gordon Sq.]** **45**
1 January 1917

Dear Miss Marshall

Your letter to Garsington was forwarded and reached me today. I am very sorry your holiday is wasted by toothache. Thank you for your news, which I am very glad to have.[1]

Here are a few French books that occur to me at the moment as suitable:

Voltaire, *Candide*
Stendal, *La Chartreuse de Parme*
Vandal, *L'Avenèment de Bonaparte*
Melchior de Vogüé, *Trois Drames de l'histoire russe* [sic].

The thing to remember in reading history is that the mad extravagant things people did are exactly what people do now. The book about Napoleon in this list tells you how Lloyd George became Prime Minister;[2] the book about Russia will enable you to understand the position of Rasputin.[3] Contemporaries know nothing. Nero was thought a saint: caricaturists alluded to his time as 'a sweeter, simpler reign'.[4] Under his successor, an unknown hand daily put flowers on his tomb, though the penalty for doing so was death. There is hope for us all. Panegyrists to this day stick up for him, pointing out that the people he murdered were his mother and his aunt, which is rather an endearing trait, seeing what elderly relatives are apt to be.[5]

However, this is irrelevant. I find myself constantly taking refuge from the present in more humane and kindly times, such as that of

---

1 Marshall's letter has not been preserved.
2 In 1799 Napoleon had been recalled from Egypt ostensibly to save the revolution from foreign invasion. In the coup of 18–19 Brumaire, he overthrew the ruling Directory with the help of two of its members. The three then installed themselves as consuls with Napoleon as undisputed leader. Russell may have intended a comparison with the way Lloyd George schemed with Edward Carson and Bonar Law to oust Asquith and establish himself as undisputed master of the War Cabinet.
3 Rasputin, the Tsar's sinister religious advisor, had just been assassinated.
4 A long tradition, starting with Tacitus and Suetonius and continued by Christian writers, has established Nero's reputation as a monster. Later scholarship, however, revealed that his reign was relatively benign. He was popular with the common people but hated by the patricians, whose views Tacitus and Suetonius represented, for bringing the imperial government into disrepute, not so much through his notorious orgies, as by his unseemly interest in poetry and music. It is not clear where the phrase about 'a simpler sweeter reign' comes from, but it was not an unreasonable opinion: the violence of Nero's reign was minor compared with that of the civil war which followed his overthrow. The story about the flowers on his tomb is widely repeated.
5 Nero's aunt, Domitia Lepida, lost a power struggle with his mother, Agrippina, and was executed in 54 AD. Nero gave evidence at her trial but otherwise seems not to have been responsible. He did, however, have Agrippina murdered in 59 AD. A ferociously ambitious woman, she had murdered, among many other obstacles to her power, a former husband and a stepson and was beginning to scheme against Nero whom she no longer controlled. With elderly relatives like this, Nero might well claim mitigating circumstances.

Nero. I wish the outlook for peace were brighter. I think we shall have peace in the autumn, after Lloyd George has drunk the blood of half a million young Englishmen in an offensive which he knows will effect nothing. I do not think Lloyd George worse than the rest of mankind – on the contrary I think he belongs to the best 10 per cent – it is the human race that is vile. It is a disgrace to belong to it. Being busy is like taking opium, it enables one to live in a land of golden dreams – I must get busy again. The truth is not the sort of thing one can live with.

Yours very sincerely
Bertrand Russell.

Marshall's reponse was brisk and clever:

> For goodness sake get busy again, quickly, and get rid of that distorted vision of Truth to which idleness – or plum pudding? – seems to have given rise. Remember *you* are a 'contemporary' of the European War and Lloyd George and this generation of the human race and are therefore wrong in your views about them.

This was sound advice, though it made no allowance for Russell's need to relieve his feelings and the remarkable extent to which writing enabled him to do so.

Russell's opportunity to get busy came on 11 January when he was elected acting chairman of the NCF, replacing Fenner Brockway who had been jailed. Hitherto, Russell's work for the NCF had been under Marshall's supervision, now he had to take on a much greater degree of responsibility for the running of the organization. He loathed the work, but knew it had to be done and applied himself to it to the best of his ability for almost a year. He appears to have been a surprisingly successful administrator. He handled matters efficiently and decisively; he had by this time a thorough, insider's knowledge of NCF and was well-respected by its members; and the effort he was prepared to put into the work remained apparently limitless. His dislike of the work led him to underrate his success at it, and criticism from Marshall, who was rarely prepared to let others work without interference, was apt to make him defensive. Vellacott assesses his work as chairman judiciously, and concludes: 'He was acutely aware of his deficiencies as an administrator, and his greatest weakness seems to have been his tendency to exaggerate them' (*Russell and the Pacifists*, p. 143). As chairman, he was involved in the daily work of the NCF's head office and in looking after the interests of COs in the Home Office camps. He was also responsible for initiating NCF policy and for writing a weekly editorial in the *Tribunal*. It cannot have been easy, especially since one of his first tasks was to put the organization's finances in order by cutting expenses.

Russell's mood at this time was also influenced, as so often in the past, by his relations with Ottoline during his vacation at Garsington. Though still drawn to her with an almost irresistible attraction, he began at last to see it was hopeless. Although he said he believed 'very little' of what Katherine Mansfield said against Ottoline, he credited his talks with Mansfield that Christmas with enabling him 'to think of Ottoline as a friend rather than a lover' (*Autobiography*, vol. ii, p. 27). The next letter shows how hard it was for him to do this.

[To Ottoline Morrell]   [London?]   46
                                                            [26 January 1917]
                                                            Saturday night

I have just got your little letter about Nicod.[1] I had not heard a syllable till he appeared on my doorstep yesterday – the proposed law under which he was to have re-examined was defeated so he is safe.[2] The letter you forwarded was from Kaufman,[3] a young Cambridge mathematician who has just been sentenced to two years in prison – a most lovable and wonderful person. He was near the end of an important piece of research when they took him.

I am no longer busy *all* day, though I am busy a good part of it. Dr. Salter (of Bermondsey) and I are going through the N.C.F. expenses with a view to reducing them by about half, as funds are low. It involves giving notice to people and doing horrid things that will interfere with the work very much. It takes a very great deal of time.

Tomorrow I lunch with Mrs Huth Jackson[4] to meet Olive Schreiner.[5] Next day I speak for the League of Peace and Freedom.[6] The whole of the two following days I have a Peace Conference – and so on. I go to the office every day if I can find a moment – generally

---

1 This letter seems not to have survived.
2 Nicod had been threatened with conscription under stringent new regulations designed to overcome the chronic shortage of manpower at the front.
3 George Kaufmann, a mathematician, apparently of German origin, who returned to Munich after the war. It is not known what work he was engaged on, but he became very interested in relativity immediately after the war.
4 Annabel Huth Jackson, the daughter of Sir Mountstuart Grant Duff. She had known Russell as a child and recalled her visits to Pembroke Lodge in her memoir, *A Victorian Childhood* (1932).
5 Olive Schreiner (1855–1920) the South African novelist, feminist, and radical, best known for *The Story of an African Farm* (1883).
6 The Women's International League for Peace and Freedom.

I spend several hours there. It doesn't matter – it is just as good as anything else I should do. I feel quite played out – I don't suppose I shall come to life again till after the war. The world is so beastly – Wilson is the one bright spot – and he is *very* bright.[1]

I am living all against impulse – my impulse is to write biting things about the pleasure men derive from having their sons killed, or about what fun it is to be a journalist of military age on the *Morning Post* – or about the Bishop of London at the Last Judgment, full of surprise to find himself not appreciated. It drives me wild that peace can so *obviously* be got and hardly anybody wants it, except the soldiers, who don't count, because there is so little affection in the world.

I have made my life more or less independent of yours, but I hate it. You could easily undo it if you cared to – but I don't know if it would be wise. I feel rather lost – and I am haunted by the feeling that you are unhappy about Lawrence and other things,[2] and it makes me utterly miserable not to be able to help you. I keep on longing for solitude, but I can't get it. I used to want sympathy when I was unhappy, but now I feel it would be no good. What I want is leisure for a new effort of will, to get over the feeling that the human race is not worth doing anything for, since it finds more pleasure in death than in life. Miss Doty's articles in the *Nation* are interesting and terrible.

I dined the other night with Captain White,[3] the lunatic. Three months in prison tamed him. He now works for the Government and lives virtuously with his wife and practices a kind of Dostoiewsky humility. I have a sort of affection for him. Do you remember how mad he was at the Caxton Hall the time you were there?[4] Goodnight.

    Your
        B.

---

1 Woodrow Wilson was attempting to convene a peace conference. Unknown to Russell, however, the German High Command had already taken the decision to resume unrestricted submarine warfare that would shortly bring the US into the war.

2 Ottoline had been reading the manuscript of Lawrence's novel, *Women in Love* (1920), in which she appears, vividly but unflatteringly, as Hermione Roddice. It is not entirely clear how she got hold of the manuscript. In her *Memoirs* she simply says 'it arrived', Lawrence having told her earlier that he was writing about her (vol. ii, p. 128). But Lawrence was annoyed that she had found out and told his friends not to tell her about the novel. However it reached her, Ottoline by her own account went 'pale with horror' when she read it. It was the end of her friendship with Lawrence, whom she never saw again.

3 Capt. J.R. White (1879–1946), a friend of Colette's. The son of Sir George White, 'the defender of Ladysmith', he had been jailed for trying to bring the Welsh miners out on strike. Jim Bricknell in D.H. Lawrence's *Aaron's Rod* (1922) is based upon him.

4 This was the occasion when Ottoline attended Bertie's *Principles of Social Reconstruction* lectures. White had spoken from the audience on 'sex and free love' according to Ottoline (*Memoirs*, vol. ii, p. 96).

Russell's misanthropic despair lasted into the spring, and was lifted only by political events. In Russia, after several weeks of strikes, riots, and mutinies, a provisional government had been formed and on 15 March the Tsar had abdicated. Russell, whose hatred of Tsarist Russia was almost as deep as his hatred of the war, was enormously excited by the new development. The March Revolution was so popular in Britain that even the government felt obliged to welcome it – recognizing, of course, that there was not much it could do about it and hoping, by its approval, to keep Russia in the war. For Russell and the pacifists, on the other hand, the revolution brought hopes that Russia might withdraw from the war, thus creating another opportunity for a negotiated peace. As soon as the news arrived in England, the NCF and various labour organizations formed the Anglo-Russian Democratic Alliance to welcome the revolution and, more importantly, to impress its lessons on the British authorities. Chief among these was the new Russian government's 'Charter of Freedom', promising freedoms which had ceased to exist in Britain since the war began, and a degree of democracy that even prewar Britain could not match. One of the first acts of the Democratic Alliance was to draw up a similar Charter for Britain – a document probably drafted by Russell. Support for the British Charter was to be stirred up a large propaganda campaign starting with a public meeting in the Albert Hall on 31 March. Although Russell was involved in organizing the Albert Hall meeting, he did not himself speak at it. The following day he wrote about it to Ottoline.

[To Ottoline Morrell]   **[London]**   47
                                                 1 April 1917
                                                     Sunday

I feel I must tell you about the Albert Hall meeting last night, because it was a really wonderful occasion, and you can find out nothing about it from the papers. The Albert Hall was absolutely packed, and 20,000 people had to be refused tickets.[1] Every person there was wanting a real absolute change in everything – not the sort of piecemeal niggling reforms that one is used to, but the sort of thing the Russians have done. There was *no* opposition. The C.O.'s came in for their due share of applause – that one had expected. But besides that people cheered for a republic, for freedom for India, for all the things one never hears mentioned. Jos Wedgwood,[2] who represented moderation, suggested that it was possible to believe that some good objects could not be

---

[1] The hall itself held 12,000.
[2] Josiah Clement Wedgwood (1872–1943), the Liberal MP for Newcastle-under-Lyme, was one of the platform speakers. Though not a pacifist, he was well to the left of the Liberals and joined Labour in 1919. Indian independence was among the causes he championed.

obtained without war, but he could only get a hearing after an urgent appeal from the Chairman. The whole atmosphere was electric. I longed to shout to them at the end to come with me and pull down Wormwood Scrubs.[1] They would have done it. The Reporters applauded, but did not take notes. A meeting of the kind would have been utterly impossible a month ago. Smillie and Williams[2] were admirable as regards Labour. The regular pacifist gang were not speaking, and the general public did not know what sort of meeting it was going to be. 'To cheer the Russian Revolution' sounded quite respectable. But speakers one and all urged that we should do likewise. The audience was largely Russian Jews.[3] I saw my little friend Tchitcherim[4] (the Secretary of one of their organizations) afterwards, beaming like a cherub. There was a lot said about Ireland – the Sinn Fein martyrs[5] were enthusiastically cheered. The Russians have really put a new spirit into the world, and it is going to be worth while to be alive.

Bertie had seen little of Colette early in 1917, and their occasional meetings were often unsatisfactory. Colette complained that a wall had arisen between them. He had written frequently enough, but his brief letters could hardly have given her much reassurance. Her own letters during this time were sad, puzzled, but forbearing. Bertie's withdrawal might compromise her happiness but not, it seemed, her affection.

It was the Albert Hall meeting, when they had stood together singing 'The Red Flag', that restored some of their closeness. Colette remembered it as 'a mighty, inspiring moment' (*After Ten Years*, p. 112). About this time, they had taken to referring to each other as comrades, and they began to picture their lives after the war as a joint enterprise. The time when Bertie had supposed that they were merely having a light affair had ended. They spent the day after the meeting walking together in the country, blissfully happy. Bertie refers to it as their 'day of day-dreams' in the next letter.

---

1 The prison in London where Clifford Allen had been held.
2 Robert Williams (1881–1936) leader of the Transport Worker's Union.
3 This can hardly have been correct.
4 Georgi Vasilievich Chicherin (1872–1936) had been a friend of Russell's Uncle Rollo. From 1904 to 1917 he was a member of the Russian Social Democratic Party in exile, and he worked with the pacifists in Britain during the war. After the Bolshevik revolution he returned to Russia and succeeded Trotsky as Commissar for Foreign Affairs (1918–1928).
5 Those executed after the Easter uprising.

[To Colette O'Niel] **[London]** **48**
5 April 1917

My Beloved

Your dear little letter came this morning. It was a great joy to get it. I shall think of you continually till we meet again – longing to know everything.

My dearest loved one, since our day of day-dreams I have realized more than ever how I cling to you and how deeply you are rooted in my heart. I want you to be always growing freely, and with the utmost happiness that one can have in such a world. And I know that there is no limit to the difference you make in my life – and you will make more and more as years go by – always in perfect and absolute freedom. I love what you are in yourself. I love the generosity of your love – when it goes to others too, not only when it comes to me. I love your fearlessness and your pride when you are unhappy – and your belief in liberty is an endless happiness to me. Dear one, I feel a *perfect* comradeship with you, spiritually and physically. I *long* to be free to give far more than I have been able to give yet – endless treasures and devotion which can't be given in odd moments between committees and meetings.

Goodbye my Darling, my heart's Joy. My very soul is yours.
B.

So far, Bertie had seen little of Colette's troubles and had tended to assume that he was responsible for most of those he saw. Her main worry, however, had nothing to do with him. After a good start, her stage career had stalled. As pacifists, both she and Miles found it difficult to get work. In April, she wrote to Bertie about her 'work despair': despite having 'done everything possible to get work', she complained, she still had 'no work at my own job, no paid work of any kind (and not a rag fit to wear)'. (Her NCF work was unpaid.) Money, however, was not the main problem: her unearned income was about £500 a year, making her better off than Bertie, although she did have debts which Bertie may not have known about. The real problem was lack of work on the stage for which she had been trained. The extent to which she was committed to this particular form of success was difficult for Bertie to appreciate. To give it up, she said, would seem like committing suicide.

Colette said afterwards that Bertie disliked the theatre and thought her theatrical ambitions worthless. This was not entirely fair. He had been an early admirer of Ibsen and Shaw and it was, after all, a reading of Euripides' *Hippolytus* that had transformed his life in 1901. The wartime theatre, however, was not inspiring – most productions tried to foster either mindless patriotism or cheerful oblivion – and Bertie did think success there was not worth having. In his attempts to redirect her interests into politics, he was also trying to be practical. To her, however, his efforts seemed prompted by his indifference to the one form of achievement that mattered to her.

49   [To Colette O'Niel]   [London?]
                                                                  1 May 1917

My darling Loved One

I am glad you were happy in the country – it *was* beautiful, and I was happy too.[1]

I am infinitely glad you wrote what you did about your 'conception of what life must be'. I don't think there is much need to worry about the money and the clothes, because they will come inevitably before long. (I will talk about this another time, but I mean it quite seriously and literally.[2]) But work is a more serious matter. I hope with all my soul that you will soon have success on the stage and get a job – but – if you don't, if that ambition has to fade, you will have to pick up your life and put your spirit into something else.

There is a sort of alchemy of defeat that one has to learn: how to turn defeat into victory. Think of Allen: imagine what goes on in his mind as he finds his body growing feebler and his intellect less alert, as he realizes that the world is passing on and forgetting him, as it slowly comes to him that perhaps here, in his prison cell, is the end of his ambitions and his hopes, the sum and conclusion of all that he will ever have done for the world. How do you feel one would deal with a fate like that? There is really only one way, and it is the way we must all come to sooner or later: to live by love, to care really and profoundly for others more than for oneself. There is no other way through the abysses of life. I have been down into the depths not once, but several times – I know how the world looks when *all* personal hope is dead, and there seems nothing at all in one's future but pain and weariness. In those moments love has come to my rescue – love of all mankind, profound longing to help, to help many if possible, but a few in any case. The faith of those moments fades away again gradually, but it remains dimly in the background, and it really does inspire one's life. It was the faith of those times that came up in me when the war broke

---

1 Colette had spent part of April at her mother's country house at Cox Green, Berkshire. Bertie must have visited her there, though there is no other reference to his visit.
2 Russell intended to give her some of his debentures. Colette refused them: 'I'll never forget your dearness, but I shall never forgive you if you don't obey' (2 May).

out. It is that that is coming to Allen, and it is that that makes all men love him wherever he goes.

I know you believe in love as an abstract doctrine, but I want you to feel it as an active principle. The world is *full* of things, valuable and important things, that you could do for mankind – political, revolutionary things, as well as helping particular people. I want you to feel in your bones that a useful life is a life worth living: you will feel that if you have enough active love.

In the winter, I lost all active love for mankind, and I sank into despair – but love came back, and life became tolerable again.

One must not be unbending in outward things, but only in the springs of one's life. And without love one cannot live a good life. You are allowing yourself to be conquered by Fear – fear of personal failure. But personal success is not the thing to live for. Think of the immensity of the world and the vastness of human suffering.

O my dearest, I love you with a consuming love. I *long* for you to be happy and to grow to your full spiritual growth. There is still a long development ahead of you, and much pain. I can't save you from it, I suffer because I can't. Goodbye, my life, my Soul. Be courageous, and be *great. You can be.*

B.

Colette, not surprisingly, was not ready for 'the alchemy of defeat' – she was young, and naturally hoped for victory instead. In her reply she conceded that she might be deficient in 'active love' but hotly disputed what she took to be Bertie's suggestion that she was indifferent to politics. Primarily, however, she tried to restate her case about the theatre: 'I do so want you to understand', she said.

Russell's work with Catherine Marshall was never easy, but at the beginning of May some sort of crisis occurred. Its nature is not known, but evidently Russell thought that only plain speaking could put things right. In the end, however, he did not send the following letter.

[To Catherine Marshall] 57 Gordon Square 50
3 May 1917

Dear Miss Marshall

Thank you very much for your kind letter.[1] I agree entirely that we *must* learn to work together without mutual irritation.

---

1 She had written to apologize for being 'horrid and cantankerous'.

I am painfully conscious of my own shortcomings. It is difficult in middle age to take up work requiring wholly different habits of mind from those that one has practised hitherto. I dislike the work so much that I should be overjoyed if I could have a painful and dangerous illness from now till the end of the war. But that is neither here nor there.

I do not think you are equally conscious of your shortcomings, and I think if you were it would be a good thing. You seem to me to have a wrong conception of how to get work out of people. You try to do it by fault-finding, which is really a militarist method. My chief trouble is forgetfulness, which is entirely due to mental fatigue. Repeatedly, after you have been scolding me, I have hardly slept a wink all night (that happened again the night before last), which makes me more tired and therefore more forgetful. Also your manner of fault-finding fills one with despair, which simply makes one want to give up the work altogether. It is not only I who feel this: every one at the office feels the same, except Miss Rinder.[1] After you have been criticizing, I have to go round consoling, and persuading people that they are not so incompetent that they ought to retire. I know this way of treating people is against your principles, and if you can become conscious of it you will amend. Your present way of treating us all is paralyzing, and is one of the reasons why we are not more full of initiative. It discourages initiative to know that anything one may attempt will only lead to destructive criticism from you.

We all have our faults; you yourself have a good deal of the faults you mind in us. Different people have different ways of working, and different capacities and incapacities. It is no use to find fault with people for things they can't help. One wants to try to understand a person before expecting things from them. But I am saying all this because I think it is only hurry and anxiety that has led you into these habits, not anything deep-seated and incurable.

I will give you an illustration of what I mean. Your way of treating General Childs has obviously been very successful: you knew you had no *power* over him, and you gradually led him on by gentle steps. Now he has developed further than any one would have thought possible. But your method of treating us is quite different, because instinctively you regard us as subject to your authority. The feeling of authority is one which a pacifist should root out from his instincts. I feel your answer, which will be to point out the need of efficiency. But that seems to me in essence the same as the argument that 'we must get on

---

1 Gladys Rinder, the devoted secretary at the NCF head office.

with the war'. Many ways of getting efficiency are incompatible with respect for other human beings.

At this point I got your note about Ammon.[1] I did not dictate my letter to Hunter at the office and I don't know how Ammon got such an absurd idea.

I still feel that, if I retain the Acting Chairmanship at all, there are only certain things I can do, namely: (1) *Tribunal* articles (2) Presiding at Committees (3) Office management, as regards Head Office. As regards (3), I feel just as strongly that your methods won't do as you feel about mine in other spheres. You have an immense amount of system, which you never adhere to; and you let all routine matters drift, because there is always a crisis.

On reflection, I realize that I shall have no initiative at all until the war is over. This is due partly to fatigue, partly to the fact that my instinct is oppressed by the sense of public hostility, partly by dread of your onslaughts, which I find absolutely paralyzing. My proper course would be to go away and live in the country, and try to recover a little vitality. I had hoped to save you from a breakdown by taking over your work, but that proved impossible, so I have no longer the same motive for attempting to do things that are unnatural to me.

Yours very sincerely
Bertrand Russell

Unlike Russell, many members of the NCF felt that relations between Marshall and General Childs were altogether too cosy. The justification for Marshall's use of Childs was that it was an effective way of improving the lot of COs, especially those held in prison or in Home Office camps. Its limited effectiveness, however, was revealed in the failure of the NCF's campaign to have the absolutists released from prison. Marshall was confident of Childs's support on this, and there is evidence that Childs encouraged her in that belief. When the War Cabinet discussed the matter on 22 May, however, Childs argued against release. Moreover, a few weeks later the policy, hitherto followed, of commuting the long prison sentences often handed to COs to 112 days was abandoned. This betrayal so undermined Marshall's position in the NCF that she considered resigning. Russell was among those who persuaded her to stay on, but it raised doubts for him about the NCF's ability to achieve its goals.

---

[1] Charles George Ammon, who, as secretary of the parliamentary department of the NCF, was responsible for lobbying Parliament. He was later a member of the Labour government. Marshall's note is missing so it is not known what the fuss was about. Ernest Hunter was a young man working in the NCF office.

For relief from NCF office politics, Russell took to reading Freud's *Interpretation of Dreams* (1899). This was, apparently, his first encounter with psychoanalysis, though his brief comments to Colette in the next letter give little indication of what he made of it. Even more interesting is his suggestion that after the war he and Colette should go to Russia to meet the revolutionaries. Colette was doubtful about Russia and even less enthusiastic about giving up the stage to become a latter-day Madame Roland and inspirer of strong men. Bertie's attempt to sweep her away with the idea, shows how little she had succeeded in her efforts to make him understand her passion for the stage. On the other hand, her tactful reply shows that she realized that Bertie's moods were apt to swing manically from despair to elation, and that the latter had to be waited out just as much as the former. 'I feel', she said wisely, 'that part of what you say is true of you but not of me and that what you say about Russia might be true for you but not for me.'

51 [To Colette O'Niel]

[London]
6 May 1917
Sunday night

My dearest Darling

I can't *tell* you (and I couldn't hint over the phone) how *terribly* disappointed I am about today.[1] I made sure that either you were away or you didn't want to see me – and I felt I couldn't do nothing all day – so I walked and walked and walked – very beautiful – but I would a hundred million times rather have been with you. A thought came to me: will you come to Russia with me when the war is over? We could get to know all the leading revolutionaries – *no* one there cares about respectability – it would be amazingly interesting – and a real refreshment to the spirit. *Do* make up your mind to come, my Darling, I *do* want you.

I am creeping back into life, but not N.C.F. life – scientific rather – I am reading Freud on dreams, most exciting. I see in my mind's eye a great work on how people come to have the opinions they have – interesting scientifically, and undermining *ferocity* at the base (*unmasking*, I ought to have said) – because it is always hidden behind a veil of morality. The psychology of opinion, especially political opinion, is an almost untouched field – and there is room for really great work in it. I am quite excited about it.

---

[1] Colette had expected him to call at her flat that afternoon – she had recently moved to 6 Mecklenburgh Square. After staying in all afternoon she had sent round a note wondering if he was well. Presumably he had just found it on returning from his walk. It is not clear how the misunderstanding had arisen.

My dear one, I get so troubled – ever since that day we had tea in Knightsbridge – wondering how your ambitions and mine are ever going to fit in with each other. It is a fearful problem. But if it is not solved somehow everything will go wrong. It is the 6 months after the war that are the difficulty.

I half think of becoming Russian after the war. Will you join me?

I long to share a life of adventure with you – high adventure – and great enterprises. I feel together we could do great things – greater and more exciting than anything on the stage. If I could believe you could be fired by the thought! You don't know how I long for you and love you and want you. I become dead without you, and the future loses all savour. I *want* you to be *great* and *glorious*, and I think I can help you to be. I think you have had too modest an ambition, and a greater one is easier of achievement. You are made to be a Madame Roland.[1] You should be an inspirer of *strong* men – you should buckle on Allen's armour – you should catch the fire from Tcheidze[2] and Lenin[3] and bear the torch here in years to come. The world needs women like you – and there are not many so fearless, so really believing in liberty. You *can* live more *greatly* than you have ever lived yet. Your despair is really because you are not living greatly enough. You have no limitations, if you would only believe it. I can imagine such a life for you and me – after the war – as shall make every moment glow with the fire of great things nobly done. You could be an orator to move thousands and sway the destinies of the world.

Tell me what you think of it my Heart's Comrade. I love you, and my spirit calls out to you to come and seek the mountain tops.

    B.

On 3 June a second mass meeting to welcome the Russian revolution was to be held at Leeds, organized by the Labour movement. Russell travelled to Leeds with the Mallesons, Ramsey MacDonald, and other Labour leaders. Russell was not among the platform speakers at Leeds, but he spoke from the

---

[1] Jeanne Manon Roland (1754–1793), the French Girondin revolutionary. During the revolution her house became the intellectual centre for the Girondins, on whose policy she exerted considerable influence. She was executed when the Jacobins came to power.
[2] Nikolai Chkheidze (1864–1926), in 1917 the Menshevik president of the Petrograd Soviet. Before that, as a member of the Duma, he had established a reputation as a politician of the far left. He had always opposed Russia's participation in the war.
[3] On 16 April Lenin had arrived from exile at the Finland station in Petrograd, where he had been welcomed by Chkheidze.

floor in support of a civil liberties motion along the lines of the 'Charter of Freedom', and received an huge ovation. Three other motions were passed: one welcoming the Russian revolution; one urging peace without annexations or indemnities; and the last, the most radical of all, calling for the formation of workers' and soldiers' councils throughout Britain. Quite how radical this motion was was a matter of some dispute. W.C. Anderson of the ILP, who moved it, said it was not intended to be subversive; Robert Williams of the Transport Workers' Union, who seconded it, said it meant socialist revolution. Russell was evidently more impressed by Williams. But what quite rightly worried him, despite the euphoria of the meeting, was the weakness of the provisional committee that was set up to implement the fourth resolution. This lack of follow-up doomed any hope of a revolutionary peace in Britain.

52 [To Ottoline Morrell] [57 Gordon Sq.] 5 June 1917

My Darling

I got back from Leeds yesterday. It was a wonderful occasion, but a little disappointing from the point of view of practical outcomes. Snowden and MacDonald and Anderson are not the right men[1] – they have not the sense for swift dramatic action. The right man would be Williams (of the Transport Workers), but he is not yet sufficiently prominent. Smillie is perfect except that he is old. The enthusiasm and all-but unanimity were wonderful – out of 2500, there were only about three dissentients. Nothing was lacking except leaders.

To my great surprise, they gave me about the greatest ovation that was given to anybody. I got up to speak, and they shouted for me to go on the platform, and when I got there they cheered endlessly. They applauded everything that had to do with C.O.'s – Allen's name came up often, and always produced a great cheer.

It was a good beginning, but a very great deal remains to be done. MacDonald, whom I travelled down with, was persuaded we should be broken up by soldiers – he has lost his nerve – he does the things, but expects disaster.

The decision of the French Chamber today is bad.[2] But I feel almost sure peace will come in the autumn.

---

1 All three were parliamentary constitutionalists.
2 Amid strikes and mutinies the French Chamber of Deputies had met in secret session to discuss Franco-Russian relations and French war aims. The socialist deputies had tried to pass a resolution calling, among other things, for peace without annexations or indemnities. In the end, however, the Chamber declared, by 453 votes to 55, its confidence in the government's ability to achieve the restitution of Alsace-Lorraine, the destruction of Prussian militarism, and the imposition of a war indemnity on Germany.

I find it hard to think of anything else. Poor Miss Marshall was there, her mind filled with niggly details of business – she seemed terribly out of place. She has gone away for a holiday now, so I can't get a holiday till August – but her absence is in itself a holiday. I wish I could come to Garsington but I don't know when I can. I go to Manchester this week-end for three meetings – otherwise I shall be here. Goodbye.
Your
   B.

Events in Russia further weakened Russell's belief in the usefulness of the NCF. In May he had gone so far as to draft a letter of resignation from his post as acting chairman in which he had explained his doubts:

> Opposition to the government is likely to be strengthened, not so much by pacifist arguments as by economic considerations and resentment at interference with industrial freedom. It is difficult for the N.C.F. as an organization to take any part in such movements, which nevertheless are more likely than direct pacifist efforts to prove effective in moving the world in the direction in which we wish to see it move.
>
> (*Papers*, vol. xiv, p. 163)

Although he did not submit his resignation, the sense that the NCF had ceased to be effective in either its immediate practical aims or in its long-term political ones dogged him through the rest of the year.

With time it had become easy for the government to ignore the lobbying of the NCF on behalf of COs. But then, in 1917, the absolutists found a most improbable ally. Margaret Hobhouse was a pro-war Conservative with close links to Lord Milner in the War Cabinet. Her son, Stephen (Milner's godchild), having become a Quaker, was jailed in 1916 as an absolutist. But this did not change her opinion of the war: in a note left among his papers, Russell said that her son 'persuaded her that Christianity and war were incompatible, so she gave up Christianity.' Her son's plight did, however, persuade her that the COs were being brutally and unjustly treated and she launched a campaign on their behalf. She took her concerns to Milner and he took them to the War Cabinet. From this stage on the NCF was surreptiously involved, providing both Milner and Hobhouse with information. Milner seems to have been quickly persuaded that the COs were being badly treated, but Hobhouse felt he was unlikely to get far with the War Cabinet unless his concerns were backed up by a public campaign. This she proceeded to organize, again seeking the advice of the NCF. Her public campaign was centred round a small book about the COs, '*I Appeal Unto Caesar*', which was published over her name, although it was in fact written by Russell. Russell's authorship was a closely guarded secret: any suggestion he was involved would have undermined the book's effect. There are a few letters from Hobhouse to Russell among Russell's papers and a copy of the following letter to her. She probably destroyed the original, and Russell's other letters, to keep the secret of the book's authorship safe. '*I Appeal Unto Caesar*' was a remarkable success. It sold widely and received favourable notices from papers that would have excoriated anything bearing Russell's name. More importantly, it had a perceptible effect in softening the government's treatment of COs.

53 **[To Margaret Hobhouse]**   **57 Gordon Square**
                                                                   6 June 1917

Dear Mrs. Hobhouse,

Your letter of the 4th June reached me yesterday. I did not suppose that the Quaker booklet would be of much use for public distribution, but the statistics at the end are useful. I quite agree with you that we cannot expect sympathy for the Tolstoyian [*sic.*] view of life, but the thing that we have to preach is that men ought not to be imprisoned for their opinions even if those opinions are such as most people think harmful.

I feel also a certain scruple in agitating for the release of these men without letting it be known what it is that they really believe. They care more about their beliefs than about themselves, and they think, rightly or wrongly, that they help the spread of their beliefs by being in prison for them. It is hardly fair to them, or even really kind, to minimise in any way their opposition to the views of the majority of mankind. I feel sure this is what your son himself would think.

As you say, the War Office is playing the very game of the men it is persecuting. This fact leads many of them and their friends to deprecate all attempts at securing their release. I do not myself take this view because I care about the conduct of the nation and not only about the C.O.s. But I think that we as well as the authorities realise that a large proportion of the men in prison and of their sympathisers outside dread nothing so much as release because they realise the immense propaganda value of their continued imprisonment. The I.L.P. has done everything it could. Its power is very limited. It was not the I.L.P. but the Trade Unions which secured amnesty at the point of the bayonet.[1]

---

1 In May there had been a wave of strikes in the munitions industries which had forced Lloyd George to launch an inquiry into their causes.

With regard to your letter of June 2. I have the pamphlet well in hand, and I think I quite understand the sort of thing you wish it to be. It will, of course, not be published by the N.C.F. since if it were it could not have the tone that you desire. I thought of making it an expansion of the previous memorandum, less official and more human in its tone, but preserving the same kind of moderation.

With regard to prison reform, I must say that I think Mr. Philip Kerr[1] is deliberately trying to divert you into a direction in which your efforts will be enormously less useful to the C.O.s. I am whole heartedly in favour of agitation for prison reform, but those who hold that the C.O.s ought not to be in prison at all do not wish this question mixed up with the quite different question of the more enlightened treatment of ordinary criminals.

I think you would do well to induce the societies for prison reform to move in that matter, but to keep that quite distinct from the question of the liberation of C.O.s. That agitation ought to be conducted by different people and different methods. Mr. Kerr's proposal seems to me intended to produce delay and to damp down an awkward agitation. I very earnestly hope that you will not fall in with it. But I am proposing to include in the pamphlet an account of prison conditions both in England and Scotland, and this will, I hope, help you in any agitation for prison reform that you may undertake.

My own view is that the prospect of securing unconditional release for the Absolutists within the next few months is very good. I think the whole tone of the world is changing so fast in the direction of greater liberality that it will soon become impossible for the Government to persist in the persecution of opinion. I do not wish to jeopardise the prospect of unconditional release by any agitation calculated to suggest that mere mitigation of punishment might be regarded as satisfactory.

I return Mr. Clark's letter.[2] The point of view expressed in it is that taken by most Quakers. I am grateful to you for letting me see it.

I hope to get the pamphlet finished early next week, and will send it to you as soon as it is typed. If you wish it to be in any definite way different from what I suggested, I should be glad to know.

Yours very truly,
Bertrand Russell

---

1 One of Lloyd George's private secretaries who was gathering information about the COs with a view to making recommendations on their treatment.
2 The letter is lost. Mr Clark was probably Roderic Clark of the Friends' Service Committee.

Though Bertie continued to visit Garsington, his relations with Ottoline became more and more strained. During a visit in late July there was clearly some mutual recrimination; it was perhaps the first time they had both recognized to each other that they were no longer in love. Characteristically, Bertie felt depressed and guilty about it when he got back to London.

54 **[To Ottoline Morrell]** [57 Gordon Sq.]
27 July 1917

I wrote you a horrible letter the other day. Today I will try to write more sincerely.

Everything that I do and feel now-a-days is the outcome of despair. Absolutely my whole being went into my love for you, but that turned to despair. I lost the belief that I could do any more philosophy, chiefly through Wittgenstein, and I lost the wish to do it through the war. The war at first raised hopes of new work in me – when I wrote *Social Reconstruction* I was full of hope. Then I realized that I had been much too optimistic about human nature. I have come to hate human life and to have hardly any belief in its possibilities. The work I do is insincere, because it expresses hopes that I really think delusive. I feel dimly that if I made a great enough effort I could find something to live for, but instinctively I put it off till after the war, because I don't want to yield to my mood and give up peace-work; and also because I am so weary that I can't think sanely. I have no real hold on life. I simply don't know how to express the utter devastation inside me. I feel that I am rotting away inwardly. The walls stand for the present, but they must fall sooner or later. The sort of thing you and I had in common depended upon faith and hope, but now I have neither. I used to want to express pain when it had not gone so deep. Now I have no impulse to say anything sincere, and I am only writing this because you wanted me to say what was going on in my mind. I used to hope you could help me to overcome the fundamental despair, but gradually I found you couldn't. I don't regard it as a revelation of the truth of the world, but merely as a morbid state I have got into. There is no cure for it except rest. But unfortunately I can't rest with you, because I can't be superficial with you. I don't think any good is done by expressing a despair which goes as deep as mine does, but my only way of not expressing it is to talk about things that don't go deep. I am profoundly dissatisfied with myself. I should like to live an austere self-reliant life, but I shirk the pain of it. I should not if I had any clear belief, or anything that I felt I could do. Meanwhile I long for death with the same kind of intensity with which I long for the end of the war.

Pain that goes beyond a certain point isolates one, because one cannot escape from it through sympathy. My whole nature has wanted you and cried out to you, but in vain – you thought you could give the sort of response I ought to want, but it was not the sort I really did want. I feel entirely without hope as regards myself. I shall go on being undermined by pain until everything crumbles. The only problem is to put it off as long as possible.

Six months ago I started to write out what I felt, hoping to find some way out. But I broke off in the middle, because it was clear there was no way out. I send you the stuff I wrote – you can throw it away.[1]

The whole trouble is lack of courage. I ought not to care how much I suffer. But things are really dreadful. These days the pavements have been chalked by the newspapers with the notice 'Kerensky shoots traitors' – all London has been gloating and hugging itself with voluptuous delight because Russian regiments that will not fight are being butchered.[2] How is one to bear such a world? I feel an alien, a being from another planet. Each fresh horror strikes at the raw place, and makes it quiver worse than before.

I know you don't like my unhappy moods because they are so self-absorbed. But what am I to do? If you have any prescription I will consider it. But I know of none – and my feeling is that it is not fair to associate with people unless I keep my despair to myself. *Please* write to me – here – I shall tell Smith[3] my address – probably I shan't stay long in any one place.

Your
B.

The very next day, however, Russell was jolted, at least momentarily, out of this mood of despair by a bit of political excitement. After the Leeds conference the provisional committee had started work setting up workers' and soldiers' councils. Russell had persuaded the NCF, though only by the narrowest margin, to seek representation on the councils. As a result on

---

1 This was probably the manuscript 'Why do men persist in living?' found among Morrell's papers. See *Papers*, vol. xiv, pp. 26–7.
2 The provisional government had not negotiated an end to Russia's participation in the war and, early in July, had started a new offensive which had now turned into a rout. Faced with mutinies, desertions, and unrest during the so-called 'July days', the government, now under the leadership of Aleksandr Kerensky, had lurched to the right and was using troops still loyal to it to put down dissent.
3 Frank Russell's butler. Russell was about to go on a holiday with Colette.

28 July Russell attended a meeting at the Brotherhood Church on Southgate Road to organize the London council. The government, which had welcomed the Kerensky revolution in March and been only mildly hostile to the Leeds conference, was now beginning to worry, and sterner measures were taken to prevent the formation of the councils. Leaflets were posted in pubs around the church denouncing the group as German spies and a large drunken mob broke into the building and attacked those inside. Several people were hurt and Russell would have been among them but for the intervention of the unknown woman mentioned in the next letter. The belated arrival of the police to save him was the result of circumstances that Russell learnt of only afterwards and gave him one of his best stories of the war:

> Two of the drunken viragos began to attack me with their boards full of nails. While I was wondering how one defended oneself against this type of attack, one of the ladies among us went up to the police and suggested that they should defend me. The police, however, merely shrugged their shoulders. 'But he is an eminent philosopher', said the lady, and the police still shrugged. 'But he is famous all over the world as a man of learning', she continued. The police remained unmoved. 'But he is the brother of an earl', she finally cried. At this, the police rushed to my assistance.
>
> (*Autobiography*, vol. ii, p. 32)

Though Russell goes on to say he went home in a mood of 'deep dejection', this was not how he described it to Ottoline later the same day.

55 [To Ottoline Morrell] [London] 28 July 1917

I got shaken out of the mood of doubt and depression I was in by the events at our meeting this afternoon which was broken up. A vast crowd of roughs and criminals (paid) led, or rather guided from behind, by a few merely foolish soldiers (Colonials) broke in – it was only due to great self-restraint on the part of the delegates that there was no bloodshed. It was really very horrible. There were two utterly bestial women with knotted clubs, who set to work to thwack all the women of our lot that they could get at. The roughs had horrible degraded faces. The crowd outside as we were leaving was very fierce – several women had almost all their clothes torn off their backs. But absolutely no one showed the faintest trace of fear. Most women would have been terrified, but ours were not even flustered.

I realized vividly how ghastly the spirit of violence is, and how utterly I repudiate it, on whatever side it may be. The mob is a terrible thing when it wants blood. The young soldiers were pathetic, thinking we were their enemies. They all believed we were in the pay of the Kaiser.

At one moment they all made a rush at me, and I was in considerable danger – but a woman (I don't know who) hurled herself between me and them. They hesitated to attack her – and then the police appeared. She showed wonderful courage.

I found the whole thing bracing. I realized that there are things that I believe in and that it is worth living for – love, gentleness, and understanding.

The mob got in by smashing the doors, before our proceedings had begun. It is strange how the world loves its enemies rather than its friends.

Goodbye. Thank you for your letter this morning. Every word of it is true.[1] I shall come back to real things in time – meanwhile one must exist somehow.

Your
B.

At the beginning of August, Colette and Bertie had a short but wonderfully happy holiday together at Ashford Carbonel in Shropshire. It was especially important for Bertie because it allowed him at last to get over Ottoline. 'After Ashford', Urch wrote, 'the power of decision had passed from [Ottoline's] hands' ('Letters', vol. i, p. 133). Colette described it as 'a grand, unforgettable holiday' (*After Ten Years*, p. 121).

While on holiday, Bertie began to think of philosophy again. Colette recalled that on one of their walks he got so carried away explaining his views on 'emphatic particulars' (Russell's term for what are now known as indexical expressions: 'this', 'here', 'I', 'now', etc.) that he lost his way and added eight miles to their journey.

After their holiday, Bertie returned to London while Colette rejoined Miles and went to Keswick to stay with Catherine Marshall's parents. During this time she and Bertie exchanged many letters happily remembering their holiday, bemoaning their present separation, and looking forward eagerly to their reunion.

---

[1] Ottoline's long (and largely illegible) reply to the previous letter.

56   [To Colette O'Niel]   **[London]**
                                                25 August 1917
                                                Saturday

My dearest Darling

Your lovely letter this morning *was* a joy – an unspeakable delight. I wish the others would go on without you often![1] It is heavenly to think of you full of joy and love up on the hills in that big free world. O my love, you are so beautiful and so dear. I love you in every way of love. I love you now immeasurably more than even a few months ago. I am yours, yours. I long for you every hour and every minute – away from you I am hardly alive – when our lips meet, life burns in a great flame between us.

Last night I dined with K. Mansfield – she was in a good mood, having accomplished a lot of writing that she thinks successful.[2] I haven't seen it yet. She talks very well about writing, and I liked her – but I did not feel I want to see her very often. However I promised to go again on Monday, as then her stories will be typed and she will read them to me. Today I go to Garsington. I shall leave on Monday before the post comes.

My head is full of schemes of philosophical work. I hope in January I shall be able to get out of the NCF – that is not very far off. Meanwhile I must possess my soul in patience – such patience as I can muster.

I shall be giving philosophical lectures every Thursday in October and November – they will start me off on the philosophical road.[3] Perhaps they will grow into a book. I long to be away from bustle – free to love and think – they seem to belong together oddly. My mind keeps going over our happy times. I think of the evening when we read Shelley – and Orleton Common – and the joy of the nights. My dear one, my loved one, I love you to the utmost limits of my being. Less than a week now!

B.

---

1 She had stayed at home while the others had gone sightseeing to Lodore Falls.

2 The previous week Virginia and Leonard Woolf had agreed to publish her long story *Prelude*.

3 This arose from Russell's earlier plans to found a school of philosophy outside the universities. He was to give a series of introductory lectures on mathematical logic at Dr Williams' Library in Gordon Square between 30 October and 18 December (actually on Tuesdays, not Thursdays). The lectures had been arranged by the secretary of the Aristotelian Society, H. Wildon Carr, with the immediate aim of alleviating Russell's financial difficulties. (Russell was paid £50 for the lectures.) His book *An Introduction to Mathematical Philosophy* (1919) was based on them.

This happy mood continued into September. At the end of August they had a joyous reunion when Colette returned to London to continue her search for work. Bertie even began to appreciate how much the stage meant to her. And now, as if to crown everything else, Colette finally got work. The film director, Maurice Elvey (1887–1967) offered her the leading role in *Hindle Wakes*, a film based on a play by Stanley Houghton about a mill girl who refuses to marry the boss's son who had seduced her. By all accounts it was a good part in one of Elvey's most successful silent movies, though not a single print of it seems to have survived. Colette was overjoyed – 'even though it was only acting for the films' (*After Ten Years*, p. 122).

As soon as she got the news, she wrote from her mother's house to Bertie whom she expected to see the next day:

> I'm caught up in a sudden wave of events, half glorious, half less so. When are you coming? Teatime I hope. I'll keep all news till then. I long for the safety of your arms, but perhaps there are worse things than a vague (probably superstitious) apprehension of disaster.
>
> (14 September)

Not surprisingly, this enigmatic message, carried to Gordon Square by special messenger, alarmed Bertie, who immediately set off for the Attic in nearby Mecklenburgh Square. Colette, of course, was not there, so he left a note which Colette found when she returned later that night. So she had to write another note to allay his fears by telling the news she had hoped to keep for the next day. Bertie wrote back:

> I'm *delighted*, my Darling, that you have got a job – I don't think there is anything really to worry about. I was afraid of some much worse thing.

What there was to worry about – the less glorious half of the wave of events – was that Colette knew Elvey, was sexually attracted to him and may well have been sexually involved with him in the past. The previous October she had told Bertie she had received a letter from Elvey (whom she always refers to as 'Paul' in the typescript of her letters):

> It turned out to be a declaration and, do you know, I thought it rather typical of him to have chosen that moment [just before he had an apparently serious operation] to make it. But perhaps I'm wrong in thinking rather badly of him. I do feel he's rather prone to sweat people and stamp on them . . . But because I don't know whether I'm right or wrong, it leaves me thinking rather badly of myself for feeling as I do.

This certainly complicated Colette's working for Elvey, and it was to cause Bertie a great deal of worry.

Typical of the film industry in those days, work was to begin immediately. Colette got the news on Friday; on Sunday she left for Blackpool to shoot the first scenes; a week's work on location was to be followed by a few weeks' studio work in London. On the Saturday she saw Bertie and left him far from certain that there was nothing 'really to worry about'. He wrote to her in Lancashire on Monday.

57 **[To Colette O'Niel]** **[London]**
17 September 1917
Monday

My Darling,

I keep in wondering about you – what you are doing, how things are going with you, whether you feel yourself a success, and everything.

I am living on a terrible anxiety myself. Our talk Saturday night left me with the impression (perhaps a wrong one) that your impulse to Maurice was so strong that you would almost certainly yield to it, and persuade yourself that there is no danger, though really there is a great deal. I cannot bear to think of your beauty destroyed, your health and happiness gone, and you shut out from the touch of love by a hideous misery. For me it would be the end of life – I should not even try to bear it. Miles is a better man than I am – he is a saint. I wish I were more like him.

B.

That Bertie was jealous is not to be denied – indeed, his jealousy grew to epic proportions in the ensuing weeks – but his main anxiety in this letter is evidently the fear that Elvey had syphilis. Urch is not so explicit in her commentary, but she does say that on their Saturday meeting Colette had 'carelessly mentioned a rumour' she had heard about Elvey ('Letters', vol. i, p. 155). Bertie's jealousy, which was rapidly to overtake his fear of syphilis, was based on, what Urch called, an 'intense, microscopic, and accurate insight which, though accurate, was also partial and prejudiced' (*ibid.*), namely that Colette was sexually attracted to Elvey. But the conclusion Bertie drew from this, that she and Elvey would become lovers while they were on location, was, Urch said, false. They did indeed become lovers – but only after Bertie had done much to alienate her.

While she was away, Bertie's anxieties grew. He lost touch with her because the film moved quickly from Blackpool to Rishton near Blackburn and then to North Wales. The production schedule was hectic and Colette's letters were infrequent but still loving. Though excited to be making the film, her description of Elvey was not flattering: she thought he was 'hard and commercial' and insincere when he 'talks in what he would call a "highbrow" way'. She gave the impression of a tough, energetic, but ignorant man. (*The World Encyclopedia of Film* declares flatly that he had 'no education'). More equivocally, she said her feelings about him 'hadn't changed at all' and that she disliked feeling so suspicious of him because there were times when 'he talks with such feeling'. It seems he was making some attempt to seduce her – but there was little to suggest he was succeeding.

It did not take much to raise Bertie's fears to fever pitch. His anxieties prevented him from sleeping and that made him even more frantic. While she was away, he spent his time with Miles ('the nearest thing to being with you', he told her on the 19th), who was taking the situation much more calmly. She returned to find the following letter waiting for her at the Attic.

[To Colette O'Niel]   **[London]**   58
[24 September 1917]
Monday morning

My Heart's Love

It has been *dreadful* not knowing your address these days – I longed to write, and it would have been a relief even to telegraph.

I am afraid you have wondered why I wrote such wretched scraps. I have been thinking about you the whole time, to the entire exclusion of everything else – except when I forced myself to think about work. I have lived a sleep-walker's life – not seeing or knowing what was going on around me, merely thinking and feeling. The outcome of it all is that I love you far more profoundly than I ever did before – but in a rather new way – with more sense of responsibility, and with a great longing to bring you into closer union with what makes up my religion – if I can.

I have been realizing, against my will, that I have been intolerably selfish towards Miles, and have encouraged you to be sometimes less tender with him than he deserves. I have a great affection for him, and I have made him go through hell – I must try to amend. I do want and need your love, but I want it as little as possible at his expense.

Thank you, my Beloved, for what you say about the thing we talked of that last night.[1] It would mean so much to me that I hardly dare to think of it in advance. I wonder if that would be cruel to Miles?

---

1 On the Saturday before she left for Blackpool they had discussed having a child. In her letter she had mentioned it again saying that a lot remained to be discussed.

Anxiety on the question of Maurice, for the reason I gave you, upset me a good deal – it robbed me of sleep, and when I don't sleep I cease to be quite sane. I couldn't write about it while I was anxious, because I didn't know your address, and then I didn't know but what it might be too late.

From something you said our last evening, I gathered you thought I idealized you – this is not so, and I began to be afraid I must have not been as fully sincere as I ought to have been. I don't as a rule see much use in telling people their faults, but perhaps I am wrong.

For all these reasons, I have lived through a great deal while you were away. It seems to me, in the end, that there are still further regions of love that we can get to know together – I want to go with you into still new worlds.

I took away from you something of what you got from Carpenter,[1] and I feel you haven't yet quite got anything to take its place. I believe together we could find something that would be truer and deeper, and take more account of what is grim in the world, but would be equally sustaining. One does want to live for the world, and one wants love to illumine the world and help one to see how to live for it. There are things to be discovered about how to live, and I feel together we could discover great things. Without you, I should feel life an empty waste – there would be nothing left to live by but naked will.

I am utterly worn out with the longing for your arms and your lips – it has been terrible – I do not know how to live through the hours that remain. Till then, goodbye, my soul cries out to you – I want you.

B.

They planned to meet the next evening, but ran into each other by chance in Whitehall two hours early and 'flew straight into each other's arms' (Urch, 'Letters', vol. i, p. 156). It might seem that the danger was past, but that would be altogether too simple. Late that evening they had a row and Bertie returned to Gordon Square more distraught than ever. The row, curiously, was over something Colette said about Miles, whose virtues she thought Bertie exaggerated.

Bertie's inability to refrain from putting his thoughts in writing was almost pathological. That he was unable to write to Colette while she was away did not

---

1 Edward Carpenter (1844-1929), the writer and reformer sometimes called 'the English Tolstoy', had been one of Colette's heroes before she met Bertie. In *After Ten Years* she said that after she got to know Bertie 'I new that Carpenter's creed meant nothing to me any more' (p. 109).

prevent him writing about her. This took the form of a moral character analysis, which he headed 'What she is and what she may become'. 'This business with Maurice', it began, 'is of the sort that results from a tangle in the soul'. Bertie's efforts to disentangle Colette's soul were not notable for their tact. Two of her good qualities – love of freedom and hatred of cruelty – were, he thought, 'not very operative', while the third – energy – was of the sort 'that makes a dog run while his master walks'. Vanity was 'the worst side of her character . . . entirely crude, seeking the applause of all and sundry . . . the dominant motive in the most important parts of her conduct'. It was responsible for her love of sexual adventure, her preference for personal success over public good, and in part for her desire to make money. 'She is at present almost entirely destitute of self-control' he concluded, rather in the manner of a schoolmaster writing a term report on a difficult child. 'Most of her impulses are good, but she yields to all, good and bad alike . . . Consequently, though her nature is full of kindness, she will do things that cause anguish to the people she cares most for.'

One might have counted it good fortune that Bertie did not have Colette's address at the time he wrote this so that he was spared the temptation of sending it to her. Little discretion arose from delay, however. On his return to Gordon Square after their row he sent it. It crossed with a conciliatory letter from her, which made him wish to soften the blow – though not, as the next letter shows, by very much.

Bertie clearly wished to lash out at Colette because of Elvey – nothing else could explain why he sent the document to her. But he found it impossible to admit this. Had he done so, he would have found himself in the grip of those possessive impulses which he had blamed, in *Principles of Social Reconstruction*, for most of what was wrong with the world. He may have told Ottoline in July that he was too optimistic about human nature when he wrote the book, but it was still his creed – indeed, the creed he wished to pass on to Colette in place of Carpenter. Admitting that he had failed to live up to his own principles would do nothing to relieve the anger and hurt he now felt towards her. Accordingly he let his feelings out in the strange form of a psychological-moral critique of her character. Having established the moral vantage point from which to rebuke her, he was not apt to reverse himself easily.

[To Colette O'Niel]   **[57 Gordon Sq.]**   **59**
                                              [26 September 1917]

My Darling,

I am much happier since your letter came. I will trust you and not worry any more. There are painful things to be gone through, but I will believe that they will have an end.

Thank you for your letter – it has brought hope. I am becoming insane through lack of sleep, so you must be tolerant if I am not wise these next days. I have sent Miss Kyle[1] to buy me something to make me sleep. If I could sleep everything would seem better.

You gave me great pain last night, not by anything to do with me, but by a tone of brutality which I have felt slightly before but never so strongly. The way you spoke of Miles hurt me through and through. But I *know* you *can* live for the world, and if I can endure I will help you. If you cannot, everything will come to an end between us because in the long run I feel competitiveness and callousness are horrible to me – in spirit they are the very same thing as militarism. I feel them physically as well as mentally.

I will remember your kiss in Whitehall and I do know you care for me. But it is impersonal things that I want most in you. I want you to live by the spirit of love – it does exist in you, and it might be dominant, but it isn't. Don't think things are insincere phrases because they don't happen to suit your mood.

I think it is true that things will be all right after these next three weeks.[2] At any rate I try to think so.

Last night I talked nonsense because truth was too difficult. I felt you a thousand miles away, even when I was in your arms. That was why I went away.

I posted some things to you before your letter came – things I had written while you were away. You may feel the analysis of your character unkind, but I felt I had been to blame for not saying these things sooner. They were not new thoughts. And I can no longer have these things in my mind without speaking of them. But I would not have posted them if I had had your letter.

My life is inextricably bound up with you. I could part from you, but I could not go on afterwards.

My child I long to be just gentle and kind and keep pain away from you. But you have got to have pain before the brutality is ground out. I remember being just as brutal at your age. I want strength these days – and I have so little. Goodbye. My love is with you.

At this point, perhaps, insanity was not much of an exaggeration. Amazingly, Colette wrote on the 27th that her love still surrounded him. Bertie was overcome with contrition.

---

1 His typist.
2 While the studio footage of *Hindle Wakes* was shot.

[To Colette O'Niel] **[57 Gordon Sq.]** 60
[27 September 1917]

O my love, it is so dreadful to think of your unhappiness – and I feel you must think of me on a sort of gaoler – if there had been more time I would not have been so rough, but I was in terror and used all weapons. Now I feel it all from your point of view, which I didn't before. Using force is horrible – I wonder if you can really forgive me. It seemed the right thing to do for your sake, but perhaps I ought to have left you your freedom whatever the consequences might be.

Nothing but the physiological terror for you could have made me do as I did.

I feel *no* impatience now. I only want to make up to you as far as I can for your pain. I ought to have spoken more frankly sooner. You sometimes begged me to criticize you more severely but I thought it wasn't necessary.

Dear One, don't be cruel and ruthless – it does hurt so. The world is so full of pain, one doesn't want to add to it. And when I feel you on the other side in the things I live for I feel so lonely and cold. I have said things that must hurt you horribly, and I think they are true, but very far from the whole truth. I do believe in you. I think you are born to live nobly, but one fights against a destiny that is full of pain. There is infinite nobility in your profile – and faces never mislead. I have been very near a breakdown, and probably foolish – but last night I slept, so I am sane now.

I love you very deeply. For a moment I thought the you I had loved was dead – but it wasn't. Goodnight.
    B.

But it was Bertie himself who was on the other side in the things he lived for – as Colette proceeded to reveal. She pointed out that it was unfair to condemn Elvey on the basis of a rumour. Miles, she said, was going to confront Elvey about the rumour and ask him to take steps to 'clear himself' – presumably by taking the Wassermann test – and she made it clear she would not sleep with him unless he did so. Apart from this, however, she refused to restrict her freedom – 'one should live by one's creed', she added pointedly. If it really had been 'only the physiological terror' that had prompted Bertie's actions, everything should now have been all right. But of course it was not.

61   [To Colette O'Niel] [57 Gordon Sq.]
28 September 1917

I have just had your letter.

I am more sorry than I can say, but I find I can't bear to see you at present.

If, later on, your relations with Maurice come to an end, let me know, and I will do my best to come back to you. In the meantime, there is nothing for us both but to try and forget each other. I wish I felt differently – but it is no use pretending.

I do not feel critical of you – you are acting according to your nature, and that is right. But I also must act according to mine. Goodbye. May all happiness be yours.
    B.

You have given me a year of happiness, for which I shall always bless you.

And that, it would seem, was that – only, again, it was not. The correspondence petered out when Colette went to recover in the country during a break in the filming. On her return, there was no letter from Bertie waiting for her. She tried again:

> I cannot understand. I cannot even attempt to put into words the immense desolation in my heart because you no longer want my love ... What is it in you that is trying to drive me to despair? I only want to be with you and watch you rest, take your hands and let the worship shine from my eyes, give you the love and energy you are forcing me to withhold.
>
> (10 October)

Bertie was unrepentant: 'I *wish* I could still care for you. I would if I could make myself – but I don't. There seems nothing more to say.' Colette gave up:

> I'm sorry I've understood so little. First, that you care nothing for me; second, that you don't believe in my love; third, that you hate my work. I've not known these things before. I know them very well now ...
>
> I've looked down eternity with you, now I've to struggle to regain it alone. You put threads of glory in my hands. Now I've to pass them on to others. How strange that we neither of us knew the

truth! I was so unobservant that I even thought you needed my love. Perhaps you thought so yourself, but it isn't so.

(11 October)

She told him she would break with Elvey (who had now 'cleared himself'): 'I went to him a free woman, with freedom to give. Now I am nothing, I've nothing to give.'

With this, Bertie relented and went to see her. It was not too late for a reconciliation even though, by now, a further complication had arisen because Bertie had made arrangements to share a house in the country with Vivien Eliot.

[To Colette O'Niel] **[London]**
[16 October 1917]
Tuesday evening

My Darling

I keep on thinking about you from morning till night, and half through the night – still in a fluctuating uncertain sort of way, with undecided moods. But I think I know now more or less what I shall come to in the end.

When I care very much, an element of possessiveness inevitably comes in. I must get rid of *all* possessiveness towards you. That means the loss of something that we have valued. I don't yet know how much, but I will do absolutely everything I can to make it as little as possible. The chief thing it takes away is the sense of rest and peace in being with you, so that if I am to do my work I can't be with you constantly, but only as much as will not leave me tired out.

I want to get back to writing books and doing real work. For this I must live in the country, and not entirely alone – otherwise I should grow too miserable to be able to work properly. I found accidentally that the Eliots don't want to go on being always together, and that she was looking out for a place where she could live alone in the country and he would come for week-ends.[1] So I suggested that, as I too wanted to live in the country, we might be less dreary if we lived in the same house. She was pleased with the idea, and no doubt it will happen. I want, for everyday, reliable companionship without any deep stirring of emotion; if I don't get it, I shan't do any more good work. I feel this plan may hurt you, and if it does I am sorry; but if I let myself grow

---

1 While they looked for a suitable place, Vivien stayed at Senhurst Farm near Abinger Common in Surrey – the farmer had been Frank Russell's gardener. Tom was now working for Lloyd's Bank in London and lecturing two nights a week in the city. He stayed in London during the week and spent the weekends at Abinger Common.

dependent on you, we shall have all the recent trouble over again next time, and I can't face that, and I don't suppose you can. So I must have a life which is not fundamentally shaken by your moods. If I once felt secure against ultimate despair, I could give you a great deal, though never again the whole of me.

I wish you could understand. I have written out what I feel on the general question – you might show that to Miles.[1] You mustn't be theoretical in your psychology. Possessiveness is my fundamental vice, as vanity is yours. We are none of us perfect, and we have to come to terms with our vices as best we may.

I still love you underneath. It is shock that has made me cold for the time being.

B.

The scheme for a quiet life in the country with Vivien Eliot never materialized. She took up her temporary residence at Senhurst Farm on 17 October, and Bertie joined her there before the end of the month. It was a disaster.

63   [To Colette O'Niel]   **[57 Gordon Sq.]**
                                                       30 October 1917
                                                       Tuesday

Your letter has helped me to see the truth of my own feelings, which I have been gradually coming to understand.

You say you would wish that we should be much together *but not as lovers* – that is impossible.[2]

I feel still all the things you speak of – the Cat and Fiddle, the Clee Hills, the moonlight nights and the sunsets.[3] Part of the shock was to find that apparently they meant very little to you, but I do know now that I was wrong about that. They are tremendously vital in me. *I love you still*. I was numb from shock – as if I had fallen off a precipice and been all but killed – and I feared you because you had pushed me over the precipice. At first I was too stunned to know what I felt; but now I know absolutely for certain that I love you, and that there is no sort of happiness without you. I still doubt how much there might be with you.

---

1 He enclosed a sheet on 'possessiveness in sex relations'.
2 Actually she had said that, *if* they could not be together as lovers, she wished that they could be together in other ways – at least if her transcription of her letter is correct.
3 She had reminded him of their happy times together.

I must now tell you what made me write such a very depressed letter the other day.¹ I told you I was thinking of taking a cottage with the Eliots. I intended to be (except perhaps on very rare occasions) on merely friendly terms with Mrs Eliot. But she was very glad that I had come back, and very kind, and wanting much more than friendship. I thought I could manage it – I led her to expect more if we got a cottage – at last I spent a night with her. *It was utter hell.* There was a quality of loathsomeness about it which I can't describe. I concealed from her all I was feeling – had a very happy letter from her afterwards. I tried to conceal it from myself – but it has come out since in horrible nightmares which wake me up in the middle of the night and leave me stripped bare of self-deception. So far I have said not a word to her – when I do, she will be very unhappy. I should like the cottage if we were merely friends, but not on any closer footing – indeed I cannot bring myself now to face anything closer.

I want you to understand that the one and only thing that made the night loathsome was that it was not with you. There was absolutely nothing else to make me hate it.

The man is going up and down the street calling 'sweet roses – sweet lovely roses' – it makes my heart ache. I always associate him with that very early morning when I sent him to you.²

O my Colette, my very Soul, the world is all grey and horrible without you.

I am sure you have a heart really, but you are young and ignorant, and you stab without knowing it. I am glad you are being good to Miles. Dear One learn to respect suffering even if you can't understand it, and not to be impatient of things you can't understand.

I have felt something new and better in your last few letters, as though there were less of the insolent triumph that used to hurt so terribly. I have felt that ever since the wonderful letter you wrote that brought me to see you.³

The plan of the cottage with the Eliots was an attempt to make myself a life more or less independent of you, but it has failed. If the plan goes through, I shall be more dependent upon you than ever.

---

1 A letter of 25 October, in which he had said: 'I am unhappy about myself – I do hate to be such a miserable creature. I feel imprisoned in egotism – weary of efforts and too tired to break through to love . . . I should like to hide away from all mankind.'
2 After their first night together, on his way back to his brother's house, Bertie had encountered the flower seller and paid him to deliver a bunch of roses to Colette. 'The words, "Sweet lovely roses",' he wrote in his *Autobiography* (vol. ii, p. 27), 'were ever since a sort of refrain to all my thoughts of Colette.'
3 Her letter of 11 October.

Apart from you, life has no colour and no joy. A sort of odour of corruption pervades everything, till I am maddened by nausea. I have to break Mrs. Eliot's heart and I don't know how to face it. It mustn't be done all of a sudden.

O Colette, I am so tortured and miserable. Should I find rest if I could lie in your arms? Would you let me creep into them and lie very still? Would you show mercy to a poor wounded suffering thing? I don't want passion – not yet at any rate. I want to come home. You drove me out and put a stranger there, and I felt it was no longer home, but I think you could make me forget, at least for moments.

When are you coming back from Manchester?[1] When can I see you? Don't cut short your time with Miles. What I want most is to see you kind, no matter who it is you are kind to. That is the one thing necessary to restore happiness.

This is not a courageous letter. Pride has led me a strange dance since you went to Blackpool, but what I am writing now is the real truth.

When I try to think calmly, it seems to me that either you or I must go under, and that it won't be you. That is because I need more than one should, certainly more than you have to give. That is why I tried to escape. I thought I had escaped, but I was wrong. Now you will despise me. If so, let me know at once, and I will try again to get free.

Do please write at once – I shall see Mrs Eliot on Thursday evening and I want to have a letter from you first. Tell me all you think – even if it hurts. I am so impatient to hear from you. Goodbye my Beloved. My heart is yours for ever and ever.

    B.

Colette replied next day: 'Beloved, my Beloved, I got your letter this morning and I'm coming straight back to you.' She was on the train to London as she wrote.

Their reunion was joyful: 'All the world's transformed for me by having found you again', Bertie wrote on 2 November. They rented a studio at 5 Fitzroy Street so they could be together. In November Colette was busy getting it ready and on 1–2 December they spent their first weekend there. The timing was unfortunate, for that weekend Clifford Allen was released

---

[1] She was with Miles, who was working there.

on medical grounds – mistreatment in prison had very nearly killed him. Catherine Marshall had spent the weekend trying to contact Bertie so they could meet him from jail and take him to a nursing home and was furious that Bertie had gone AWOL when he was needed. Though Bertie felt guilty and disappointed to have missed Allen, the weekend otherwise seemed to have gone well: 'You were *wonderful* . . . and I came away feeling *very* full of love' Bertie wrote on leaving, but he added ominously: 'Don't give another thought to the things I said in the night.'

Inevitably, however, it was the latter that came to dominate his recollection of the event. The truth was that, with Colette still seeing Elvey, Bertie could keep his jealousy down only by act of will – and his will seemed often to fail him at night. 'The only thing you don't give me', he had told her on 31 October, 'is what I ought not to want – the sense of possession.'

In the new year he wrote to Colette in Cornwall, where she had a small part in a film being made of J.M. Barrie's play *The Admirable Crichton*. Elvey, fortunately, was not involved.

[To Colette O'Niel]   **[London]**   64
                                    4 January 1918

My sweetest dearest Love

I feel so full of love and tenderness that I must write once more before you go – a letter to go with you in the train and make you feel my spirit travelling with you.

I think I have at last come to a real understanding of the whole situation, and it has made me happier. Tell me if you think I have got it right. I have to understand things in order to acquiesce in them.

It seems to me that your nature has two sides which are very separate. One is the side that has made me love you, the side that made you a pacifist, that made you love Carpenter, and give him up with anguish, that admires Allen and hates prisons and cruelty, that sees visions of a happier world and loves the beauty of sunsets and the sea, and is moved to terrible pain in moments of passion. It is all this that makes me love you with a love that your beauty and vitality could not call forth of themselves.

Then there is another side: The side that goes into your work, and into your more boisterous pleasures, the only side that you show to most people, aiming at personal success, rather harsh and ruthless, fond of enjoyment and full of vigorous youth. This side is partly indifferent to me, partly disagreeable. Owing to the fact that it includes your work, it is a very important side of you. As I do not care about it, I was bound to leave you unsatisfied, and your instinct naturally led you to Maurice, who likes in you just what I like least – or so I imagine.

I respect people's work when I feel that it is rooted in something impersonal, like love of man or truth or art. But though I have tried hard, I have not succeeded in believing that your work is rooted in any feeling of that sort, though those feelings come in as *controlling* it, but not *inspiring* it. I may be wrong about this, very likely I am. It is largely because I feel this that I fail to satisfy you, and you need Maurice. If it were not him, it would be somebody else.

I had felt that the side I do not care for was growing stronger and the side I love was growing weaker; but the night before last you made me feel that what I love in you is as much alive as ever. I fear that it will grow weaker with time, because your work will bring out the opposite more and more. But I hope I am wrong.

I realize now why it was such a long time before I felt sure of the depth of my love for you. I did not feel sure till last summer, because I was aware of the other side, and it made me a little uncertain as to the reality of the side I cared for.

It is a failure of perfect love that I do not love the whole of you, and I deserve Maurice as my punishment. But there is a curious difficulty: all that I really profoundly believe about what is best in you, and about what is less good, and about how to try to be of use to you morally, has got mixed up with jealousy, so that I no longer have the pure heart that one needs for such things. This is a misfortune.

I wonder whether all this is true. I long to know whether you think it is or not.

Forgive me for having said you were lacking in tenderness and affection. There are times when you have both to a wonderful degree. But there are other times when you want to go your way, and I appear oppressive. It is my fault. I must try not to have any views as to what you ought to do and be.

My Beloved, I have an immense tenderness towards you, and a feeling of something infinitely precious in you, which I want to watch over and keep from extinction. Perhaps I ought to have more faith, and not fear such a possibility. But I see horrible visions of your being driven to desperation by desire for work and worries over money, gradually compromising with your instinct as to what is decent, and gradually losing the straightforward simple determination to live according to your own beliefs. I cannot think of you twenty years hence without apprehension. Vanity and extravagance are what I chiefly fear; in the long run, they may lead far. Forgive me for saying this.

This is not the letter I meant to write. I am such a miserable failure myself morally that I do not know how I dare to speak of moral things to you.

I only meant to say I love you, and I understand about Maurice. If my love were larger and more full of sympathetic understanding, I should satisfy you more fully. I was happy in your arms the last two nights, and I felt all that sense of infinite rest and peace that I used to feel. Goodnight my dearest Darling. I love you, love you, love you.
    B.

Many thanks for the £5.[1]

'The year that is just over', Russell lamented to Ottoline on New Year's Day 1918, 'is the first since I grew up during which I have written nothing to speak of.' He had, in fact, published one book (*Political Ideals*, written in 1916) and seventy-four articles that year; but most of this was journalism and he was anxious to embark on something philosophical. On 22 January he began a series of eight weekly lectures at Dr Williams' Library in Gordon Square. These lectures, the philosophical counterparts of his earlier course on mathematical logic, constituted a retrospective of his philosophical work to date, together with an account of problems still remaining. (The chief problem was the need for a new account of belief to replace one Wittgenstein had demolished nearly five years earlier.) Russell lectured without a prepared text, but a stenographer recorded the lectures and they were subsequently published as 'The Philosophy of Logical Atomism', still one of the best general introductions to his work. Financially, however, the lectures were a failure; Russell seems to have cleared no more than £10 from them.

    The NCF, at this time, was in the doldrums. In part this was due simply to the battle fatigue which had overtaken its most active members, including Russell. There had been cruel disappointments in 1917: the opportunity for a negotiated peace at the beginning of the year had been lost; the absolutists were still in jail; and neither the Kerensky nor the Bolshevik revolution had brought the war to an end. Moreover, the relative success of the book he wrote for Mrs Hobhouse, emphasized the ineffectiveness of opposition to the war through the NCF. In December, therefore, he resigned as chairman (Alfred Salter replaced him) and in the new year began to wind down his pacifist activity.

    At this moment, however, the authorities moved against him. The first mention of impending trouble occurs in the next letter to Clifford Allen who was convalescing in Yorkshire. Allen's health had been permanently damaged by his time in prison and it was many months before he was able to resume an active role in politics, though his interest remained undiminished.

---

[1] Colette was repaying a loan from Bertie in instalments.

65 **[To Clifford Allen]** 57 Gordon Square
2 February 1918

My dear Allen

I have been meaning to write to you, but I have been seedy and have had no spare energy. I agree very strongly with all you say about the need of an informal group rather than our old N.C.F. Committee, and about the importance of your getting in with the big work that Labour has to do.[1] I don't agree with your gloomy view about the prospects of peace. I feel pretty confident that peace will come this year, owing to hunger. The nations at present are for peace in proportion to their food shortage. The change in common opinion in this country is amazing. The talk one hears in trains and buses etc. is all for immediate negotiations. I don't doubt that the present strikes in Germany will be suppressed[2] and that the engineers' threat here will fizzle out;[3] but both will revive before long.

The police are on the track of the *Tribunal*. Two detectives visited me yesterday morning when I was in my bath, and asked me if I had written an article (about a month ago) called 'The German Peace Offer', and in particular a certain sentence about the American garrison being useful for intimidating strikers. So I said I had. They then asked me if I edited the *Tribunal*; so I said I didn't. I thought they would ask who did, but they didn't; they went away, after saying it was about the *Tribunal* they were inquiring.

I wrote C.E.M[arshall] a long letter today. I am afraid she is still in a very worrying frame of mind.[4]

Presumably you have heard about Harry Davies:[5] that he has been had up for embezzling £1000, and pleads guilty. I could never have believed such a thing. It shows how hard it is to judge people – also how queer the Welsh are.

The world grows more full of hope every day. The Bolsheviks delight me; I easily pardon their sacking the Constituent Assembly, if it

---

1 Allen had written on 15 Jan. that he did not intend to go back to pacifist work, but would work for Labour after the war on things that the pacifists would not do. He thought that the affairs of COs in prison and in the Home Office camps should be handled by an informal group rather than the NCF, presumably because the NCF was so hated by the government that it did more harm than good for the COs it tried to help.
2 Both Germany and Austria had been hit by waves of strikes in January. In Germany the strikes were suppressed as Russell predicted, but in Austria the government had to make concessions.
3 The British government was engaged in a new recruiting drive, taking men from hitherto protected industries. The engineering unions threatened to strike against conscription unless the government examined the possibilities for a negotiated peace. Lloyd George managed to talk them out of it.
4 Marshall, never in robust health, had been close to a nervous breakdown since December. Much against her will, she was no longer active in NCF affairs.
5 The Welsh representative on the NCF National Committee.

at all resembled our House of Commons.¹ Although in theory they are orthodox Marxians, in practice they tend to be Syndicalist. How they succeed! They seem to have won Finland and the Ukraine, with every prospect of winning the Cossack regions.² They have stirred revolt in Austria and Germany; they have even made some English people think. But they will never make America think. Wilson's friendly words about them were obviously due to his not knowing what they are after.³ Rumania has allied itself with Austria to resist them, so we support Rumania against them.⁴ The class-war is in being, and is forming an alliance between Lloyd George and Kühlmann.⁵ Probably in the end all the governments will combine against Russia; then none need abandon annexations, because all can take bits of Russia.

I hope your weight is better,⁶ and that the nervous twitchings have not developed. I have joined with my friends the Eliots in taking a house at Marlow.⁷ Won't you come there when you are tired of Scawby? Mrs. E. is kind, and you would like Eliot★ – and I do want to see more of you. *Do* come.

Yours ever,
B.R.

★ Did I show you his *vers libres* about me, written when he only knew me as a Harvard teacher? I enclose them for your amusement. (No time.)⁸

---

1 Elections to the Constituent Assembly had been planned by the Provisional Government before it was overthrown. The Bolsheviks went ahead with the elections, and lost. On 19 Jan., after Bolshevik members had failed to persuade the assembly to subordinate itself to the Soviets, the assembly was dissolved.
2 In 1917 Finland, the Ukraine, and the Cossack areas which stretched along the southern borderlands of the old Russian empire had declared or been granted their independence. In the Ukraine and Finland, however, civil wars had broken out following attempted Bolshevik coups. At the beginning of February Bolshevik forces seemed poised for success in both places, though later the Whites gained the upper hand by calling in German troops (and in the Ukraine, the Allies as well). The situation with the Cossacks was more confused. Cossack troops eventually formed the nucleus of the White army in the ensuing Russian civil war.
3 On 8 January Wilson had addressed congress outlining his famous Fourteen Points as the basis for peace. In doing so he had referred favourably to the Bolsheviks' renunciation of conquest at Brest Litovsk.
4 Romania, under Austro-German control, had annexed Bessarabia with allied approval.
5 Richard von Kühlmann (1873–1948), German foreign minister, who negotiated the Treaty of Brest-Litovsk with Russia in March 1918. Russell's view here is very similar to that expressed by Trotsky in a speech to the third All-Russian Congress of Soviets in January 1918.
6 On 5 January, Allen had recorded in his diary that his weight was now over 8 stone (112 lbs) for the first time since he had been released from prison.
7 The studio in Fitzroy Street with Colette had not been a success and in December, despite the previous failure at Senhurst Farm, Russell and the Eliots had revived the idea of a joint household in country and had taken a five-year lease on a house in Marlow, Buckinghamshire.
8 Russell refers to Eliot's poem 'Mr Apollinax' (1915), an affectionate picture of Russell as Apollo's son (which is what the title means) whose 'dry and passionate talk devoured the afternoon' to the confusion of his hosts at Harvard in 1914.

Contrary to Russell's belief, Scotland Yard was mainly interested in his article. (Not that they left the *Tribunal* untouched: on 22 April the NCF's printer was raided and printing equipment destroyed. The pacifists, fortunately, had a second press in reserve and a special issue appeared under the cheeky headline: 'Here we are again!'). Russell had ceased to write regularly for the *Tribunal* by the end of 1917, but when the editor was ill he was asked to write something for the issue of 3 January. The article he wrote urged the Allies to take seriously the German peace offer to the conference at Brest-Litovsk; failure to do so, he argued, would prolong the war with tragic consequences. Describing the world which would result, he wrote:

> The American Garrison which by that time will be occupying England and France, whether or not they will prove efficient against the Germans, will no doubt be capable of intimidating strikers, an occupation to which the American Army is accustomed when at home.
> *(Collected Papers,* vol. xiv, p. 399)

For this remark he was charged on 4 February with having made 'statements likely to prejudice His Majesty's relations with the United States of America'. On the 9th he was found guilty and sentenced to six months' imprisonment in Second Division. It was a particularly harsh sentence. Russell made what he could of the trial, but it did not lend itself to propaganda as his trial in 1916 had. Naturally he appealed and he remained free until the appeal was heard on 1 May.

It is difficult to suppose that Russell's statement was actually likely to prejudice Anglo-American relations – the American embassy could not even locate a copy of the *Tribunal* when its opinion was sought. Establishing that the American government had not been offended by the article was to be an important part of Russell's appeal. For this he enlisted the help of an old undergraduate friend, William H. Buckler (1867–1952), an American then at the US embassy in London.

66 [To William H. Buckler]

57 Gordon Square
27 Februaury 1918

My dear Buckler,

As regards my prosecution, I should wish to assure you, and all Americans who may be interested, that I had not the faintest intention or desire to cause bad blood between this country and the United States, or to say anything that could be regarded as insulting. The one sentence on account of which I was summoned was taken out of its context, and was made to seem to bear a meaning quite different from that which it obviously bears to any one reading the article as a whole. The article was a plea for the initiation of peace negotiations at no very distant date, and in order to enforce this plea it drew a picture of what may be expected to happen years hence if the war is prolonged indefinitely. I did not say 'These things *will* happen'; I said 'These things will have to happen unless peace is made'. But I fully expect that peace will be made before matters come to such a pass.

One of the things that must happen if the war continues is labour unrest. It seemed to me that our Government would be likely to station troops in disturbed areas with a view to making labour reluctant to strike; and that among such troops there might be Americans. I presume that the distribution of such American troops as are in this country is mainly a matter for our own authorities, certainly not a matter in which the American Government would be likely to take action. The matter was not dwelt upon; on the contrary, the article proceeded at once to suggest to the more fiery spirits that a revolution is by no means a thing to be desired.

It is absurd to suppose that I could wish to injure the relations of Great Britain and America. I desire good relations between *all* countries, and by no means least between these two. I have been the recipient of much kindness in the United States, for which I entertain a grateful memory. Indeed it was chiefly in order to prevent any possibility of such a disastrous event that I thought it wise to mention it; and I fully believe that it has become impossible, in view of the action that our Government have taken against me.

Yours sincerely
Bertrand Russell.

P.S. I enclose a copy of the article in question.

Buckler did his best. He asked the American government to request a pardon for Russell or, failing that, a reduced sentence. The American ambassador, however, would do nothing without prior approval from Washington, so the correspondence was sent there. The authorities in Washington sought the opinion of William Wiseman at the British embassy, who offered a venomous assessment of Russell's letter. If Russell was expressing his real opinion, he said, he should be locked up as insane and if he was making mischief he should be shot. With this, hope of official American intervention came to an end.

Through the first half of 1918 Russell was exceptionally busy. Apart from his philosophy lectures and work for the NCF, he was contracted to write *Roads to Freedom* for an American publisher and was determined to have it finished before he was jailed. The book compared socialism, anarchism, and syndicalism, and involved Russell in a good deal of reading, especially about anarchism, which he had not previously studied. Colette caught the measles early in March and Bertie took the opportunity to finish the book while she was ill. Their relationship thrived under the threat of jail as it had not done since the previous summer, and on 20 March they went back to Ashford Carbonel, the scene of some of their happiest times in 1917, for a week's holiday. Bertie took the manuscript of his book to read to her. For once they were not disappointed by an attempt to recapture happy times.

67   [To Colette O'Niel] [London]
[28 March 1918]
Thursday night

My dearest Darling

I miss you already so terribly that I don't know how to last till Monday night – and how to get through the months without you in prison I can't imagine. I used not to miss you half so much in short times. I really care for you more than I have ever done before – you have been more wonderful to me than ever before – so gentle and tender. I feel sure you are still rough sometimes with other people, but with me no one on earth could be more loving. My dear dear one, I bless you. It is wonderful to be so loved – you have made me cease to hate myself. Hating oneself is very painful. I used to spend my time running away from my own spectre, from something grim and jabbering and horrible, grinning at me out of corners. The last time I felt that was that awful night in the Studio – you have driven away the spectre – he daren't come within the circle of your arms. Deep, deep down in me is the sense of failure – of somehow not having reached something I ought to have reached – but when I feel your love that sense leaves me: I feel that at least in our love I have touched something of what I seek through the world. I have lived through sacred moments with you. Loneliness is the worst thing: you used to make me feel less lonely last summer, and then after Blackpool that came to an end, but now it has come back more fully than ever, especially since I have been going to prison. Passionate love by itself does nothing for loneliness; it has to be combined with immense affection and tenderness.

I want to give you henceforth always the kind of love that relieves loneliness. I hope I can – but there will be difficult times – they will be the times when you don't need me.

I feel that we have come much nearer together lately than we ever were before – I must remember that in future troubles. I want most of all to have the sense of comradeship and intimacy grow more and more between us. I want you to feel that in the real vital impulses of your life

I shall be with you, feeling as you feel. One thing which has brought us nearer is that I now realize you must have acting as your work – until Blackpool I hoped gradually to turn you aside from it; after that, seeing you couldn't be turned aside, I felt there was no hope of your ever making any serious attempt to live a decent life – because a decent life requires work that isn't wholly selfish. But now I believe your impulse to live in a way that is some use to others is too strong to die, and will insist on finding scope sooner or later in your work – it is easy to see how it could find scope, if you achieve success without selling your soul. I do respect you now, because I don't think you will sell your soul, and I think when you get success you will use it for good things. That makes me really care about your career. And that brings us much closer together than when I was all against your work.

All this sounds horribly priggy, but I can't help it. I do feel in all my instincts that one's work *must not* be just for oneself, and when I think you don't feel that, it troubles me. But your despair lately, and all our talks, made me feel happy about all that – particularly Clee Hill.

The real reason for all this moralizing is that I am dreading prison – ever since I saw Morel[1] – one never moralizes except as the result of some evil passion, and the evil passion that is driving me is fear. Some of the effort one has to make spills over and becomes morality. Fear is a beastly thing – one feels so ashamed of it. There is talk of raising the military age to 50, which might mean five years in gaol: fear at once fastens on it and thinks of it as if it had happened. What worries me is the thought of having my brain spoilt, just when I am ready to do a lot of really good work. One wouldn't mind the mere disagreeableness, if one could be sure there would be no permanent damage. At least so I tell myself, but it isn't true, because I shouldn't mind death as much as 5 years in prison, though it would be more damaging to my power of work.

Your letter-card has just come – such a joyful surprise. Bless you, my Sweetheart – my Heart's Comrade, I love you, love you, love you. Goodnight Beloved.
    B.

This is your writing block which I packed by mistake.[2]

---

1 E.D. Morel had spent six months in Second Division for sending pacifist literature to Switzerland. He had been released in January and Russell had seen him on 26 March to learn about prison conditions. The meeting was far from reassuring. Russell was shaken by the change imprisonment had wrought in Morel, who had broken down mentally and physically.
2 He meant that he was using Colette's letter block – not that he was returning it.

Despite the bravado of the next letter, Russell was seriously worried about prison. Talking to Morel had disabused him of the idea that it would be a time for study and meditation. The government, moreover, desperate for cannon fodder, was about to raise the maximum age for military service to fifty-one. (*The Times* had carried an editorial on the subject on 27 March.) Under this legislation Russell would be conscripted as soon as he had served his sentence and returned to jail as an absolutist. The revolving door policy which had been used against Allen could then be expected to keep him jailed at least until the war was over. There was good reason for him to be concerned about the effect that prolonged imprisonment would have on his health.

The situation was the more depressing because Russell no longer felt going to prison would serve any useful purpose. (Hence his remarks on 'unsuccessful martyrdoms' in the next letter.) He thought that pacifists were now best employed preparing themselves to play an effective role in the postwar reconstruction. In Russell's case, this meant doing philosophy and writing books like *Roads to Freedom*. In 1918, unlike 1916, Russell would have happily avoided jail.

It may seem ironic that the government should prosecute Russell just as he was abandoning pacifist propaganda, but governments are rarely as stupid as they often like to appear. Russell could have been charged over any one of scores of things he had written since 1916. He had even made the same claim about American troops, in even more inflammatory terms, in a *Tribunal* article the previous August (*Papers*, vol. xiv, p. 298). The government knew that Russell intended to give up pacifist work, and Russell himself believed that they prosecuted him now because it was their last chance to do so. But vindictiveness is probably not the explanation.

Russell's arrest was part of a stepped-up campaign of harassment against pacifists occasioned by the growing unpopularity of the war and the government's fear that Labour would join the pacifists in calling for a negotiated peace. In Russell's case, it seems that the government hoped that, since he was giving up pacifist work anyway, the threat of jail might induce him to make some kind of recantation or at least promise to stay out of politics until after the war. Negotiations along these lines between the government and some of Russell's friends did in fact take place. In this, however, the government had misjudged its man – and so, too, Russell occasionally feared, had some of his friends. He was quite prepared to state that it had been his intention to give up pacifist work, but under no circumstances would he promise not to resume it.

The remark which got Russell into trouble was not as far-fetched as some commentators have maintained. The American Army had recently been used to break strikes at home, and Russell was able to quote in court from official US documents admitting as much. He made a point of including the necessary documentation in *Roads to Freedom* (pp. 89–90).

[To Clifford Allen]   **[London]**   **68**
                                                 [2? April 1918[1]]

My dear Allen

Thank you for your letter. All that you say does help one. Meanwhile I feel that what I shall have to face will be of the utmost triviality – not worth a thought.

I am having some difficulty in restraining my philosophical friends from committing me behind my back. So I have written out an authorized statement of the facts about my retirement, to be used if necessary; and I am instructing Counsel not to mention the fact that I retired. I can't wholly control what my friends may say, but I can prevent their committing me, by making my own statement.[2]

The Government seems to be getting into difficulties. I think as regards Ireland it seems little short of sheer insanity.[3] But the trouble resulting will not, I fear, be of a kind to do any good.

Please thank CEM[4] for her letter, received this morning, and prospectively for the parcel. I look forward to being joined by Dr S[alter][5] but as he is already a Government official (in his capacity of panel Doctor) I fear I may be disappointed. I should entertain him with examples of unsuccessful martyrdoms. What caused Christianity to grow was episcopal organization and promiscuous charity on a large scale. Every persecution caused a great set-back. You should read Chapter XV of Gibbon.[6] No one who has not done so is competent to take an intelligent part in the Labour movement.

My case is not till Monday, or perhaps later. Tell C.E.M. I like the idea of a laughter strike. I *loved* being with you – it was the greatest joy and refreshment.

    Yours ever
    B.R.

All we talked of is being done.[7]

---

1 Allen had visited Russell in London on 31 March and this letter was plainly written shortly afterwards. Allen had been coaching Russell on how to survive in jail.
2 He made two statements: see *Papers*, vol. xiv, pp. 406–7.
3 Conscription was being introduced in Ireland.
4 Allen was now staying with Marshall in Scotland.
5 With the change in the age of conscription, Salter would now be liable for military service.
6 Chapter XV of Edward Gibbon's *Decline and Fall of the Roman Empire* (1776–1788), on the rise of Christianity.
7 This caginess was no doubt intended to thwart the government spies who opened Russell's mail.

Russell's conviction brought many friends to his defence, including many, like Gilbert Murray, who disagreed with him about the war. Russell had hardly been kind to Murray since the war began, but when Murray wrote offering to help their friendship was renewed. Murray did what he could to help Russell's appeal, but the main concern was now the government's decision to raise the maximum age for conscription. This seemed to make jail inevitable, however the appeal went.

69   [To Gilbert Murray]   57 Gordon Sq.
                                                                        [2 April 1918]

My dear Gilbert,

Many thanks for your letters. It seems decided that the military age is to be raised, and that being so, I fear it is necessary for me to be prepared before I go to prison. As you know, I have been a supporter of the Absolutists, and I could not conscientiously accept alternative service. But if the Tribunal chose to recognize my work in philosophy as of national importance (!) I could simply go on doing it, and avoid prison without compromise. I don't the least mind a definite 6 months' sentence, but I do mind being in indefinitely for perhaps a number of years, as I believe I should be no good for work after that. And there is a lot I want to do still, in directions to which the Government would have no objection.

The easiest way from the point of view of the Government might be if the National Service Representative were instructed not to object to exemption in my case. Then there would be no need of a fuss. And the Government would be perfectly free to withdraw my exemption at any moment if they found me again obnoxious. This is a question of pulling strings; I don't know whether you would see any way of doing it.

I am sorry to bother you with all this, but when I am once in prison I shall have no means of attending to the matter, and it is really important for my whole future.

Perhaps you might send this letter to Carr,[1] if it turns out that he is willing to act. I am overwhelmed with business and have little time to spare.

       Yours ever,
           B. Russell

---

[1] Herbert Wildon Carr, the secretary of the Aristotelian Society, who was organizing a petition among philosophers on Russell's behalf.

It soon became clear that, unless Russell undertook to abandon pacifist propaganda for good, the government would not reduce his term of imprisonment. Murray then drew up the following petition in the hope that Russell would be able to serve his term in First Division where conditions were much easier:

> The undersigned, while in no way sharing Mr Russell's views on the war or seeking to palliate the gravity of his offence against the Defence of the Realm Act, beg respectfully to urge that, in view of the extraordinary value of his work as a philosopher and mathematician; the danger of his powers being injuriously affected by any extreme strain; and the fact that he had already, before his prosecution, ceased his political activities and returned to philosophy, he be allowed to serve his imprisonment in the First instead of the Second Division.

Russell felt this still conveyed an implicit commitment.

[To Gilbert Murray]   57 Gordon Square   70
                                                       4 April 1918

My dear Gilbert

    I saw Miss Rinder this morning and gave her various messages in regard to my affairs. But there is one point which struck me after she was gone. In the petition which you are getting up, you speak of my having given up pacifist work before the prosecution. This is perfectly true, and I have no intention of resuming it. But I do not wish to feel that I am in honour bound not to resume it later on, if new circumstances should make it seem desirable. It is for this reason (among others of less weight) that I will not give any undertaking. I have an uncomfortable feeling that the phrase in your petition, left unqualified, would bind my future actions. Perhaps it would be better omitted, and instead you might inform those for whose signature you ask that *you* know I do not intend to work at pacifism at present, and had retired, but without committing me as to the future. The distinction in my mind is that between an intention and a promise. I will give no promise, express or implied.

    My warmest thanks for all you are doing.

    Yours ever
        B. Russell

Russell's appeal was finally set for 1 May. He spent his last ten days of freedom happily with Colette at the Cat and Fiddle. Just before he went back to London and jail, he wrote to tell her of what her love had meant to him.

71   [To Colette O'Niel]   [The Cat and Fiddle]
                                            April 1918

My Darling
   I find when I am with you that I can't say the things that are in my heart, but when these days are over I want you to know as much as I can tell you of what you have given me – I want to tell you very quietly, very simply, so that you will know it is the exact truth.
   Ever since Falmouth, there has been something new and more wonderful between us. You have made me feel your love as I never felt it before – a protecting love, which seems to have made you really understand the dark terror of loneliness, so that you have dispelled it altogether. I have always wanted to be loved as you love me, and I have never been loved in that way before. I go about all day with the sense of your spirit enfolding me – I say to myself 'nothing matters, because Colette loves you' – and that will stay with me through prison, and keep me fundamentally happy through it all. The need of love is the greatest need I have – more even than for work. It is a need to give, just as much as a need to get – and with you I am happy in both, because you don't mind my giving you a very great deal of love.
   I should like to tell you all the things I love in you, but they are so many that a lifetime would not be long enough. You have sometimes a look of an innocent child, which catches at my heart, and makes me long that you should be happy, and kept from hurt, and not turned cynical. It rouses such tenderness that it makes me at moments almost afraid to touch you – and desperately afraid of how the world may touch you. Then you have a look of sad wisdom, like one seeing suddenly deep into the hidden pain of the world; that look makes me believe in your destiny, and that you cannot let your life be wasted. Then there is the look I live for – when your eyes shine from sheer joy. It is rare, but worth waiting and waiting for. Perhaps I shall see it when we are together again after prison. But most wonderful of all is the look of love. . . .
   What first drew me to you was your beauty and your vitality, and I love both as much as I ever did, though there is so much besides now. It is almost strange that I am as much 'in love' with you as I have ever been – creeping into your arms after a time away from them is still a thing of holiness and wonder. I never even begin to get used to you – the joy of you, and the sense of peace that you give me, are still a miracle to me every time. The feeling of your arms round me is such a happiness that it makes all the world stand still.
   I have a great tenderness to you now, and a real care for you that I used not to have – I used to love you almost entirely selfishly, for the happiness you brought me. Through the Maurice trouble, and through

what your deep love has called out, I do now love you in other ways besides. I feel I could live through fifty Maurices now, if you still wanted me. The only thing that would bring despair would be if I became nothing to you, and my love grew useless to you – or if I felt that what you call the prayer in you had grown dead. But it won't.

Through you I have grown young again. I have infinite energy and endless new ideas, and if the law allows I shall do mountains of new work. I have been strangely slow in realizing all that your love is. But I do realize now. It is my life – everything else is built on it, and it makes everything else easy. Your love is the most wonderful thing that has ever come to me, and makes me thankful to have lived till now.

The time of separation will not be really long. Do not sink into despair, my Heart's Comrade. Remember that my spirit will be with you always, enfolding you in love and tender thoughts. And our love is a living, growing thing, with a soul of its own, and with most of its life still to be lived. I shall count the hours, but I shall know that we shall live again with new life when the time of separation is over. All blessings on you, my beautiful, my tender love.

On 1 May the magistrate dismissed Russell's appeal, but did direct that the sentence be served in First Division since 'it would be a great loss to the country if Mr Russell . . . were confined in such a form that his abilities would not have full scope'. This was not the result of a deal with the Home Office – the magistrate was subsequently reprimanded for his leniency.

The difference between First and Second Division was important. In Second Division prisoners worked long hours sewing mail bags. They were allowed books but had little time to read them and were not allowed writing materials. Diet was poor, privacy non-existent, and conversation was not permitted. In First Division work was not compulsory and prisoners were allowed unlimited reading and writing materials (subject to the governor's approval). Russell could receive and send one letter a week to a designated correspondent (Frank Russell) and receive three visitors each week. Russell had a large cell (for which he paid 2/6d a week) and had it cleaned by another prisoner for 6d a week. He had his own clothes and furniture (provided by his sister-in-law), was allowed flowers, snuff, and chocolate (provided by Ottoline), but no tobacco. All this was standard in First Division – as Vellacott says, it had a 'remarkable eighteenth-century aristocratic flavour to it' (*Russell and the Pacifists*, p. 237).

After a week inside, Russell's first official letter was taken up with practical arrangements. The chief problem – which would recur – was that he had already almost run out of books to read. It took the best efforts of all his friends to keep up with his voracious appetite for reading material. The prison governor had to read and approve all outgoing communications (including the manuscript of *An Introduction to Mathematical Philosophy*) and the brisk tone of Russell's official letters from jail was no doubt at least partly for the governor's benefit. The letter is written on a letter form provided by the prison. To save space, Russell often abandoned paragraph breaks. They have been inserted here as required by changes of topic.

72 [To Frank Russell]   Brixton Prison
                                                         6 May 1918

Dear Frank,

All goes well with me – everybody treats me kindly, from the Governor downwards. I hope soon to have writing materials: then I shall write first a book called *Introduction to Modern Logic*, and when that is finished I shall start an ambitious work to be called *Analysis of Mind*. Conditions here are good for philosophy. I am quite happy, though soon I shall be very bored – but as yet I am not even that. I am proving the truth of what Goethe says as to the soul which alone is happy.[1]

Practical matters: (1) You said there was an arrangement about washing but didn't tell me what. (2) There are still very few books for me. Please see that more come. Philosophy books: ask Miss Wrinch; write P. Jourdain Esq., Basingbourne Road, Fleet, saying I want everything published by his firm on principles of mathematics;[2] tell Whitehead I want to write a text-book to the *Principia* and will read anything he thinks relevant; Mrs. Whitehead (97 Coleherne Court, S.W.5; or telephone) will recommend books (especially memoirs) on *French Revolution*. Tell her I am reading Aulard,[3] but want something less official. Books for me (except on philosophy) need not be bought but can be got for me from London Library by Miss Kyle (Putney 2062; 1 Arundel Mansions, Fulham Road S.W.) who has to go there anyhow on my behalf. (3) I should like my *Nation* and *Common Sense*[4] forwarded here, but I don't know whether I shall get them if they are sent by post? I *now* get the *Times* regularly.

My existence here is regular and wholesome; I shall cultivate my mind enormously. Please tell Lady O. Morrell that it is impossible she should send me too many books. She is very good at selecting books –

---

1 A reference to Klärchen's lyric 'Freudvoll und Leidvoll' in Act III of Goethe's *Egmont* (1788): 'Glücklick allein / Ist die Seele, die liebt' ('Happy alone is the soul that loves').
2 Jourdain was the English editor of *The Monist*, a journal owned by Open Court, an American publisher which published mainly philosophy.
3 Presumably Alphonse Aulard's four-volume *Histoire politique de la révolution française* (1901).
4 A radical journal edited by F.W. Hirst.

but they had better be supplied through Miss Rinder to avoid duplication. But I want a few *as soon as possible* from somewhere.

Life here is just like life on an Ocean liner; one is cooped up with a number of average human beings, unable to escape except into one's own state-room. I see no sign that they are worse than the average, except that they probably have less will-power, if one can judge by their faces, which is all I have to go by. That applies to debtors chiefly.

The only real hardship of life here is not seeing one's friends. It was a great delight seeing you the other day. Next time you come, I hope you will bring two others – I think you and Elizabeth both have the list. I am anxious to see as much of my friends as possible. You seemed to think I should grow indifferent on that point but I am certain you were wrong. Seeing the people I am fond of is not a thing I should grow indifferent to, though thinking of them is a great satisfaction. I find it comforting to go over in my mind all sorts of occasions when things have been to my liking. Impatience and lack of tobacco do not as yet trouble me as much as I expected, but no doubt they will later. The holiday from responsibility is really delightful, so delightful that it almost outweighs everything else. Here I have not a care in the world: the rest to nerves and will is heavenly. One is free from the torturing question: What more might I be doing? Is there any effective action that I haven't thought of? Have I a right to let the whole thing go and return to philosophy? Here, I *have* to let the whole thing go, which is far more restful than choosing to let it go and doubting if one's choice is justified. Prison has some of the advantages of the Catholic Church.

Miss Rinder is away: the Mallesons, 6 Mecklenburgh Square, know her address. Send this letter, just as it is, to them, and they will attend to all the matters, which would be a bother to you – or rather she (Miss R.) will: I don't know her address at the moment.

I am infinitely grateful for the bed and furniture, and for all the endless trouble you and Elizabeth have both taken on my behalf. Otherwise I should have had a much worse time. I feel this letter ought to be full of sublime thoughts, but alas they won't come! My only really strong desire is to be able to do some philosophical work while I am here: in that case the time won't seem very long, and will not be wasted from the point of view of public usefulness.

The *Times*'s of last week have just come – you were right in saying there was nothing in them[1] – also some handkerchiefs, for which many thanks.

---

1 This is not a comment on the quality of journalism. Colette had arranged to send messages to him via the personal columns. Hence Russell's concern that he get his copy on time. Colette's first message, using the code name 'G.J.', appeared on 7 May.

Tell Murray and Carr and others how very grateful I am to them: clearly it was their exertions that got me put in the first division. Murray has been very magnanimous. I am grateful for so many kindnesses from so many people that I can't thank all by name — please convey thanks somehow, where you can. I am remarkably happy; more so than I had been for years until quite lately. Love to you and Elizabeth and whoever else it is appropriate to.

Yours affectionately,
B. Russell.

Gladys Rinder took over as official correspondent when Frank was away (or seemed slack in his duties). Prison afforded Russell not only an opportunity for philosophical work but time for reflection. Reading Lytton Strachey's recently published *Eminent Victorians*, for example, led him to reflect on the differences between the Victorians and the moderns, and by implication, between Strachey's generation and his own. Without friends to talk to, his musings filled his letters.

73   [To Gladys Rinder]   Brixton Prison
                                             21 May 1918

Dear Miss Rinder

Not having received a letter from my brother when it was due, I have decided, especially as he is likely to be much away, that it will save trouble and worry all round if I make you my correspondent. So will you have the kindness to answer this letter on Saturday, and write in future every Saturday, or Friday night if more convenient? If you haven't time, don't trouble; my brother will continue when he can; but regularity and reliability in one's weekly letter is important, otherwise one suffers from sleeplessness and headache through anxiety. Please always send my letter itself on to Percy,[1] and relevant extracts to whoever they concern. My brother and others will tell you what they want you to put in. Remember that what one wants is news of one's friends. I get politics from the papers, and can manufacture sentiments and jokes on the premises, but news I can only get through visits and letters, and you know many friends of mine whom my visitors hitherto have not known. Tell my brother I wish *you* to be one of any visitors next week (Tuesday or Wednesday) — I have not asked for you before as I thought you were away on your holiday.

---

1 'Percy' was one of Colette's code names.

Messages. To Miss Smith:[1] From Washburn, *The Animal Mind* p. 187: 'Some very interesting behaviour was observed by Garrey in a school of the little fish called sticklebacks. He noted that if any object was moved along the side of the aquarium containing them, the whole school would move along a parallel line *in the opposite direction*.' (Italics in original). *To Wildon Carr*: I have asked leave to see him and to send him MSS. but have not yet had any reply. He might perhaps approach H[ome] O[ffice]. I have written about 20,000 words of *Introduction to Mathematical Philosophy* to follow lines of lectures *before* Xmas. Shall then work over lectures *after* Xmas (which I have, thanks).[2] For the moment, shall probably not attempt to *write* on *Analysis of Mind*, but to read and think. Thanks for number of *Psychological Review*: read with great interest.[3] No behaviourist so far as I can discover tackles any of the difficult parts of his problem. If any of them have written intelligently on analysis of *belief*, I wish to read them. Hope to finish *Introduction* in another month or so. Prison is all right for reading and easy work, but would be impossible for really difficult thinking. All this is equally to *Whitehead*.

Tell G.J. I want more definite news. And who is G. who has the privilege of being right?[4] Happy mortal – wish I were like him. I came across a letter from Buzot[5] the Girondin to Madame Roland which is

---

1 Probably Lydia Smith, a Quaker schoolteacher who was editing the *Tribunal*. The passage about sticklebacks is an inside joke arising from Russell's appeal. His counsel, Tindal Atkinson, had pointed out that a letter criticizing America's war effort had been published in *The Times*, yet *The Times* had not been prosecuted. According to the *Tribunal* (9 May 1918, p. 2), he said that 'It appeared like a case of catching the minnow and letting the whale go free. He thought perhaps the word "minnow" was hardly the right one – he might almost have said "stickleback". This remark caused great amusement in court, as some present thought he was referring to Mr. Russell.' M.F. Washburn's *The Animal Mind: A Text-Book of Comparative Psychology* (1908) was among the many books on psychology Russell read in prison.
2 These were his lectures on 'The Philosophy of Logical Atomism' which were being published in four instalments in *The Monist* (Oct. 1918 to July 1919). Russell did not edit the lectures for publication, a typescript was prepared from the stenographer's transcript and sent to America to be set. Most probably, Russell had received proofs (since he asks later in the letter if Jourdain planned to start publication in the July issue) and planned (when the *Introduction* was finished) to develop the lectures into a book, working from the proofs. This never happened, either because he did not receive all the proofs before he was released, or because his new theory of belief turned his work in a different direction.
3 In prison Russell read several articles from volumes 18–23 (1911–1916) of the *Psychological Review*. See *Papers*, vol. viii, pp. 326–8 for a list of his reading in prison.
4 Colette had placed the following message in *The Times*: 'G. is right. Happy beyond words. Work improving too. Earning extra £2 a week.'
5 François Nicolas Léonard Buzot (1760–1794) a far-left Girondin Deputy in the French National Assembly. His love affair with Madame Roland started in 1792, a few months before she was arrested and he had to flee for his life. They smuggled letters to each other while she was in jail and he in hiding. He committed suicide to avoid arrest six months after she was executed.

of such great historical interest that I am copying it out for G.J. to add to his collection.¹ I might in time come across others of equal interest if he desired. Here it is: 'Me voici, ma bien-aimée, privé de la joie de votre société et de la douce volupté de vos baisers. On pourrait me supposer encore d'autres ennuis, mais en cela on se tromperait. La seule chose qui me gêne, c'est l'interruption de l'amour qui m'a soutenu pendant les temps difficiles et pénibles par lesquels il a fallu passer. A part les griefs d'ordre personnel, on a eu à souffrir l'angoisse qui dérive de la ruine de la patrie par des ambitieux furibonds, et du danger de la destruction de la civilisation entière dans cette guerre qui devient de jour en jour plus atroce et plus acharnée. De tout cela, j'en ai souffert dans les temps passées. Comme tout esprit généreux, j'ai eu des rêves de bonheur universel; comme tout homme capable de droiture intellectuelle, j'ai dû abandonner rêves. Après une période de désespoir, j'ai appris à supprimer les émotions causées par les affaires publiques, et à trouver toute ma joie dans la sympathie, l'amour, le généreux courant vital, qui me sont venus de vous. Encore maintenant, c'est l'idée de vous, c'est le souvenir de nos temps heureux (surtout à l'avenue chez la Boismaison)² qui me soutiennent. Je me plais à me figurer vos journées, remplis de travail et de succès, donnant lieu à l'espoir que vos amitions se réaliseront. Mes journées aussi, malgrès l'endroit où je ne trouve, ne sont pas sans utilité. Mais je suis en proie à une impatience croissants, dévorante, pour le moment qui nous réuunira. Ne m'oubliez pas, ô mon âme. Rappelez vous que je ne songe qu'à vous nuit et jour, que c'est l'image du moment dans lequel je vous reverrai qui fait l'unique bonheur de mes méditations. Vos communications, surtout au jour de ma fête, m'ont causé une joie inexprimable; je baise le papier sur lequel ils se trouvent. Mon coeur est à vous entièrement. Toute la passion, tout le dévouement de mon être se donnent à vous. Au jour de la réunion et de la liberté! Votre amant, B.'³ The resemblance of past and present is amazing! End of message to G.J.

---

1 What follows is not one of Buzot's letters, but a love letter from Bertie to Colette.
2 Ashford Carbonel. The owner of the farm at which they had stayed was a Mrs Agnes Woodhouse. The farmhouse was called 'The Avenue'.
3 *Translation*: 'Here I am, my beloved, deprived of the joy of your company and of the sweet, sensual pleasure of your kisses. You might suppose I still had other worries, but in that you would be mistaken. The only thing that concerns me is the interruption of the love that has sustained me during the difficult and painful times through which it has been necessary to pass. Apart from personal griefs, one has to suffer the anguish caused by the ruin of one's country by ambitious madmen, and of the danger of the destruction of the whole of civilization in this war which becomes more atrocious and more fierce day by day. From all that, I have suffered in the past. Like every generous spirit, I had dreams of universal happiness; like every man capable of thinking rightly, I have had to abandon dreams. After a period of despair, I have learnt to suppress emotions caused by public affairs, and to

Message to Lady Ottoline: Many thanks for Michelet,[4] etc. I do hope I shall see her again before long at one of my weekly visits. My thoughts go very often to Garsington — I long to be sitting on the lawn discussing a million things. Please give Lytton my very warmest thanks for his book — I *devoured* it with the greatest delight — I read again all the parts I had heard before. It is brilliant, delicious, exquisitely civilized. I enjoyed as much as any the Gordon, which alone was quite new to me. I often laughed out loud in my cell while I was reading the book.[5] This to him; to you, also, some farther reflections. He judges men by an artist's standard, by whether they are delightful to contemplate; this places sincerity high among virtues, and makes the Victorians disgusting. But they had immense energy, and they had genuinely (in spite of cant) a wish to improve the world, and they did improve it. I prefer them to Bernhardi[6] or Northcliffe,[7] who are sincere but evil; I prefer them even to Lytton who is sincere but indifferent to the rest of mankind. He does not sufficiently consider men as social forces. At the beginning of the Victorian era, starvation and ignorance were almost universal, at the end, there was little starvation and much education. Our age is pursuing the opposite course, and we shall need a set of Victorians to put us right. The useful man is not the same as the delightful man. Lytton punishes Florence Nightingale for killing Herbert,[8] but he was one, for thousands she saved. End of message to Lady O.

---

find all my happiness in sympathy, love, the abundant living stream that has come to me from you. Even now, it is the thought of you, the memory of our happy times (especially the avenue at the Woodhouse's) which sustains me. I delight in imagining your days, filled with work and success, giving room to hope that your ambitions will be realized. My days too, even though I'm not where I want to be, are not without use. But I am tortured by a growing, devouring impatience for the moment when we will be reunited. Do not forget me, O my soul. Remember that I dream only of you night and day, that the only happiness in my thoughts is in picturing the moment at which I'll see you again. Your messages, especially on my birthday, have given me an inexpressible joy; I kiss the paper on which they are found. My heart is entirely yours. All the passion, all the devotion of my being pours out to you. To the day of reunion and liberty! Your lover, B.'

4 Probably Jules Michelet's *Histoire de la révolution française* (7 vols., 1847–1853).

5 Lytton Strachey had read parts of *Eminent Victorians* to his friends (including Russell) at Garsington. In jail Russell read the four debunking portraits of Cardinal Manning, Florence Nightingale, Dr Arnold and General Gordon with so much amusement that the warder came to his cell to remind him that prison was a place of punishment.

6 General Friedrich Adam Julius von Bernhardi (1849–1930), an extreme Prussian nationalist. In 1912 he published *Deutschland und der Nächste Krieg* (English transl. *Germany and the Next War*, 1914) which advocated German expansion through wars with France, Britain, and Russia.

7 Alfred Charles Harmsworth, first Viscount Northcliffe (1865–1922), the press baron.

8 As Minister for War Sidney Herbert had been responsible for sending Florence Nightingale to the Crimea. After the war he had taken up her ambitious plans for reforming the War Office. She drove him mercilessly until, caught between her irresistible will and the unbudging inertia of the War Office, his health broke down. He died in 1861 of overwork at the age of 51.

To Eva:[1] Sincerest commiseration. *To P. Jourdain*, Basingbourne Rd., Fleet, Hants.: Is he going to print two of my logic lectures in July and two each subsequent quarter? I hope so. And can he guess how much money I shall get from him for them *during the present year*?

Life here is very monotonous. If any little thing goes wrong, or if any worry settles on one, it is difficult to shake it off. For the first time in my life almost, I am seriously reflecting how poor I am! This is a sign of vigour that can't find its proper outlet. I try not to think much about public affairs, as one is cut off from action. I like reading about the Amazon, or anything remote and free. I am tired, but the life here is restful. I read enormously, and write a good deal. But it would be impossible to do really good writing here, because one dare not get excited. There is no denying that I shall be glad to get out – I sincerely hope it may be before the whole six months are over. But it is only boring, being here; I can't pretend it does any real harm, though it would if anything happened to start one worrying.

I hope you had a good holiday and are finding Adam Street not un-home-like. Tell *Miss Mackenzie*[2] I am very glad West is to be published; and tell *Miles* I am glad about *Young Heaven*[3] and sorry about *Second Thoughts*,[4] though the latter had a longer run than I expected. Love to everyone.

Yours very sincerely,
　　Bertrand Russell.

While Russell was in prison, Murray and Carr were trying to collect money to establish a fellowship for him so that he could teach philosophy when he came out, since no university could be expected to employ him. The main point of this was to secure his exemption from military service, since teachers over 45 were exempt. To assist their efforts Russell set out his philosophical plans in greater detail.

---

1 Probably Eva Kyle, his typist. She had neuralgia.
2 Dorothy Mackenzie, the fiancée of Graeme West, a soldier who had written to Russell from the front about politics. Russell got to know Mackenzie after West was killed in action in April 1917. *The Diary of a Dead Officer*, a collection of his letters and memorabilia edited by Cyril Joad, was published in 1918.
3 *Young Heaven* was a one-act tragedy by Miles Malleson and Jean Cavendish about a touring actress whose brother was killed in the war. The play, with Colette as the lead, was put on many times well into the 1920s. Bennitt Gardiner, who followed her career closely, thought it one of her best roles (*Russell*, nos. 23–4, pp. 31–2).
4 Not a play, but a booklet by Miles published by the National Labour Press explaining why he had had second thoughts about the war and become a CO. It seems to have been banned but not as quickly as Russell expected, which explains his reference to its long 'run'.

[To Frank Russell] **Brixton Prison** 74
27 May 1918

My dear Frank,

They won't allow me to use the nice paper you sent, so you will have to endure this. I am *very* sorry I was so cross last week – *please* forgive me – it was only a prison fuss. One lives here in constant irritation from lack of liberty, and as it is useless to visit it on the authorities one has fits of visiting it on friends. The irritation passed as soon as I got your letter – I had forgotten Witsuntide.

Letter from Miss Rinder arrived today, full of news. Please thank her for it. Tell her I greatly regret her removal, and it mitigates my sympathy for Miss Ellis. Nevertheless I wish her to convey my sympathy to her and her accomplices. I suppose she won't pay?[1]

I don't want my ordinary letters circulated – they are not worth it. I had thought of a monthly manifesto, but a weekly scrawl is different. I am not sending many messages to you or Miss R. or Lady O. as I hope to see you all Wednesday but please thank Lady O very warmly for her message.

Please thank Eliot for message – tell him I hope his wife is better.[2] If he ever had time, I should like to see him, but probably he couldn't manage it. Tell him I am getting on with work – writing a text-book of the *Principia* to begin with, but that will soon be finished, and then I shall begin more serious work such as I sketched to him. Love to him and Mrs E. – I should like to see J.R.M.[3] when convenient, tell Miss R. – I want particularly to see Wildon Carr some time before long. I asked to be allowed an extra visit from him but have not heard. Would he apply too? If not granted, I must see him at an ordinary time. I continue to speculate as to my position when I emerge from here. I think he may have something to say on it, as Murray hasn't. I gather he has, from Miss R. It is important, and I wish I had something to rely on. Tell Carr the following is my scheme of work, which he may show to any philosopher except Santayana.[4]

I. I have nearly finished an *Introduction to Mathematical Philosophy*, 70,000 words – prelude to *Principia*.

II. I shall then immediately begin on *Analysis of Mind*, before going on with logic. (a) I want to tackle first the analysis of belief, and shall

---

[1] Gladys Rinder's letters have not survived and it is not known what this was about. 'Miss Ellis' was probably Edith Ellis of the Friends' Service Committee.
[2] Eliot had inquired about Russell's work. He had also said that Vivien had been 'in very bad health'.
[3] Ramsey MacDonald.
[4] The reasons for Santayana's exclusion will emerge shortly.

be grateful if he will send me any book I ought to read bearing on this. For purposes of logic, I *must* know whether there are atomic facts containing two verbs, such as beliefs *appear* to be.[1] (b) I want to be clear as to the relation of symbolism to psychology, and generally the status, in relation to the real world, of what logic calls the 'proposition'. (c) I want a precise theory of the nature of vagueness.[2] These three problems I want to solve for the sake of *logic*; there are others, which I wrote to Carr about before,[3] which are rather *metaphysical*, i.e. concern the question 'are there specifically mental entities?'. I expect to take several years over this work, as there is a lot of reading to be done before I can begin writing. (N.B. I don't know *what* reading.) Then I shall be free to turn to:

III. Elements of Logic. This will set forth logical basis of what I call 'logical atomism', and place logic in relation to Psychology, mathematics, etc.

IV. Then I must do a metaphysic: as it were an *Encyklopädie* – summing up results, in criticism of Physics, Psychology, mathematics, etc.

V. When too old for serious work I should like to write a book like Santayana's *Life of Reason*,[4] on how to behave reasonably in this preposterous world. I hope by then I shall know.

As always hitherto, I shall occasionally abandon philosophy for a short spell of other work or mere holiday: I have found that in that way one's thoughts remain fresher. I become more and more fixed in the determination, which I came to last autumn, to do no more pacifist work. The situation does not admit of it: America is now in control. It seems to me that since Brest-Litovsk there has been nothing for pacifists to do; on the other hand my philosophical interests are very keen.

Please give my love to Whiteheads: say I haven't yet had any French Revolution Memoirs, and should like names sent to Miss Kyle for her to get from the London Library. *She* got me Morse Stephens,[5] not the *sort* of book I want, an old stager history which I have read

---

1 Two verbs are required to state a fact involving belief (e.g. that Othello *believes* that Desdemona *loves* Cassio). Russell's question is whether this is merely a matter of linguistic form or whether it reflects a feature of the fact being stated. The question was of considerable importance for his philosophy. See 'Philosophy of Logical Atomism', Lecture IV (*Papers*, vol. viii, pp. 191–200).
2 See his paper 'Vagueness', *Australasian Journal of Philosophy* (1923) (*Papers*, vol. ix, pp. 147–54).
3 Cf. his letter to Carr, 17 April 1918 (*Coranto*, 1975, p. 18).
4 A five-volume work by the American philosopher George Santayana published 1905-6.
5 *The Principal Speeches of the Statesmen and Orators of the French Revolution, 1789–1795*, edited by H. Morse Stephens (2 vols, 1892).

before. Tell Lady O. I have been reading the two books on the Amazon: Tomlinson I *loved*; Bates bores me while I am reading him, but leaves pictures in my mind which I am glad of afterwards.[1] Tomlinson owes much to *Heart of Darkness*.[2] The contrast with Bates is remarkable: one sees how our generation, in comparison, is a little mad, because it has allowed itself glimpses of the truth, and the truth is spectral, insane, ghastly: the more men see of it the less mental health they retain. The Victorians (dear souls) were sane and successful because they never came anywhere near the truth. But for my part I would rather be mad with truth than sane with lies.

Please tell Miss Rinder to give the following message to G.J.: I am glad the bit of Girondin history was found interesting. I will send more when I come across it. I haven't anything to send this time but I probably shall next. Say Boismaison was a place where one at least of the agents in that drama derived much of the strength and vigour required, and there is evidence that the recollection and hope of it was a source of inspiration. Delighted by G.J.'s last message. I want also the following message sent by Miss Rinder to Percy: I am glad he is getting on so well and always exceedingly glad of news of him: amazed to hear he is economizing – congratulations![3] Please tell (or get Miss Rinder to tell) Lady Constance it was a *great* pleasure to see her, and I am sorry I was rude to her parasol: it is only because the *slightest* change in old friends is vexing, even though really it may be for the better.

I remain quite happy, except for the feeling of being always on the verge of exasperation, only kept under with effort. I work a lot and read a lot. I get occasional worries, which are hard to shake off; and I get self-absorbed. I review the past, see where I have made mistakes etc. But I don't waste time on remorse: I note the fact that I was a fool, and try to think of ways of escaping from the consequences of my folly. I feel the main duty of all who care for the world is to reach the end of the war alive and vigorous, so as to be useful in building up again. This is the thought that would govern my conduct. In places, the behaviour it inspires has an unheroic appearance, but I can't help that, I feel sure it is right from the point of view of the world's welfare. Love to

---

1 The books were: *The Naturalist on the River Amazons* (2 vols, 1863; with an introduction by Charles Darwin) by the Victorian naturalist Henry Walter Bates (1825–1892), who discovered 8,000 new species during eleven years in Brazil; and *The Sea and the Jungle* (1912), a travel book based on an expedition up the Amazon, by the novelist and essayist Henry Major Tomlinson (1873–1958).
2 Joseph Conrad's novella of 1902.
3 Colette had said (via Rinder's official letter) that she was living on milk puddings and saving all her salary.

Elizabeth. I enjoy *joint* letters: each gives things the other wouldn't.[1] Love and gratitude to you.

Your loving brother,
Bertrand Russell.

I am bankrupt: Please send some money or bring it Wednesday.

Colette had told Bertie (via *The Times*) that his Buzot letter had made her 'whole world radiant'. Although Russell was allowed to send only one letter a week, there was no restriction on the other writings he could send out. So he started writing letters to Colette in French, disguising them as letters from Buzot to Madame Rolland which he had copied from a book.

75 [To Colette O'Niel]
Lettre [*sic.*] from Buzot to Madame Roland, James Guillaume, p. 403[2] (G.J.)

Savez-vous, ma bien-aimée, combien le manque d'action contribue à clarifier les idées? On vit d'habitude dans une espèce de fièvre où les affaires du moment prennent une telle importance que l'on ne sait plus distinguer ce qui est permanent et ferme de ce qui n'est que passager et fluide. Depuis que j'ai eu le temps de réfléchir, j'ai su bien plus nettement qu'auparavant l'importance sans bornes que vous avez pour moi. Je possède heureusement votre portrait, qui est toujours devant mes yeux pendant que je travaille; il m'arrive souvent de le porter à mes lèvres, tandis que mon imagination me présente les délices distinctes des yeux, des lèvres, des joues, du cou: tout vit dans ma mémoire, si clairement que j'ai presque l'illusion de la réalité. Votre communication au sujet de la Boismaison m'a transporté au ciel, je n'ai guère pu m'empêcher de chanter sous l'echo des mornes murailles qui m'entourent. Je songe continuellement aux temps heureux que vous promet l'avenir – si tout s'arrange bien. N'ayez aucun souci sur mon compte. Grâce à vous ma jeunesse sa renouvelle, et je me sens la force d'accomplir des travaux énormes, pourou que mes affaires s'arrangent. Faites moi savoir si vous croyez qui je suis en danger de faire trop pour me dérober à la persécution. Je souffirais volontiers, sans essayer d'y

---

1 Frank and Elizabeth had written their last letter jointly.
2 James Guillaume was a French historian of revolutionary movements. Russell had evidently been reading his *Études révolutionnaires* (2 vols., 1908–1909) which includes a number of letters and documents from the French revolution of 1789 – though no letters from Buzot.

echapper, si j'y voyais la moindre utilité; mais je ne désire pas sacrifier mes trauvaux futurs sans rien accomplir. Cependant, quand j'essaie de faire ce calcul, votre image et le désir toujours croissant de vos bras m'obsèdent à un tel point que la pensée honnête n'est pas facile. Car vous avez porté le bonheur jusqu'au fond de mon âme – les démons ne me poursuivent plus, votre amour les a chassés. Seul, je n'est plus l'âme isolée; entouré d'indifférents, la tendresse m'enveloppe comme le doux vent d'ouest à l'approche du printemps. Vous revoir dernièrement, c'était en même temps une joie et un supplice – un supplice parce que je ne pouvais vous faire sentir tout l'amour qui bouillonait en moi, parce que je ne pouvais pas même vous serrer la main comme je l'aurais vouler, parce que le moment était passé presqu'avant qu'il n'eût commencé. Mais la joie l'emporta mille fois sur la tristesse. J'ai senti toute la force de votre amour, toute la merveilleuse vitalité que vous me communiquez. J'ai vu les larmes dans vos chères yeux, et je n'ai pas pu les embrasser! Mais j'ai su que c'étaient des larmes d'amour, non pas des larmes amères. Je ne puis vous dire combien je voulais faire sentir l'intensité de mon amour. Ma chérie, ma douce amie, mon âme, il n'existe aucune limite à mon amour: c'est un amour sans bornes, fort comme la mort, profond comme la mer. Au revoir bientôt, ma belle colombe. Le temps passera, et le bonheur vous attend. Soyez heureuse, comme moi je le suis. Votre amant, B.

Translation

Do you know, my beloved, how much lack of action contributes to clarifying ideas? Usually we live in a type of fever, where the events of the moment take on such an importance that we no longer know how to distinguish what is permanent and fixed from what is passing and fluid. Since I've had the time to reflect, I know more clearly than before the limitless importance that you have for me. Fortunately I have your picture, which is always before my eyes while I work; I often bring it to my lips, while my imagination conjures up for me the individual delights of your eyes, your lips, your cheeks, your neck: everything is alive in my memory, so clearly that I almost have the illusion it is real. Your message on the subject of Boismaison transported me to heaven.[1] I could hardly stop myself from singing under the echo of the thick, gloomy walls that surround me. I dream continuously of the happy times that you promise in the future – if all goes well. Have no

---

1 In *The Times* on 27 May, Colette had said she was 'longing and longing' for Boismaison. (They planned to return to Ashford on his release.)

worry on my account. Thanks to you my youth has been restored, and I feel strong enough to accomplish enormous works, provided that my affairs go well. Let me know, if you think that I am in danger of doing too much to escape from persecution. I would willingly suffer, without trying to escape, if I saw the least utility; but I don't desire to sacrifice my future work without accomplishing anything. However, when I try to do this calculation, your image and the ever-growing desire for your arms obsesses me so much that honest thoughts aren't easy. Because you bring happiness to the bottom of my soul – the demons no longer pursue me, your love chased them away. Alone, I am no longer a lonely soul; surrounded by indifference, tenderness envelops me like the soft westerly wind at the start of spring. Seeing you again last time was both a joy and a torment – a torment because I can't make you feel all the love that seethes in me, because I can't even hold your hand as I would have liked, because the moment had passed almost before it had started. But happiness lifts me a thousand times higher than sadness. I felt all the strength of your love, all the marvellous vitality that you bring to me. I saw the tears in your dear eyes, and I couldn't kiss them! But I knew they were tears of love, and not bitter tears. I can't tell you how much I want you to feel the intensity of my love. My dear, my sweet love, my soul, there exists no limit to my love: it's a love without boundaries, strong as death, profound as the sea. Goodbye, my beautiful dove. Time will pass and happiness awaits you. Be happy, as I am.

Your lover,
B.

The ruse of disguising love letters as copies of historical documents was limited: it could not be used frequently without arousing suspicion and the content of such letters was necessarily restricted to generalities. Before long, however, Bertie discovered that he could smuggle letters out between the uncut pages of a book. He tried this first by sending Ottoline a volume of the *Proceedings of the London Mathematical Society* and telling her, via an official letter, that she would find it more interesting than she might think. After puzzling over the volume, Ottoline at last discovered the hidden letter. She returned the volume with her own letter inside, saying, via the official letter, that she hoped her notes would prove her mathematical ability and asking for another lesson. Once this trick was discovered, long letters flowed freely in both directions and the weekly official letter ceased to be important.

The letters which resulted are curious documents, consisting usually of several sheets possibly written over several days, often unnumbered and undated, and sometimes lacking (so far as we can tell) the usual salutation and conclusion. Inevitably, sheets got jumbled and some were missed by their recipients. Indeed, well into the 1920s letters were falling out of books that had been with Russell in prison. It is often impossible, therefore, to be sure that the original letter has been fully and correctly reconstructed. Indeed, these documents strain all the usual criteria for individuating letters.

[To Colette O'Niel] **[Brixton Prison]** 76
[20 or 27 July 1918[1]]
Saturday

My Darling, my Heart's Love,

I *do* so understand that you dare not let your imagination dwell on things that bring impatience: I find I *can't* keep my thoughts away from you, so I make *plans* endlessly, I think them out, I compel them to be businesslike and sensible, and I get joy from their solidity – it makes the future seem real. Since I have been here, I have thought a great deal in the way of plans, You would hardly believe how *everything* for me is bound up with you. Almost for the first time in my life, I find I really *want* to live – if I found I was going to die in a month, I should be horribly annoyed – it is quite a new queer feeling. I am full of plans for philosophical work – I hope to do a really big piece of original thinking (of which the rough outline is in my head) between now and the end of the war: during this time I can't do *other* work. After the war is over, I should like to spend some months travelling, and then divide my year into two parts; in winter, *unofficial* teaching at Cambridge and in London, and writing on social questions; in summer, work on philosophy. I foresee a chance of a very delightful life that way. I must have some kind of teaching. My idea would be to go to Cambridge one night a week. In that way I could be as effective in the place as if I lived there, and yet keep the rest of the week for London. If we were rich enough, I would spend the summer in the country (somewhere where there is a late train). I find my ambitions don't run to political things. I want to be an intellectual leader to the young, and I can be, after the war, and you will be a help to me in that (yes you will). I had become at Cambridge before the war just the sort of thing I mean; but in future I should not want *any* official post, however humble. I want to stand for life and thought – thought as adventure, clear thought because of the intrinsic delight of it, along with the other delights of life. Against worldliness, which consists in doing everything for the sake

---

1 Colette suggested these dates for the letter.

of something else, like marrying for money instead of for love. The essence of life is doing things for their own sakes. That is why one hates commercialism, because it means doing things for the sake of something else, and that is devitalizing, like Duty. And that is really why one loves Freedom, which is really the same thing.

And through all my thoughts of the future, however business-like and however technical, it is always the thought of you that sustains the whole and makes me believe in it – otherwise I should not have the hope or the energy and the vitality to think of such things. Two years ago my only day-dream was to sit in the sun and do nothing – now I have day-dreams of activity.

It is all but a year since our first time at the Avenue.[1] You have a far deeper hold on me now than you had then, though I know you infinitely better. Clee Hill – O my love, my dear love, my Heart's Comrade – I am yours, yours, yours.

I hope you found the letter in Elizabeth's French book last visit.

With little else to occupy his time, his letters to Ottoline grew to extraordinary length.

77   [To Ottoline Morrell]   [Brixton Prison]
                                                                                  25 July [1918]

Dearest O,

It was *most* delightful finding your letter – *so* exciting not knowing whether one has come to the last sheet, going on, and finding another! I loved your letter. Thank you 1000 times for it. I thought P's letter about S.S. in the *Nation* very good.[2] Thank you for looking after mine. Murry is mean. I don't like it. Jealousy is at the bottom of it. (Not only *simple* jealousy, but a much more complex kind: see further on). Oh why are people so petty? Katherine's *Prelude* seemed to me worthless.[3]

---

1 Ashford Carbonel.
2 On 13 July the *Nation* had published an anonymous and very critical review of Siegfried Sassoon's *Counter-Attack and Other Poems*. Ottoline had befriended Sassoon in 1916, and in 1917, when Sassoon refused to return to his regiment after being wounded, she and Bertie had organized publicity which probably saved him from a court martial. Ottoline was especially mortified by the review because she knew it was by Middleton Murry – she had asked him to write it. Philip Morrell sent an angry letter to the editor which was published on 20 July. Bertie also had written a letter (under the pseudonym 'Philalethes') which he had smuggled out to Ottoline, who sent it on to the *Nation* taking care that Russell's authorship should not be known. It appeared on 27 July (see *Papers*, vol. xiv, p. 428).
3 Mansfield's collection of short stories, *Prelude*, had been published by the Woolfs' Hogarth Press in July.

I hate endless descriptions of things so trivial and devoid of significance that it is bad enough they should happen, and merely adding to the horror to record them. Katherine hates you because Murry has liked you; hating you, she hates S.S. because you don't. Therefore Murry also has to hate S.S. They two are almost a repetition of the Lawrences, a little toned down. You will hate my saying all these things, but they are correct. You will find them proved in the 3rd Book of Spinoza's *Ethics*! Prop. 42, I think, from memory.[1] Please tell S.S. that I admire his poems *very* much. Those that have appeared in *Cambridge Magazine* etc. I have read as they came out. They convince me, as the authentic truth of war. I like the bitterness, I like the absence of ultimate reconciliation of discords in some higher harmony which can enable us to enjoy our neighbour's torment with a good conscience. I like their passion and concentration. I thoroughly understand his having gone back.[2] As he says, 'Love drove me to rebel, Love drives me back to grope with them through hell.'[3] But it is a love too limited – if he remembered the Germans and loved them, he *could* not spend his time killing them. 'O German mother dreaming by the fire, While you are knitting socks to send your son, His face is trodden deeper in the mud.'[4] When one has once had that thought, one ought not to go on treading it in the mud. But I do understand that he could not bear the ignominy of safety in the hospital. Tell him what you think fit of all this – but not what is critical. I don't care to criticize what is not going to be changed. I suppose his wound is *good* news as things go.[5]

I am so glad of all you say about you and me. Next Sunday it will be just four years since you and I stood on the platform at Slough and saw the announcement 'War between Austria and Servia'. 'War is mad' you said – and we knew so little that we planned to go to Burnham Beeches again the next Tuesday, which was August 4th.

I know precisely what was the cause of our failure with each other – a thing so simple that you never could believe it important. The

---

[1] In fact, Prop. 35: 'If anyone conceived that an object of his love joins itself to another with closer bonds of friendship than he himself has attained to, he will be affected with hatred towards the loved object and with envy towards his rival.'
[2] Sassoon's refusal to return to his regiment in 1917 was an embarrassment to the government for he was well-known as both a poet and a war hero. Unable to hush the case up, the government acted with unexpected subtlety and declared Sassoon to be suffering from shell shock and locked him up in a mental hospital. Faced with this pioneering use of psychiatry for political repression, Sassoon had decided to return to the front.
[3] From 'Banishment' (1917).
[4] From 'Glory of Women' (1917).
[5] On 13 July Sassoon had been wounded in the head – 'half an inch between dead or dotty', in the words of the military doctor – and was convalescing in Britain.

whole and sole cause was that I have and require a great deal of physical affection, and you have and require almost none. I don't mean physical *passion* – I mean physical *affection*, something which is strongest when passion is in abeyance. You have so little that I don't think I ever made you understand what it was I missed. I remember at Churn telling you I was unhappy – I wanted you to take my hand and stroke it – if you had, my unhappiness would have vanished – but you didn't, so it grew – and to this day all that region, to me, is filled with anguish from that one cause.

You know I divide people's being into instinct, mind, and spirit. You and I belong together in spirit, amazingly; in mind, more or less (there is a clash of cruelty on my side against sentimentalism on yours); in instinct, not at all. All the harshnesses and criticisms and tiresome persistences that you disliked in me came *entirely* from the clash of instincts. It was not from not *trusting* you that I did not speak of C.M.; it was quite a different feeling. Your influence over me was so strong that, if I spoke, even if you said nothing, my growing feeling for her would wither and die; and I didn't want it to. Your influence is a thing you can't help and are unconscious of. I *had* to get free of it or perish – it was because getting free of it was so difficult that I was so full of resentment for such a long time. Now all that is over and as you say there are no resentments or sharp points left. All that I have been saying is purely scientific, by way of analysis.

You won't forget, will you, that if you die before me I am to have Mother Julian's Bird.[1] I shall want it but it is not a thing I could ever speak of to ask for it if you had not mentioned it – it is the sort of thing about which I am secretive.

I feel quite happy about our future. When I first come out from prison, for a short time I shall be rather absorbed by C.M. but that will quickly pass. I should *hate* to lose you out of my life and I never meant to. But you are far more despotic than you know, and it took time for me to regain inward freedom – now that is done and everything is all right.

Do you remember how I used to think and talk about Matter, first at Churn and then at the Beetle and Wedge? I am in the same stage now as regards Mind. But it is a bigger job. Matter I got done just before the war.[2] Mind will probably take about five years. It is delicious having a big new problem to play with – and it is heavenly to

---

[1] Mother Julian, an Anglican nun, had been Ottoline's spiritual mentor. She had given Ottoline a painting of a dove, which became Bertie's when Ottoline died.
[2] In *Our Knowledge of the External World* (1914).

find I am still capable of new ideas. They are the supreme ecstasy – but oh how rare – I have had perhaps one hour of it in my life. The rest, effort or retrospect. I am *intensely* impatient to get out. I mind being taken away from affection and from intelligent talk – but I don't want to be like Chappelow[1] on his 'dear ones' – and in these days one is ashamed to mind anything. But in fact it is *very* hard to work well here, and I have ideas I desperately want to work out. They did not tell me of the aspirin, but now I have spoken to the medical officer and he says I shall have it if I need it, but I don't at the moment. It *was* good of you to send it. I expect when my head is worst it is better than yours ever is – mine is only just bad enough to make good work difficult, not enough to hurt appreciably if I don't try to work. The chocolates reached me – 1000 thanks. Thank you *ever* so much for the poems of Charlotte Mew: who is she?[2] They interested me greatly. I must read them again. They gave me a mood, but my mind was wandering and I don't know what they were about. I only know the mood they produced.

Very interesting all you say about wounded officers – Snowdens – etc.[3] Isn't it sad how few virtuous people have quality? They spend themselves on others and in the end have nothing left; but one can't say they ought to do otherwise. – I don't believe in peace till the year after next. We shall wait now for America to show what it can do. – I heard the *Magic Flute* a very short time before coming in here – it is divine.[4]

I am very much interested about your new woman doctor – if only they didn't all start off by hurting you! I remember the agony to your nose at the end of your first visit to Lausanne.[5] But I *do* hope this woman will be really successful.

I heard Santayana give his lecture on American philosophy – very brilliant and polished.[6] – Lady Bessborough interested me enormously.

---

1 Eric Chappelow, a poet and CO (see Letter **28**). Russell described him as 'unduly sentimental'.
2 Charlotte Mew (1869–1928) a poet whose bitterly unhappy life ended in suicide. She published very little and Russell must have been reading *The Farmer's Bride* (1916), her only book. The main themes of its poems are loneliness, death, madness, and the fragile consolations of religion.
3 Each week Ottoline and Philip had five wounded soldiers to stay at Garsington. She had recounted how one of them had seen the Snowdens' names in the guest book and said: 'Sound stuff he writes in the *Labour Leader*.'
4 Mozart's opera was in repertory at the Theatre Royal, as part of Thomas Beecham's 'Summer Season of Grand Opera in English'. Ottoline had just been to hear it.
5 In 1912 Ottoline had gone to Lausanne to be treated by a Dr Combe who had operated, most painfully, on her nose. Ottoline's new woman doctor had decided that her headaches were caused by troubles in her nose and throat.
6 'The Genteel Tradition in American Philosophy', published in Santayana's *Winds of Doctrine* (1913). It is not clear when Russell heard it; it was originally given in California in 1911.

When I saw the picture of Lord Granville in Vol. 2 I no longer wondered at her being in love with him.[1] She is a delightful woman – so clever, warm-hearted, courageous – she constantly reminded me of you. She must have had a very great deal of unhappiness. – I knew nothing of Lady Caroline Lamb.[2] I so hate Byron that I know very little of his concerns except where they touch Shelley's. I was interested in the glimpses of Lady Hester Stanhope, whom I only knew from *Eothen*.[3] Some time I should like to read a life of her. Just now I am absorbed in a three volume *Mémoire* of Mirabeau[4] and want no more serious books. *The Desert*[5] came from you, but you had already sent it and I had read it with much delight – so I will return.

I have kept my respect for you *absolutely* – it *never* was more than now. (I always thought you a tyrant! I remember telling you so in the woods at Peppard.) But first the war and then the way you took your trouble last year[6] both made me think even more of you than ever before – the splendid proud indomitable quality that both wrings one's heart and makes one feel reverence – but I feel almost impertinent saying such things. I have now absolutely *no* grievances towards you. My mood is rather hard, because of the pain of the war: my thoughts are angular, and my feelings are like a hedge-hog's bristles – and I *dare* not *realize* the war – one has to set one's teeth and endure – and I find it sometimes makes me harsh – but none of that is personal, it is merely the tenseness of will. As far as personal things go I am happy and I am happy about my own mental powers, which is a great relief. Ever since I have

---

[1] At Ottoline's suggestion Bertie was reading the *Private Correspondence* of Lord Granville Leveson Gower, edited by his daughter-in-law (2 vols., 1917). Lord Granville (1773–1846) was a Tory politician and diplomat. Many of the letters included were between him and Henrietta Francis, Lady Bessborough (1761–1821), his mistress with whom he had two children. Her letters reveal all the virtues Bertie mentions. She was evidently devoted to Granville who, from his letters, appears superficial and foppish. Bertie had wondered (14 July) how she could love 'such a stick'. The frontispiece of volume ii gives the answer: he was very good-looking – though a contemporary thought he had 'too much of a fair, soft, sweet sort of beauty'.
[2] Lady Caroline Lamb (1785–1828) was Lady Bessborough's daughter by her marriage to the Earl of Bessborough. She married William Lamb, Viscount Melbourne, in 1805 but is best-known for her affair with Byron in 1812–1813.
[3] Lady Hester Stanhope (1776–1839), English traveller and eccentric. Adopting Eastern dress, she travelled with the Bedouin and eventually settled on Mt Lebanon, where she created her own religion based on astrology. The tribes among whom she lived thought her divinely inspired and, towards the end of her life, she seems to have agreed with them. Her life on Mt Lebanon is described by Alexander Kinglake in *Eothen, or Traces of Travel Brought Home from the East* (1844).
[4] Honoré-Gabriel Riqueti, Comte de Mirabeau (1749–1791), a French aristocrat rejected by his class, he became, despite his moderate views, an important leader of the revolutionary National Assembly. It is not known which *Mémoire* Russell was reading.
[5] Probably *Mogu, The Wanderer, or The Desert* (1917) a play by Padraic Colum.
[6] In 1917 Ottoline had learnt for the first time of Philip's infidelities, when her maid and his secretary were both pregnant by him. The crisis completely unnerved Philip who had to be put in a nursing home.

been here, you have been unbelievably good to me, and it has been a very great happiness. I do value your marks of affection more than I can say. Goodbye dearest O. till Wednesday – with much love
   Your
      B.

The aspirin that Ottoline had thoughtfully left with the prison doctor was to treat the headaches that began to plague Russell during the second half of his imprisonment. By late July his stay in jail had ceased to be philosophically productive. The major works he wrote in prison – *An Introduction to Mathematical Logic* and a long review of Dewey's *Essays in Experimental Logic* – were finished in June. Extensive reading in psychology produced new ideas on the philosophy of mind in the first half of July, but after that he wrote only fragmentary notes. The problems he wanted to work on now, belief and the nature of propositions, were more difficult than his earlier prison work, but the long months in prison had sapped his powers of concentration. He also began to run out of suitable philosophical reading material and he missed the opportunity to discuss his ideas with other philosophers. Moreover, now he could write freely, he spent more of his time writing letters.

[To Ottoline Morrell] **[Brixton Prison]** 78
1 August 1918

It *was* delightful seeing you yesterday, dearest O., and you wouldn't believe how I loved your letter. I was sorry you had such a dreadful cold. All the doctors who ever go at you begin by making you worse, however they may end. The flowers you brought are *glorious* – they glow like sunshine, and put off the coming of twilight, they are so bright. I do love bright, bright colours – what a comfort it is to have got past the aesthetic days of subdued tints. I loved your bright dress. Being here, I have *time* for delights of that sort – generally I am too full of things I want to accomplish. You are quite right that it has been good for me being here. For two years I had lived in a continual bustle – no time to read or think, a great deal of misery made bearable by excitement, not by rising above it. When I came here, I had reached a creative mood, in which I was no longer haunted by horrors to the verge of madness. The quiet, the reading and thinking, the absence of excitement, have done me a world of good. Earlier, I could hardly have stood it, but now it is fruitful. However, I have had enough of it. I have had time to think out everything I can think out in here, and now I need the stimulus of talk. I want to discuss philosophy in order to get on with my new notions. And I want refreshment – in here one gets tired for lack of change. But not in a way to matter; on the whole, being here will have done me good.

I am glad you met Littlewood[1] at last. I wonder what you made of him. I love him. Ouf! I hate all the Bloomsbury crew, with their sneers at anything that has live feeling in it. *Beastly* of them to be down on S[iegfried] S[assoon]. They put up with me because they know I can make any one look ridiculous – if I had less brains and less satire, they would all be down on me – as it is, they whisper against me in corners, and flatter me to my face. They are a rotten crew. I wish you had more congenial 'friends'. But I don't know who.

You are wrong, dearest O, to feel as you do about Julian. It is right she should be as she is at her present age, and right the school should keep her so. Remember that if one's spiritual life is as constant as yours, it wears one out as it has you. It is really important to have long times in which it does not appear. I remember myself at J's age – hard and utterly [un]feeling, vexing my people just as she vexes you, and instinctively resenting any attempt to awaken what was dormant. It is a peculiarly hard age, about 12. I think perhaps it is a weakness of yours to dig at people too much, to want too frequent evidence of their best – and when you feel responsible, as with J., your self-depreciation comes in, which is hard on the child. You altogether over-estimate what a parent can do. I remember your objecting to my praise of the Chinese doctrine of Tao because it seemed to you too passive. But in actual fact it comes very near the truth. The child will grow and develop by the process of nature, and what you can do (beyond material care) is almost wholly confined to *example*. Don't let your affection for the child be anxious and moral – you should want it to be natural and rather animal. Oh forgive me – I have such a terrible realization of children and what they need, I *do* want you to realize too. You want to do *too much*. If you don't *like* the child, you can do very little. If you do like her, that is enough. But have patience with phases – they pass, but are necessary at the time.

One mustn't let the war wear one down too much – it is really important to enjoy things and keep alive. One can do so little good to people if one is depressed beyond a point. I wish all the flowers in your garden gave you half the joy that I get from the ones you send me. The human race will survive, and the things we value will flourish again. One must be ready to take one's part in revivification when the time comes. The world is rather horrible – it always was, though we didn't realize it so clearly; but the good things are real. There is poetry and beauty and delight in the world, and it is possible for human spirits to

---

1 The mathematician J.E. Littlewood, see Letter **6**.

come close one to another. We hoped too much, but it is right to hope *something*, and to live for that. The life of the world is oddly instinctive in me. I hardly knew how much until the war came. And I feel *sure* that after the war things will revive quicker than we expect. Twenty to forty years hence there will be a wonderful period. We may not live to *see* it, but we can live to help it to come.

I'm afraid these long letters will cease when I am out of prison. Here I have such infinite leisure. When one is out there never seems leisure for long letters, though yours are *fairly* long, for which I am more grateful than I can say. But my life is bound to have less leisure than yours at Garsington. When I am out I see such millions of people, and do so much altogether – no one has the least idea how much I get into a day. But it gives a *hurried* feeling to everything, which is a pity.

I *am* so glad you have made friends with Elizabeth. She *loves* you. I am very fond of her, but embarrassed by the necessity of not rousing my brother's jealousy, which is quite oriental. I wonder what you will make of Miss Wrinch.[1] She seems to have blossomed out since I have been here, but I should think it would be rather theoretical. I wonder if you will find her so academic that you can't take any interest in her. I *hope* not. I like her *very* much – she has *very* good brains. I am delighted about Ka Cox and Arnold Foster[2] – she is just right for him. And he will afford full scope for her maternal impulses. I wonder how P's speech went off – I hope it was a success.[3] I hear America says the war is to end in January 1920. I daresay that is about right, though I think September 1920 more likely. I believe it will end in *complete* defeat of Germany – like 1814. We are in 1810 now, after Tilsit.[4]

Here is an idea for a book: all the letters one can find written after Austerlitz[5] by people who were there. I read lately Napoleon's to Joséphine[6] and Lord Granville's to Lady Bessborough.[7] The point of both was their triviality. 'How it struck contemporaries.' Then one

---

1 Dorothy Wrinch was going to Garsington.
2 Katherine ('Ka') Laird Cox (1887–1938). Before the war, as a student at Cambridge, she had been one of the group of 'Neo-Pagans' around Rupert Brooke, with whom she fell in love. In September 1918 she married William Arnold-Forster (1885–1951), a painter in the Royal Naval Reserve.
3 Ottoline had said that Philip was to give a pacifist speech on 30 July.
4 The collaboration between France and Russia which began with the Treaty of Tilsit in 1807 ended in 1810 when Russia withdrew from Napoleon's blockade of Britain.
5 The Battle of Austerlitz (1805), one of Napoleon's great victories, in which he decisively defeated Austria and Russia.
6 Letters of 3, 5, and 7 December, 1805. See J. Haumont (ed.), *Lettres de Napoléon à Joséphine et de Joséphine à Napoléon* (Paris, 1968), pp. 187–90.
7 Lord Granville, *Private Correspondence 1781–1821*, (London, 1917), vol. ii, pp. 151–2 (letter of 6 Dec. 1805).

would show how a modern person sees an event of that sort through newspaper headlines, with a historical sense which is oddly vulgar and not fundamentally true, though much more like history than what people used to feel. I commend it to you.

I am convinced that by studying the secretions of the glands we might discover how to modify character artificially. I hope we shan't, because the characters which the Education Authorities would order schoolmasters to produce would be much worse than God's unaided efforts. I used to welcome advances in knowledge, because knowledge is power; now I dread them for the same reason. Everything good is due to chance, and the area of chance is continually diminishing. There is nothing for it but conscious principle, in future; and it is a fearful battle to keep one's end up as regards that. Reading so much 18th Century has made me want to be sharp and clear, *net*.[1] I like words to cut like a scimitar, clean, deep cuts, further each time than you would think such an apparently easy blow could penetrate.

I long to be out. Happiness and work both call me. My mental powers are renewed, and I long to do a really big piece of exploring work once more. I thought it was over for ever. I bless that doctor. Queer thing mind and body – who could have thought the seat of intellect was there?[2] So far I have only hit on a number of new hypotheses probably none are right, but they afford material for work, and should lead to something. I *do* feel so happy about you and me. Goodbye dearest O. with much much love,

   Your
     B.

In late July Frank Russell had been to see the Home Secretary, Sir George Cave, in the hope of securing an early release for Bertie. He tackled Cave with confidence: 'Of course, young Cave will have to do it', he told Bertie, 'because he was my fag at Winchester.' It seemed to work: Frank told Bertie he would probably be released in August, but certainly no later than 18 September. On 8 August, however, Bertie got Cave's formal response, refusing early release. Bertie was bitterly disappointed, though a visit and a letter from Colette on the same day helped keep his spirits up for a while.

Bertie's enthusiasm for making plans for after his release was given plenty of scope in trying to decide who would live where. A very complicated

---

[1] French for 'clear-cut', 'distinct'.
[2] The doctor had cured Russell of piles.

chain of tenancies was involved, made worse by the fact that not all of those involved knew of the relationships between the others. Frank, surprisingly, did not know of Bertie's relationship with Colette, though, as Colette reported, he had 'formed his own opinions'. (Bertie, throwing caution to the winds, thought of telling him, but in the event his courage failed him and he told Elizabeth instead.) Colette and Miles had now separated: Colette stayed at the Attic and Miles moved into the Studio, which he now wanted to leave. Bertie's apartment, 34 Russell Chambers, was sublet to (of all people) Helen Dudley, who was now preparing to return to America for good. Frank was not anxious for Bertie to return to 57 Gordon Square, because his marriage had turned bad (in a remarkably short time even for him) and Bertie was inclined to take Elizabeth's side in what was becoming a fierce dispute. In addition, Bertie still had a share in the Eliots' house at Marlow though he now wished to extricate himself from that arrangement.

Bertie applied his mind relentlessly to these problems, producing more plans and instructions than would precede a medium-sized military operation. His main idea was that Colette should move into 34 Russell Chambers when it became vacant. In part this was an economy measure, but it would also give them the opportunity to be together without arousing the censure of his landlord (who in those days had considerable power over the domestic arrangements of his tenants). Elizabeth facilitated this by renting the Attic from Colette with the intention of lending it to Dorothy Wrinch and using it occasionally herself as a place to write. (Elizabeth was the only one with plenty of money, since *Elizabeth and Her German Garden* had become a best seller. Frank, who should have had plenty, was as unfortunate in his business ventures as in his marriages.)

In an earlier letter Bertie had advanced the thesis (using Mirabeau as his example) that unusual energy arose either from unusual vanity or from unusual love of power. Colette, whom he had once accused of vanity and who now no doubt wondered whether this might not have some redeeming value in his eyes, had asked him to expand on the relation between vanity and energy. Instead, he wrote on the relation between vanity and sex.

[To Colette O'Niel]   **[Brixton Prison]**   79
                                                8 August 1918
                                                Thursday

My dearest Darling

You are gone and I have read your dear dear letter – such a wonderful letter. O my Heart, I do do love you. Don't talk about wishing to be worthy of my love. You *are* glorious, my Beloved – you are beautiful and strong and with a wind of greatness blowing through you from the outer world. That is why you can love. O Colette, my dear and tender love, my very soul of swift and noble passion, I don't believe you know the thousandth part of the wonder and beauty of you and your love. My dear, you know that my spirit is a burning flame – scorching to whatever is not as burning – you know that till I met you I had come to fear the contact with others because of the pain they suffered – and with you it was different: an equal flame leapt up in you. Don't be ignorant of what is great in you. Passion, force, will, the power to feel great things greatly – heart, not yet full-grown, but existing – truth – and knowledge of the ultimate sadness – all these you have. And your beauty of face grows, and your voice becomes richer and more tender. And there is no limit to the wisdom that will be yours as the years pass. And for all these things, and above all for your love, I love you – and having found you I have found my home.

I *am* so thankful that you are working at the Experimental Theatre.[1] Oh I *do* hope it will go and flourish; it must be uphill work for a long time. It is such an *infinite* joy to me that you will have work that I can feel worth while, that is not *merely* personal to you. With your dual nature, you would never have a satisfactory life unless your work were both useful and more or less satisfying to your vanity. Neither alone would do. The plan of spending half your work on the ordinary theatre and half addressing envelopes for Miss Rinder was not satisfactory; it was like hopping on one leg for an hour and then hopping on the other for the next hour, instead of walking on both; you needed something that *combined* both impulses and now you will have it.

Vanity – yes you have lots. Almost all energetic people have. It doesn't matter, but one wants to use it as a spur to work and ambition, and as suggesting possibilities of human relations, not as a *passion* thing, or a thing making truth about oneself unbearable and flattery indispensable. Vanity and sex are very closely akin, especially in women. In many women, there is nothing of sex except vanity: they want to be admired, but if they can secure that, they desire nothing further. Women of that sort exist to drive men insane. You are not of that sort, because you have actual sex instincts well developed, thank heaven. Vanity is the *beginning* of every sex impulse in women, I should say; it ought, later to develop beyond vanity, but often doesn't. In men, vanity comes in but love of power comes in too, and sheer physical desire plays a larger part than is common with women. Rape, for example, clearly affords no satisfaction to vanity, yet most men would commit rape if it were safe.

---

1 Colette and Miles were trying to establish an experimental little theatre in London. Although the 'little theatre' movement, which spread repertory theatres to many provincial towns, was beginning at this time, this particular effort seems to have been short lived.

To a man, there is an added pleasure when the woman is unwilling, because it enhances his sense of power. I should say that is the basis of Sadism. This sort of satisfaction is impossible to a woman, by the physical nature of things. And therefore the desire to be feared is rarer among women than among men. Are these the sort of reflections you wanted? If not, tell me what you want and I will try again.

I was bitterly disappointed by Cave's letter, and to find I had even been robbed of the two weeks I thought my brother had secured. It is *so* difficult to talk when you come, there is so much one wants to say and can't, and one has such a feeling that moments are precious. Eight weeks more of this place – but that is not much in a lifetime. And of course the longer I am here the better is my chance of not being called up. Still, it *is* a blow. *October 2 is the date.*

If Miles gives up the Studio, I will take it on. It would suit me very well. One big room is just what I want. I could work there admirably. And then I shan't mind being turned out of Gordon Square, if I am. If you are going to feed at home for economy, let me join you. I have been resolving in my mind that food is the best thing to save on – we can feed at home together for very little. I *think* I shall be fairly comfortably off for the rest of this year, and at any rate able to keep us both from starving. Your having got the Attic let is grand. I am glad it is Elizabeth.

Is Miles taking the separation well? Your letters don't tell me enough of the sort of things I long to know – all sorts of intimate events. His letter seems very friendly. I *am* so glad you are going to be working with him, as it ought to keep you friends. Try to read Ottoline's letters.[1] I send two more with this, containing bits about you. I *am* so glad you feel as you do about them – the things she says about you are generous and good. Don't ever let her know you have seen her letters. I doubt if you and she could be friends, but it is worth attempting if she makes a move.

I never knew Lafcadio Hearn[2] – he is *very* interesting in his writing. I wonder what Priscilla's brother turned out to be like.[3] It's interesting your doing *Wuthering Heights*.[4] You should read Mrs Gaskell's *Life of the Brontës*. I do hope you will be able to sell it.

---

1 Along with this letter to Colette, Bertie smuggled some of Ottoline's letters to him out of prison for safe keeping. Ottoline's handwriting in her letters to Bertie is virtually indecipherable.
2 Lafcadio Hearn (1850–1904) an American journalist who was sent to Japan by *Harper's*, stayed there and became a citizen. He wrote several books explaining Japan to the West. Colette had been reading him and asked if Bertie had known him.
3 Colette's mother's 'black sheep brother from Australia' was expected.
4 Colette was preparing a screenplay of Emily Brontë's *Wuthering Heights*, but it was not filmed.

My heart, your last sheet has troubled me so – you wanting to lie in my arms and cry – it is what I want to do – it fills my eyes with tears to read what you have written. My Colette, I have found with you the love I sought – I might so well have died without finding it – and now I know the dream I had in my heart was not vain imagining, but a creative dream – and with you it has taken substance, no longer haunting, maddeningly, in the night but walking beside me in the morning sun. I bless you, Beloved, every moment. Goodbye, my lovely one, my Soul, my laughter in this dark world.

B.

Bertie's disappointment over Cave's letter coincided with disturbing news from Colette. In a letter written in late July or early August she had told him of recent meetings with Elvey and also of a lunch with her mother and six others including an American army colonel (whom she identified as 'Col. J.B. Mitchell' in her autobiography, but only as 'Col. J.' in the typescript of her letters). From what she told Bertie, it was plain the colonel interested her:

> [T]he Col. is the sort of person one gets to know instantly. So I dined with him that evening . . . He told me all about himself and his wife . . . and finally confided a good deal about his young woman acquired over here (his wife consenting): a blond war-widow with small daughter. I then felt I'd known Col. J. all my life. We went back to the house off Park Lane which he shares with four brother officers, one a very tough guy . . . I felt rather tongue-tied with them and was glad when J. saw me home.

Although Bertie carefully refrained from mentioning this in the previous letter, it helps explain why, when asked to write about vanity and energy, he wrote instead about vanity and sex. By 15 August, however, he could stand it no longer.

80 [To Colette O'Niel] [Brixton Prison]
 15 August 1918
 Thursday

My Dearest

It was a great relief to get your letter today – the one yesterday was such a wretched scrap that it made me very unhappy, and I expected to remain so at least a week.

Dear one, will you be very patient and kind with me the 7 weeks that remain, and bear with me if I grow horrid? It has been difficult after the hopes of release. I am very tired, very weary. I am of course tortured by jealousy; I knew I should be. I know so little of your doings that I probably imagine more than the truth. I have grown so nervy from confinement and dwelling on the future that I feel a sort of vertigo, an impulse to destroy the happiness in prospect. *Will you please quite calmly ignore anything I do these next weeks in obedience to this impulse.* As yet, I am just able to see that it is mad, but soon it will seem the only sanity. I shall set to work to hurt you, to make you break with me; I shall say I won't see you when I first come out; I shall pretend to have lost all affection for you. All this is madness – the effect of jealousy and impatience combined. The pain of wanting a thing very much at last grows so great that one has to try not to want it any longer. Now here it is: *I want everything as we planned it – Ashford, then Rinders' if you can.*[1] *If later I say I don't want this, please pay no attention.*

If you possibly can, write me longer letters, with more *definite* news, and answer my letters enough for me to know if they have reached you. Don't leave answering till the last minute. Remember what it is like being shut away here, thinking, imagining, seeing how much you don't tell, noticing the faintest sign of coldness, fearing that by the time I come out all your passion will be going elsewhere, as it did after Blackpool. If I were not in prison I could get rid of profitless thoughts of this kind, but in prison it is fearfully difficult. And the result is a mood in which one sees nothing happy in the future either.

It is a blow that Miles is coming 2 nights a week to Russell Chambers – but no doubt it is right, at least for the present. I have never at any time had the very faintest jealousy of Miles. I *shall* be glad when you have a flat of your own. The transition period will not be satisfactory.

There is a letter to Helen Dudley elsewhere, which you are welcome to read. (I would rather you read it.) I dare say it will astonish you, as it did me. Till I heard she was going I did not realize how much affection I have for her.[2] – Please thank Miss Rinder for letters.

Tell *Miss Rinder* I want to see Miss Silcox[3] September 15. Also ask her to tell Lady O[ttoline] that it was *pure imagination* on her part thinking I didn't enjoy seeing her. Only warders etc. are embarrassing, and letters can say more, and I felt bound to be polite to Littlewood. But I *loved* seeing her and much looking forward to her on 28th. I was tired when she came last and forgot for a moment where I was and what was happening – it took me a little time to recover from bewilderment.

Various letters in other places. Read all that interest you.

---

1 When he was released, they planned to go first to Ashford and then to stay at Gladys Rinder's family's cottage at Winchester.
2 She had been to visit Russell before leaving for America.
3 Lucy Silcox, an old friend of Russell's. She was headmistress of a school in Southwold.

I suppose it is due to the heat, but I am collapsed, and very unhappy – I want you. And I am worried about you. I wish my brother had succeeded with Cave. These last weeks will be very difficult. Thanks for *Madge*[1] etc. Be kind Darling – *I need you so dreadfully*.

Please send Paterne Berrichon on Rimbaud[2] to Ottoline – it is hers and she wants it.

Miss Dudley says *Tuesday*. Please do your utmost to get my letter to her before then.

Miss Rinder says C.A. is 'not in Cumberland' and adds 'Oh these secrets'. Where is he? Gretna Green?[3] Tell her I shall assume that is the answer when I hear to the contrary.

Two guineas a week for my flat?[4] If you give me a meal there when convenient, I will pay for it, i.e. you can take it out of the rent. Will you pay my brother till I come out, weekly? After that we can keep an account and you can pay when you are rich. Delightful about spare room – just what I should wish.

In his *Autobiography* (vol. ii, p. 37) Bertie says unequivocally that Colette fell in love with someone else, but the account which follows runs together Elvey and Mitchell as if they were one person. Colette, on the other hand, wrote merely that she 'saw a good deal of the American Army at that time' and that 'Colonel [J.B.] Mitchell . . . became a friend of mine' (*After Ten Years*, p. 127). In the typescript of her letters, she denied that she had an affair with Mitchell. It is difficult to know which version is true. Many of Colette's letters for this period are missing and passages have even been cut from some of Bertie's letters. Bertie's jealousy was not made easier to bear by his belief that it was 'an abominable emotion' (*Autobiography*, vol. ii, p. 37). Colette replied on the 19th:

> Oh Beloved, why have you let blackness swallow you up now – when we're nearing the end of this separation? . . . *Don't don't* let all those old bad feelings get hold of you again to torment you.

It was advice he tried to take.

---

1 A play by Miles Malleson.
2 Either Paterne Berrichon, *La vie de Jean Arthur Rimbaud* (1897) or his *Jean-Arthur Rimbaud, le poète* (1912).
3 Allen was supposed to be with Catherine Marshall in Cumberland but there were rumours that she was courting him. Russell's suggestion is that they had eloped to Gretna Green, the village in Scotland where English couples traditionally went to marry under the easier conditions of Scottish law.
4 Colette had asked how much rent he wanted for his flat. This paragraph was written in the top margin of Russell's letter.

By September plans for when he got out were taking up most of Bertie's attention. He would be released at 8 a.m. and take a taxi to Gordon Square to pick up his overnight things. Then he would go on to his flat at Russell Chambers where Colette would be waiting. The next day they would go off to Ashford for a holiday. After that, he would have a round of visits – outlined in the next letter – after which normal life would begin. Everything was planned in detail for when he was released on 2 October.

[To Colette O'Niel] **[Brixton Prison]** 81
Wednesday evening
11 September 1918

My dearest Darling

Your letter is *such* a joy, Beloved. Less than 3 weeks now. I shall breakfast here that day. And I shall ring your bell and you will open your door and we shall be together. And all this long weary time will shrink into a moment, and we shall begin the real life together. I do *love* your having this work and feeling like C.A. with the N.C.F. Yes, I can quite imagine that you and Gordon[1] have to put all the driving force into it. But it is splendid having something one believes in to put one's force into. I gather indirectly from Gladys that you can manage the plans I suggested, as regards dates. I have suggested October 22 to Ottoline, and she suggests Lulworth Cove – so I shall take that as settled. The intervening week-end I suppose I ought to spend with my brother. Probably I should be only two nights at Lulworth – then come back for two nights and then go to C.A. at Leith Hill for week-end. He is to be there two months at least, as you will have heard. I think he has escaped C.E.M. He was subdued before my brother but it was lovely seeing him. I do love him.

I must stick to leaving N.C.F. Committee.[2] I can't be just a perfunctory member; I know they will do things I shall disagree with, and I would rather resign without disagreement. If I stay on, I shall not be able to get absorbed in philosophy. If Salter writes to suggest reconsidering, I will write him a long letter. How amusing to think of old Voltaire so bacchanalian![3] When those things come from Marlow, you can put the Persian bowl on its ebony stand in the place where Voltaire is now. And there should also be two candlesticks from

---

1 Capt. Stephen Gordon, the treasurer of Colette's experimental theatre. He was a civil service lawyer in London.
2 Colette was disappointed he was resigning.
3 This was a bust of Voltaire which Colette had put on the mantlepiece in the flat. She had placed rowan berries behind him and said he looked 'wildly bacchanalian'.

Marlow to go on the mantlepiece. I feel V. is not appropriate to you so much as the Persian bowl, which always was there for years until I got V. But of course you will have which you like best. I *love* to think of you there only I keep feeling apologetic and afraid you won't like it or won't be comfortable or something. Oh what heaven it will be to be there with you. You must tell me *all* the business of the new theatre and let me enter into it fully.

These last weeks, every day that passes lifts off something of the weight of separation. When I first came in here, I felt that I had got into a tangle through recklessness – risk of being in prison till the end of the war, risk of poverty, great expenditure of energy on pacifism without anything achieved. I spent the first month or more thinking out how to avoid unfruitfulness. Thanks to the amazing kindness of friends, it seems as if that would be all right. When I had got everything thought out, I fretted because I couldn't get to work at once, and because I wanted so terribly to be with you – and then I got morbid fears about you. Now I have *no* troubles, I am utterly happy as regards you, and I see that work and money will be all right. Henceforth I will be less reckless: it is time to gather the fruit. I have had experience of various kinds, and I have believed in various creeds; now I feel I have got to what suits my nature, and I must think more of giving out what I have learnt than of learning more. Otherwise I shall be dead before I have expressed what is in me. I have these last weeks a great strength – the strength that comes of a perfectly clear purpose. I see the way clear before me to the realization of a great ambition, the ambition to create and express a well-rounded whole of philosophy, theoretical and practical, in a form interesting to all sorts of people, and with really important bearings on politics and how to live. To bring this to birth, I need: Perfect health; no anxieties about money; a life of routine during half the year, when I read and write; real holidays; and above all personal happiness. There seems no reason why I shouldn't have all these things now. If so, in the next 10 years I will actually achieve the sort of thing that has floated before my mind as a vision ever since I was a boy. It is to that that all my efforts are directed now.

The war has made me feel the terrific importance of being *constructive*, building up positive things. You will be doing that with your theatre. I mean to do it too: I mean to give expression to the philosophy that I believe in, and that I feel sure is appropriate to the world that will exist. I do not want to remain a voice crying in the wilderness: I want to be a voice that is answered and echoed, saying things men care to hear. And I am sure the young men, when peace liberates them, will care to hear what I wish to say.

This is a lot about myself – but I want you to know how full of life I am, and how full of real creative energy. It all centres in you and rests on you. Happiness in your love sets everything free in me.

My Beloved, every hour and every minute I think of you with joy and longing. You are beautiful my dear one, your eyes are like the morning star and your soul is like the sunlit sea. I seem to stand beside you at the edge of the world looking into the depths and mysteries of unexplored abysses – all that is strong and triumphant in me feels you my comrade – and the wiser being beneath, the child, that knows its weakness and the vast cold power of the world, turns to you too, for warmth and shelter. Dear one, it is only through love, great love, that truth can be endured – and you give me the love that makes truth endurable, and by that you make me strong. Goodnight Beloved – I love you, love you.

B.

You *have* been angelic to Eliot.[1] Thank you 1000 times.
Thursday morning
One more word of love, Darling. A very short time now and then joy. I am full of happiness, more every day. Your letters are an *infinite* delight and comfort to me. All my heart is with you every moment. I send you 1,000 kisses and all the tender thoughts that ever were in the world.

Letters for Gladys and Ottoline and Miss Wrinch and from Eliot further on (read any that interest you).

When Russell wrote the previous letter, he still expected to be released on 2 October. He apparently did not realize that some of his time would be remitted for good conduct, for, much to his surprise, he was released on Saturday, 14 September. As it turned out, this was not unalloyed good fortune. Bertie's friends were as surprised as he and their preparations to welcome him were incomplete. Prison had made him oversensitive and he began to feel that they were less than overjoyed to see him. No one was less prepared than Colette, for she had a date with Col Mitchell that evening. Inevitably, there

---

[1] With America now in the war, Eliot was liable to be called up. He was exempted from combatant service on medical grounds but, rather than wait to be called up, he wished to receive a non-combatant commission because the pay was better. This proved a most complex endeavour. Bertie had suggested to Colette that Col Mitchell, who seemed to have some influence in the American army, might be able to help him, and she had duly introduced them. Nothing was achieved for Eliot – the war ended before the red tape was sorted out – but, given Bertie's jealousy of Mitchell, it is odd that he should enlist Colette's help in a task that would throw the two of them together.

was a row. Bertie accused her of having an affair with Mitchell. She denied it. Bertie stormed back to Gordon Square. Colette went to her date.

Sadly, after so many declarations of love and so much planning for an ecstatic reunion, it was Bertie's mood of black jealousy on 15 August that most accurately reflected their actual reunion. It is difficult to know exactly what happened, since Colette's typescript does not include her letters for the next three months. They never did return to Ashford, but they did not lose touch with each other. After a few days tempers cooled. Colette promised not to see Mitchell again, but now even this caused problems.

82 **[To Colette O'Niel]**   **Telegraph House,[1]**
                                                                        Chichester
                                                                    26 September 1918

My Dearest

I cannot clip your wings and put you in a cage. What we planned won't do. Go back to Mitchell if that is what you feel right. Do everything that your impulse tells you is good. I will try for the next 6 months to grow used to it. If I can't, we will consider things afresh. What we thought of is brutal, it comes of force, it is a sin against reverence. It would be better to part than do that. That would ruin the beauty of our love, the shining quality of morning dew – and without beauty love has little worth. I do not believe we shall be able long to avoid parting, but when it comes to that I should wish to have avoided sin by the way and to have unsullied memories.

If you had felt for yourself that a quieter and less exciting life would be better for you (which I still believe) things would have been different, but I cannot force you into it against your own judgment.

I love you, and shall love you as long as I live. But I see no issue to our difficulties. I will struggle with myself but I have not much hope. However, the next 6 months will show.

I will not try the plan we had adopted, unless at some future date you come to it of your own accord. I cannot make myself your gaoler.

Deepest Love, my Darling, now and for ever,
    B.

Meanwhile the war ended almost as suddenly as it began. The Germans, trying to exploit their advantage after Brest-Litovsk, had launched an impressive spring offensive. It might even have succeeded but for the generals' determination to

---

1 Frank Russell's country home.

pursue tactics which were not working rather than those which were. Once it had petered out, however, US troops began arriving in large numbers and the German defeat became inevitable. The final Allied offensive was launched in late September and breached the Hindenburg Line, the main German defence line. The German Chancellor resigned and the new Chancellor sued for peace. The Allied terms amounted to unconditional surrender. Germany prevaricated but in the end had to capitulate. An armistice was signed on 11 November.

Meanwhile, revolution had broken out in Germany, starting with a naval mutiny at Kiel. The Kaiser abdicated and a provisional Social-Democratic government was formed, while the German communists, led by Karl Liebknecht, started to establish soviets in preparation for a Bolshevik seizure of power. Russell, now back in London from a holiday in Lulworth with Colette, was stunned.

[To Ottoline Morrell] **[5 Fitzroy Street?]** 83
[9? November 1918]
Saturday

My dearest O.

Thank you for your letter. I shall *certainly* call my place the 'Snuggery' – the name is irresistibly attractive. *Do* come *Tuesday* as soon after 4 as you can – you will see a large label on the front door showing which bell to ring.

Yes Lulworth was most beautiful and a great success. I am well into my work now – it is nice to be back at it.[1]

Was anything ever so dramatic as the collapse of the 'enemy'? The collapse of Napoleon was very slow in comparison. 'Sceptre and crown come tumbling down . . . only the actions of the just smell sweet and blossom in their dust'[2] – as Liebknecht's triumphs show. Is there going to be Bolshevism throughout Central Europe? If so I suppose we shall have to shoot down Berlin mobs to make the world 'safe from democracy'. Was ever such a whirligig? It is really very horrible – one feels Austria destroyed for civilization for ages to come. And we sit gloating and making it worse. One remains very lonely in the world – but for the moment the drama outweighs everything else. Sorry about Friday – but you would have found it a long and tiring day.

Goodbye
Your
    B.

---

1 He was working on *The Analysis of Mind*.
2 Lines from James Shirley's *The Contention of Ajax and Ulysses* (1659). Russell would likely have known them from Palgrave's *Golden Treasury* where they appear under the title 'Death the Leveller'.

Russell was sent to prison in 1918

PART II
WRITINGS

Russell's Defence of the Realm Permit Book, stamped by the Metropolitan Police E Division.

Page 7 of Russell's Permit Book, duly cancelled for the Newhaven Special Military Area, although 'special arrangements' will be made for him to attend Clifford Allen's Court Martial.

War: The Cause and the Cure
Rulers Cannot Be Trusted with Peace Negotiations
(1914)

Throughout Europe millions of ordinary, peaceable citizens, who had no wish to be disturbed in their daily pursuits, have suddenly left their homes and their work and been sent to distant places for the purpose of killing each other. This action is universally praised, and it must be confessed that it involves courage and willingness to face a horrible death with little hope of personal gain. Nevertheless it is an action whose results are immeasurably disastrous, and have not been desired by the men who bring them about. The actual fighting men have no quarrel with each other: they never saw each other before, they are all members of the same human family, differing little one from another except in external accidents, such as their speech. Yet all of them, obedient to the will of a few prominent men not themselves subjected to the dangers of war, rush into battle as though killing and maiming and wounding were the noblest thing a man can do.

The business of war, like a ghastly game, is nominally subject to certain arbitrary rules. In the absence of an umpire, each side accuses the other of infractions of the rules, which are called 'atrocities'. The rules are roughly these: A man must only fight if he belongs to a regular army, and must confine himself, in the main, to fighting people who belong to another regular army, and who are called the 'enemy', and he must only kill them so long as they are still fighting; but if a man who is not in a regular army attempts to defend his home, he may legitimately be shot in cold blood after he has been disarmed, though to shoot him when he has not made such an attempt is an 'atrocity'. As, however, there is no power to enforce obedience to the rules of war, it inevitably happens that each side disregards them when there is any military advantage in doing so. Disregard by one's own side is concealed, while disregard by the other side is at once reported and magnified. In this way it comes to be thought by each side that the other side are inconceivably wicked, enemies of the human race, and richly deserving of the extermination which it is intended to inflict.

When an army succeeds in inflicting greater losses upon another army than it suffers, there are rejoicings, and thanks are given to God. But when it kills men not belonging to an army, whether in accordance with the rules or not, no one rejoices, and it is not suggested that the Deity has any share in the matter.

Incidentally, in order to facilitate the actual fighting, towns and villages are burnt, women and children are driven out to starve, crops and stores of food are destroyed, and the utmost possible destitution is inflicted upon those who are not fighting.

The work of destruction costs, every day, about as much as would provide that day's food for the whole population of the countries involved. And even to the victors, for many years to come, the result will be poverty and want, hatred and fear, crime and brutality, a general lowering of the whole standard of civilization and happiness.

This state of things has been brought about because it has been decreed by a handful of men: the three Emperors, and the Cabinets of London and Paris.

Why do ordinary citizens obey their insane commands, and even obey them with enthusiasm, with the utmost degree of devotion and heroism?

Except in Russia, where loyalty, race, and religion are sufficient incentives, the universal motive to obedience is fear – not a craven or personal fear, but fear for home and wife and children, for liberty and the national life. Such horrors can be inflicted by a conquering army that each nation is willing to endure any effort in order to be the conqueror rather than the conquered. And by this very willingness the horrors of war are multiplied a hundredfold.

In every nation, by the secrecy of diplomacy, by cooperation of the Press with the manufacturers of armaments, by the desire of the rich and the educated to distract the attention of the working classes from social injustice, suspicion of other nations is carefully cultivated, until a state of nightmare terror is produced, and men are prepared to attack the enemy at once, before he is ready to inflict the ruin which he is believed to be contemplating. In sudden vertigo, the nations rush into the dreaded horror; reason is called treachery, mercy is called weakness, and universal delirium drives the world to destruction.

All the nations suffer by the war, and knew in advance that they would suffer. In all the nations, the bulk of ordinary men and women must have dreaded war. Yet all felt the war thrust upon them by the absolute necessity of preserving themselves from invasion and national extinction. Austria-Hungary, a kind of outpost of Western civilization among the turbulent Balkan States, felt its existence threatened by revolutionary Slavs within its own borders, supported by the aggressive and warlike Servians on its frontier. Russia, being of the same race and religion as the Servians, felt bound in honour to protect them against Austria. Germany, knowing that the defeat of Austria would leave it at the mercy of Russia, felt bound to support Austria. France, from dread of a repetition of 1870, had allied itself with Russia, and was compelled, for self-preservation, to support Russia as soon as Germany was involved. And England, believing that the German Navy was designed to secure our downfall, had felt impelled through fear to form the *entente* with France and Russia.

All these nations, fearing that they might at any time be exposed to sudden attack, perfected the machinery for rapid mobilization, and allowed their Governments the power of putting this machinery in motion at a moment's notice. Thus the issue of peace or war rested, not with the people, who have to suffer the evils of war, but with men who would not suffer by war, who, on the contrary, would gain in importance and prestige. These men, by the constant practice of diplomacy, had become filled with the spirit of competition between rival States, and had come to think it more shameful to their country to allow a diplomatic triumph to another country than to bring about the devastation of Europe. By playing upon men's fears through a Press which knew only what they chose to reveal, they were able to bring all their different countries to acquiesce in war, although, if time for reflection had been allowed it is almost certain that the voice of sanity would have compelled a peaceful adjustment of the rival interests.

If, when this war is ended, the world is to enjoy a secure peace, the nations must be relieved of the intolerable fear which has weighed them down and driven them into the present horror. Not only must armaments be immensely reduced, but the machinery of mobilization must be everywhere rendered more cumbrous and more democratic, the diplomacy must be conducted more publicly and by men more in touch with the people, and arbitration treaties must bind nations to seek a peaceful settlement of their differences before appealing to brute force. All these things can be secured after the present war if the democracy is insistent; none will be secured if the negotiations are left in the hands of the men who made the war.

This article was published in the socialist paper, The Labour Leader, *on 24 September, 1914. It gives a good summary of Russell's views during the early years of the war. He evidently felt that little could be done to shorten the conflict, or even to alter the way it was conducted, and his main practical concern was to ensure that, once peace was restored, diplomacy would be conducted in a way that would make a repetition unlikely. Russell did not choose the title of the article. It was chosen by Fenner Brockway, the editor of* The Labour Leader, *then a very young pacifist and socialist who, in November 1914, founded the organization which eventually became* The No-Conscription Fellowship. *Russell lamented to Helen Flexner (see p.32) that in the early years of the war* The Labour Leader *was the only paper 'willing to print what I want to say'.*

Source: **Prophecy and Dissent. 1914-16, The Collected Papers of Bertrand Russell**, edited by Richard A Rempel with the assistance of Bernd Frohmann, Mark Lippincott, Margaret Moran, Routledge, 1988, pages 16-19

Letter to President Wilson
(1916)

To the President of the United States

SIR – You have an opportunity of performing a signal service to mankind, surpassing even the service of Abraham Lincoln, great as that was. It is in your power to bring the war to an end by a just peace, which shall do all that could possibly be done to allay the fear of new wars in the near future. It is not yet too late to save European civilization from destruction; but it may be too late if the war is allowed to continue for the further two or three years with which our militarists threaten us.

The military situation has now developed to the point where the ultimate issue is clear, in its broad outlines, to all who are capable of thought. It must be obvious to the authorities in all the belligerent countries that no victory for either side is possible. In Europe, the Germans have the advantage; outside Europe, and at sea, the Allies have the advantage. Neither side is able to win such a crushing victory as to compel the other to sue for peace. The war inflicts untold injuries upon the nations, but not such injuries as to make a continuance of fighting impossible. It is evident that, however the war may be prolonged, negotiations will ultimately have to take place on the basis of what will be substantially the present balance of gains and losses, and will result in terms not very different from those which might be obtained now. The German Government has recognized this fact, and has expressed its willingness for peace on terms which ought to be regarded at least as affording a basis for discussion, since they concede the points which involve the honour of the Allies. The Allied Governments have not had the courage to acknowledge publicly what they cannot deny in private, that the hope of a sweeping victory is one which can now scarcely be entertained. For want of this courage, they are prepared to involve Europe in the horrors of a continuance of the war, possibly for another two or three years. This situation is intolerable to every humane man. You, Sir, can put an end to it. Your power constitutes an opportunity and a responsibility; and from your previous actions I feel confident that you will use your power with a degree of wisdom and humanity rarely to be found among statesmen.

The harm which has already been done in this war is immeasurable. Not only have millions of valuable lives been lost, not only have an even greater number of men been maimed or shattered in health, but the whole standard of civilization has been lowered. Fear has invaded men's inmost being, and with fear has come the ferocity that always attends it. Hatred has become the rule of life, and injury to others is more desired than benefit to ourselves. The hopes of peaceful progress in which our earlier years were passed are dead, and can never be revived. Terror and savagery have become the very air we breathe. The liberties which our ancestors won by centuries of struggle were sacrificed in a day, and all the nations are regimented to the one ghastly end of mutual destruction.

But all this is as nothing in comparison with what the future has in store for us if the war continues as long as the pronouncements of some of our leading men would make us expect. As the stress increases, and weariness of the war makes average men more restive, the severity of repression has to be continually augmented. In all the belligerent countries, soldiers who are wounded or home on leave express an utter loathing of the trenches, a despair of ever achieving a military decision, and a terrible longing for peace. Our militarists have successfully opposed the granting of votes to soldiers; yet in all the countries, an attempt is made to persuade the civilian population that war-weariness is confined to the enemy soldiers. The daily toll of young lives destroyed becomes a horror almost too terrible to be borne; yet everywhere, advocacy of peace is rebuked as treachery to the soldiers, though the soldiers above all men desire peace. Everywhere, friends of peace are met with the diabolical argument that the brave men who have died must not have shed their blood in vain. And so every impulse of mercy towards the soldiers who are still living is dried up and withered by a false and barren loyalty to those who are past our help. Even the men hitherto retained for making munitions, for dock labour, and for other purposes essential to the prosecution of the war, are gradually being drafted into the armies and replaced by women, with the sinister threat of coloured labour in the background. There is a very real danger that, if nothing is done to check the fury of national passion, European civilization as we have known it will perish as completely as it perished when Rome fell before the Barbarians.

It may be thought strange that public opinion should appear to support all that is being done by the authorities for the prosecution of the war. But this appearance is very largely deceptive. The continuance of the war is actively advocated by influential persons, and by the Press, which is everywhere under the control of the Governments. In other sections of society feeling is quite different from that expressed by the newspapers, but public opinion remains silent and uninformed, since those who might give guidance are subject to such severe penalties that few dare to protest openly, and those few cannot obtain a wide publicity. From considerable personal experience, reinforced by all that I can learn from others, I believe that the desire for peace is almost universal, not only among the soldiers, but throughout the wage-earning classes, and especially in industrial districts, in spite of high wages and steady employment. If a plebiscite of the nation were taken on the question whether negotiations should be initiated, I am confident that an overwhelming majority would be in favour of this course, and that the same is true of France, Germany, and Austria-Hungary.

Such acquiescence as there is in continued hostilities is due entirely to fear. Every nation believes that its enemies were the aggressors, and may make war again in a few years unless they are utterly defeated. The United States Government has the power, not only to compel the European Governments to make peace, but also to reassure the populations by making itself the guarantor of the peace. Such action, even if it were resented by the Governments, would be hailed with joy by the populations. If the German Government, as now seems likely, would not only restore conquered territory; but also give its adherence to the League to Enforce Peace or some similar method of settling disputes without war, fear would be allayed, and it is almost certain that an offer of mediation from you would give rise to an irresistible movement in favour of negotiations. But the deadlock is such that no near end to the war is likely except through the mediation of an outside Power; and such mediation can only come from you.

Some may ask by what right I address you. I have no formal title; I am not any part of the machinery of government. I speak only because I must; because others, who should have remembered civilization and human brotherhood, have allowed themselves to be swept away by national passion; because I am compelled by their apostasy to speak in the name of reason and mercy, lest it should be thought that no one in Europe remembers the work which Europe has done and ought still to do for mankind. It is to the European races, in Europe and out of it, that the world owes most of what it possesses in thought, in science, in art, in ideals of government, in hope for the future. If they are allowed to destroy each other in futile carnage, something will be lost which is more precious than diplomatic prestige, incomparably more valuable than a sterile victory which leaves the victors themselves perishing. Like the rest of my countrymen, I have desired ardently the victory of the Allies; like them, I have suffered when victory has been delayed. But I remember always that Europe has common tasks to fulfil; that a war among European nations is in essence a civil war; that the ill which we think of our enemies they equally think of us; and that it is difficult in time of war for a belligerent to see facts truly. Above all, I see that none of the issues in the war are as important as peace: the harm done by a peace which does not concede all that we desire is as nothing in comparison to the harm done by the continuance of the fighting. While all who have power in Europe speak for what they falsely believe to be the interests of their separate nations, I am compelled by a profound conviction to speak for all the nations in the name of Europe. In the name of Europe I appeal to you to bring us peace.

German peace feelers at the end of 1916 led Russell to hope that the war might soon be ended by negotiation. To help bring this about Russell appealed to President Woodrow Wilson to bring the contending nations to a peace conference. This is the text of the open letter to Wilson that Katherine Dudley smuggled into the US on Russell's behalf. She made it public at a pacifist conference in New York on 22 December, 1916. It was widely reported in the US press. See p 108.

Source: **Pacifism and Revolution, Volume 14, The Collected Papers of Bertrand Russell**, *edited by Richard A Rempel, Louis Greenspan, Beryl Haslam, Albert C Lewis, Mark Lippincott, Routledge, 1995, pages 398-399*

For Conscience Sake
(1916)

This war, as the Allies have caused the world to know, is being fought for liberty and democracy; devotion to these principles, we are assured, has mobilized the legions of the Tsar no less than the armies of the Western powers. This language was not insincere, but the logic of events has shown that it was short-sighted. Cromwell's Ironsides fought for democracy, and established a military tyranny. Our soldiers, who volunteered with generous enthusiasm in the early days of the war, are horrified, when they return wounded or on leave, to find what 'patriots' at home have made of the country which was once the land of freedom.

My own treatment, though very lenient compared to that of less conspicuous offenders, illustrates the loss of freedom essential to the prosecution of a great war. It is from that point of view that I wish to deal with it, not from the point of view of personal complaint. Personally, I have gained by the Government's blundering efforts at suppression – gained in influence and reputation and in the power of getting a hearing.

From the very beginning of the war I have protested against it. I believe that all wars between civilized states are unnecessary, and that if men had sufficient courage they could achieve by peaceful means whatever is legitimate in the things for which they fight. My opposition to war is based not upon religious grounds, but upon common sense and common humanity. I came to the conclusion during the early days of the war that if I had been of military age I could not conscientiously have taken part in the fighting. This feeling was not based upon any sympathy with the German Government; on the contrary, I should have felt it even more strongly if I had been a German. When conscription was introduced into this country, I felt bound to champion the cause of those men of military age who refused on conscientious grounds, as I should have done in their place, to enter the army or to help in the prosecution of the war. Some fifteen or twenty thousand of these men were combined in an organization called the 'No-Conscription Fellowship', whose members undertook not to enter the army whatever might be the penalties for their refusing. Some of them were Quakers, some belonged to other religious denominations, some were international Socialists, some were men who, like myself, without the support of any definite creed considered war a folly and a crime against which it is the duty of sane men to protest by every means in their power, I threw in my lot with the No-Conscription Fellowship, and gave them such service as it was in my power to render.

Under the military service acts men who have a conscientious objection to combatant service are nominally exempt. In fact, however, the conscience clauses in the acts have proved largely illusory. Claims to exemption are heard by tribunals consisting, naturally, of men entirely out of sympathy with the conscientious objectors, whom they believe to be merely cowards in disguise. The tribunals have to decide whether a man's conscience is genuine or merely an excuse for shirking. If they decide that it is genuine there are three forms of exemption which they may grant: (1) They may grant absolute exemption, which leaves a man free to direct his own life as hitherto. This form of exemption is hardly ever granted. (2) They may grant exemption conditional upon undertaking some work which in the opinion of the tribunal is of national importance. (3) They may grant exemption from combatant duties only, on condition of the applicant entering what is called 'the non-combatant corps', which is part of the army and performs such military duties as do not consist in actual fighting. The intention, when the acts were passed, was that the tribunals should grant whichever of these three forms of exemption was necessary in order to meet the conscience of the applicant.

No one realized at that time how impossible it would be for members of tribunals to understand a point of view so alien to their own as that of the conscientious objectors. Many of the most genuine were declared not to have a conscience within the meaning of the act. In early days those who were recognized as genuine were almost always placed in the non-combatant corps. It should have been obvious that a genuine objection to warfare involves an objection to the operations subsidiary to the actual fighting just as much as to actual participation in battle. But the tribunals were so firmly persuaded that all conscientious objectors were really cowards that they supposed they would be giving satisfaction in merely relieving them from the dangers of war. This, of course, was soon found to have been a complete misunderstanding. The men who had been placed in the non-combatant corps refused to perform the duties assigned to them. They were court-martialled and sentenced to varying terms of imprisonment. Up to the present some thousands have suffered in this way. Thirty-four of them were sentenced to death, but the sentence was commuted to ten years penal servitude.

One of the first to be condemned was a school teacher named Everett. As it was impossible to induce the newspapers to publish the facts concerning the prosecution of conscientious objectors, the No-Conscription Fellowship decided to secure publicity by means of leaflets, and I wrote for them a leaflet upon the subject of Everett. This leaflet in its entirety was as follows:

Two Years' Hard Labour for refusing to disobey the Dictates of Conscience. This was the sentence passed on Ernest F. Everett, of 222 Denton's Green Lane, St. Helen's, by a Court Martial held on April 10th. Everett was a teacher at St. Helen's, and had been opposed to all war since the age of 16. He appealed as a Conscientious Objector before the Local and Appeal Tribunals, both of which treated him very unfairly, going out of their way to recommend his dismissal from school. They recognized his conscience claim only so far as to award him non-combatant service. But as the purpose of such service is to further the prosecution of the war, and to release others for the trenches, it was impossible for him to accept the decision of the Tribunals. On March 31st he was arrested as an absentee, brought before the magistrates, fined £2, and handed over to the Military Authorities. By them he was taken under escort to Warrington Barracks, where he was compelled to put on uniform. On April 1st he was taken to Abergele, where he was placed in the Non-Combatant Corps, which is part of the Army. He adopted consistently a policy of passive resistance to all military orders. The first morning, April 2nd, when the men were ordered to fall in for fatigue duty, he refused, saying: 'I refuse to obey any order given by any military authority.' According to the Corporal, who gave the order, Everett 'said it in quite a nice way'. The Corporal informed the Lieutenant, who repeated the order, and warned Everett of the seriousness of his conduct. Everett still answered politely, but explained why he could not obey. The Lieutenant ordered the Conscientious Objector to the guardroom, where he remained all night. The Captain visited the prisoner, who stated that 'he was not going to take orders'. The Captain ordered him to be brought before the Commanding Officer on a charge of disobedience. Everett was next brought before the Colonel, who read aloud to him Section 9 of the Army Act, and explained the serious consequences of disobedience. But Everett remained firm, saying, 'He could not and would not obey any military order.' The result was that he was tried by Court Martial on April 10th. He stated in evidence in his own defence: 'I am prepared to do work of national importance which does not include military service, so long as I do not thereby release some other man to do what I am not prepared to do myself.' The sentence was two years' hard labour. Everett is now suffering this savage punishment solely for refusal to go against his conscience. He is fighting the old fight for liberty and against religious persecution in the same spirit in which martyrs suffered in the past. Will you join the persecutors? Or will you stand for those who are defending conscience at the cost of obloquy and pain of mind and body? Forty other men are suffering persecution for conscience sake in the same way as Mr. Everett. Can you remain silent whilst this goes on?

Issued by the No-Conscription Fellowship. 8 Merton House, Salisbury Court Fleet Street, London, E.C.

(The last two sentences were not mine, but were added while the leaflet was in the press.)

A quarter of a million copies of this leaflet were distributed, and very shortly after its publication Everett's sentence was reduced to 112 days. I do not think any of us imagined at the time that the leaflet could be regarded as illegal. In this, however, we were mistaken. Men engaged in distributing the leaflet were prosecuted and sentenced to varying terms of imprisonment with hard labour. As soon as I found that this was happening I wrote to *The Times* to state that I was the author of the leaflet. A prosecution naturally followed, in which I was charged with contravening the regulation that 'no person shall in writing or in any circular or other printed publication make statements likely to prejudice the recruiting and discipline of His Majesty's forces'. The case was heard before the Lord Mayor on the 5th June of this year. I conducted my own defence and was fined £100, a sentence which was upheld on appeal to quarter sessions.

This sentence had two consequences. First it led the Government to refuse me permission to fulfil my engagement to lecture on philosophy at Harvard. This refusal was conveyed in a letter from our ambassador at Washington to the president of Harvard, dated June 8, when my case was still *sub judice* owing to my appeal. (The conviction before the Lord Mayor was the only ground alleged for the refusal of a passport.) The second consequence was my dismissal from my lectureship at Trinity College, Cambridge, also explicitly based on this ground. The college, however, showed more sense of justice than the Government, since it waited until the sentence had been confirmed on appeal.

The next stage in the proceedings arose out of a series of meetings in South Wales, at which I spoke in favour of the initiation of peace negotiations, always with the all but unanimous approval of the audience, even when I spoke in the open air to perfectly casual crowds. This series of meetings seems to have alarmed the war office. They were misled by inaccurate reports from casual reporters, which they did not show to me, and which I only saw long afterward. After thinking the matter over for some six weeks they served a notice on me forbidding me to enter 'prohibited areas'. The power of serving such notices was given to them for the purpose of dealing with spies. Prohibited areas are for the most part places near the sea. They include the whole coast, and a good many whole counties abutting on the sea. The object of the regulation permitting such orders was to prevent suspicious characters from being able to signal to German submarines, or give notice of the embarkation of troops, or otherwise afford help to the enemy. The war office was good enough to state that it did not suspect me of such activities. Nevertheless, a power only intended to guard against them was used by the military authorities to hamper my movements, and to restrict my opportunities for propounding arguments which they evidently did not know how to answer except by force.

Some amusing results followed from this prohibition. I had arranged (mainly for the innocent purpose of earning my living) to give a course of six lectures on the philosophical principles of politics in various large towns. Some of these happened to be in prohibited areas, and I was, therefore, unable to fulfil my engagements in those towns without the express permission of the war office. I stated publicly, in print, that my lectures would not be concerned with the war, but this was not enough to satisfy the war office. They asked me to give an honourable undertaking that I would not infringe the defence of the realm regulations. This I could not do, since these regulations are so framed that every one who speaks or writes must necessarily infringe them.

The result of the war office prohibition has been, of course, to afford an immense advertisement to my lectures, causing them to be much more widely attended, where I can give them, than they would otherwise be. In prohibited areas, they have been read by friends to crowded audiences. The first lecture of the course, on 'Political Ideals', was read before one thousand people in Glasgow by Robert Smillie, president of the Miners' Federation of Great Britain, a man whom the Government dare not offend because of his power in a vital industry. The matter has been repeatedly debated in Parliament, and ministers have had such a poor case that they had to descend to statements directly contrary to the facts, as for example, that they had asked me to give an undertaking not to do propaganda in America, and that I had refused. No hint of such a request ever reached me. The publicity which they dread, and which in other cases they have usually succeeded in avoiding, has been forced upon them in my case, largely owing to the fact that my proposed visit to Harvard was prevented. If they had permitted this visit, my time would have been occupied in preparing and delivering lectures on ethics and mathematical logic. As it is, most of my time has been free for the activities which they dislike. So much for the wisdom of interference with free speech.

The authorities have recently made repeated offers to me to withdraw all orders against me if I will cease to agitate for better treatment for the conscientious objectors. But this I cannot do. I have never urged any one not to enlist, though the authorities say and most people believe that I have done so. The principle for which I stand is liberty of conscience – a principle universally accepted before the war, even by those who now attack me. I have urged the Government not to prosecute men for their genuine convictions, and I have urged the public to bring pressure to bear on the Government to this end. At first those who stood for a reasonable treatment of the conscientious objectors were very few. Gradually, as these few succeeded in making the facts known in spite of the penalties for so doing, public sympathy largely changed, until even the Archbishop of Canterbury demanded less cruel penalties. Solitary confinement, dark cells, irons, bread and water, brutal insults from commanding officers, and often gross physical ill-treatment, proved the courage and genuineness of the victims. Now, the worst features of the persecution are at an end. The men who have come before the tribunals recently have usually been awarded civil work of national importance, not work in the non-combatant corps, and a revision of sentences has extended this change to those who were sentenced earlier. The proportion of shirkers among those who claim to be conscientious objectors is very small, because the obloquy which has to be endured is, for most people, much harder to bear than the trenches, and this fact has gradually come to be recognized. The chief problem remaining is as to those who will not accept what is called 'work of national importance'. Among such men are included most of the leaders of the movement, and probably a majority of those who realize the full implications of resistance to participation in war. They argue that they are already doing the work for which, in their own opinion, they are best fitted, and that if they are asked to change their occupation, it is with a view to organizing the nation's resources for war.

Is it to be supposed that, under such circumstances, I can pledge myself to do nothing further on behalf of the conscientious objectors? The agitation in which I have borne a part has already achieved a very notable success. Those who are willing to do civil 'work of national importance' are now allowed to do so, whatever may have been the original sentence of the tribunal, provided their subsequent conduct has given evidence of their genuineness. They are a very large section, and in regard to them the main battle is won. I think it is fair to claim that this measure of toleration, imperfect as it is, reflects credit on the British nation and the British Governments; no continental power, I am convinced, would have hesitated to shoot men who refused military service at such a time as the present. But the work remains incomplete so long as those whose consciences can only be satisfied by absolute exemption are kept in prison. The success of the agitation hitherto is an encouragement to persistence in it, and the sufferings of those still in prison (including many of my personal friends) make it quite impossible to withdraw from the agitation until they are set at liberty. Until that day comes, it is impossible for me honourably to enter into any compact with the Government.

What further developments may be in store I cannot tell, but I make no doubt that, as hitherto, they will do more damage to the Government than to their intended victims. And in the end it will have been established that belief in the brotherhood of man is not in itself a crime.

This article, written late in 1916 and published in The Independent, *a New York weekly, on 15 January 1917, is Russell's most extensive summary of his struggles with the British authorities during the first half of the war. In it he reprints the 'Everett leaflet' for which he had been fined in 1916 (see pp 78-85).*

Source: **Pacifism and Revolution, Volume 14, The Collected Papers of Bertrand Russell**, *edited by Richard A Rempel, Louis Greenspan, Beryl Haslam, Albert C Lewis, Mark Lippincott, Routledge, 1995, pages 37-43*

Freedom or Victory?
(1917)

We are sometimes told that this is a war for freedom; at other times, with more sincerity, that it is a war for victory. Let it be conceded at once that freedom and victory are both very good things, but it would be well if people recognized that they are not compatible and that, though freedom would probably result from a peace made now, victory, even if it could be attained some three years hence, would be purchased at the cost of freedom and of everything else that makes life worth living.

What has happened to freedom at home during the war we all know. Men have been sent to prison over and over again for refusing to abjure profound religious and moral convictions. It has become a crime to circulate, or even to possess, any literature dealing with the war or with the peace after the war in a spirit not wholly acceptable to the Government. Appropriately enough, Mill's *Liberty* has been seized by the police. I have not so far heard of a man being sent to gaol for mentioning Magna Charta, but doubtless that will come. By the law of the land as it now exists, any man or woman can be kept in prison for the duration of the war without any charge being formulated or any trial being held. Those of us who are still at large owe thanks to the Government for its clemency.

In America, since the United States became a belligerent, the state of affairs is even worse. The leaders of the I.W.W. were imprisoned by the fiat of the Government for no discoverable reason except that their opinions were adverse to the war. Conscientious objectors, except when they are Quakers, are treated even worse than they are with us. Troops have been called in to disperse Pacifist meetings, and there has been no hesitation to stimulate mob violence.

Meantime the attitude of the Western Powers towards the new-born liberties of Russia has been a mixture of bigotry and folly, which it would be hard to parallel in the annals of statesmanship. It is said that our Government desires to see democracy in the Central Powers, but that certainly is the only place where our rulers can tolerate it. One is tempted to suppose that they regard democracy as a curse and wish to inflict it upon Germany as part of the price of defeat. In Russia, by forcing Kerensky into his ill-starred offensive by refusing to allow Stockholm or to revise their war aims, they secured the victory of Lenin and made a separate peace inevitable. It is not for a moment to be supposed that our authorities desired this result. But it is the result which their actions were bound to produce, as all intelligent people foresaw. It is absurd to accuse Lenin of treachery. Russia is too distracted, too worn-out, too destitute of supplies, too near famine to be physically capable of carrying on the war. Ever since the Revolution Russia has spared no efforts to bring about a general peace. These efforts having failed, sheer stark necessity has compelled the attempt to secure a separate peace. Probably Lenin's advocacy of peace is the chief source of his strength. It is clear that as part of the terms of peace, the Finns and the Poles, whom the Tsardom oppressed, are to recover their liberty. Although we are the champions of small nations, we have not displayed any extravagant joy in this partial realization of our programme. Our newspapers have been filled with lies about Lenin; that he is a Jew, that he is a German, that he is in the pay of the Kaiser. The fact is that he is a Russian aristocrat who long ago sacrificed everything to his principles. Meanwhile our newspapers, in their moments of optimism indulge in the hope of a military domination by the Cossacks under the leadership of Kaledin, which we are given to understand might be as intelligent, as enlightened and as free from corruption as the Tsardom of blessed memory.

Amid the clamour of the Never-Endians in our own country Lord Lansdowne's letter has come as a sudden gleam of sanity. His suggestion is, in brief, that we should make it clear that we are fighting for security against future wars, not for territorial aggrandizement. The outburst of mad rage with which this suggestion has been received shows how far it is from representing the mind of Lord Northcliffe and his wage-slaves in the 'Government'. The German and Austrian Governments, in their replies to the Pope's peace note, have made it clear that they favour international arbitration and progressive universal disarmament. Can we suppose that our militants desire these things? Is it not clear that militarism, conscription, and the fear of war are at all times the great assets of the rich in resisting the claims of Labour? Can anyone doubt that disarmament and international security, if they could be brought about, would lead to an economic reconstruction in which profiteering and capitalism would receive short shrift? Can anyone suppose that Lord Northcliffe would welcome such a state of affairs, or that he would favour a policy likely to bring it about?

Mr. Lloyd George, in his famous Paris speech, alluded to the 'impenetrable barrier' in the West. I should be liable to prosecution if I endorsed his opinion, but merely to quote it can hardly be considered illegal. Yet, with Russia out of the war, the fighting must be more and more confined to battering against this 'impenetrable barrier'. America cannot have a large army in France until the year after next, and if I were not afraid of being unpatriotic I should suggest that there is no reason to expect American troops to succeed where British troops have failed. The war is being carried on partly from inertia, partly because it gives power and wealth to certain persons who may not improbably find themselves in a less enviable position after the conclusion of peace. There is no reason whatever to expect that we shall be able to obtain better terms two years hence than could be obtained now. It is clear that we could obtain now the restoration of Belgium and Northern France with international agreements for arbitration and progressive disarmament. The objects with which our soldiers enlisted in the early days of the war could be achieved tomorrow. The territorial objects which our Government professes to have in view can probably not be achieved either now or later. The nation, deluded by a lying press, has remained for the most part blind to these patent facts, but there are signs of awakening, especially in the Labour Party. Upon the Labour Party at this moment a heavy responsibility rests. They have the power, if they will, to bring the Government to reason. Will they use that power, or will this opportunity, like so many others, be allowed to pass?

By 1917, war-weariness was endemic in Britain. It affected even Lord Lansdowne, the former foreign minister and chief architect of the 1904 Entente with France that had brought Britain into the war, who surprised the Government by calling on it to make a clear statement of war aims as a necessary prelude to peace negotiations. As disgust with the war mounted, the Government redoubled its efforts to suppress dissent and Russell redoubled the vehemence of his denunciation. This article, published on 15 December 1917 in The Pioneer, *the weekly organ of the South Wales branch of the Independent Labour Party, shows him at his most scathing.*

Source: **Pacifism and Revolution, Volume 14, The Collected Papers of Bertrand Russell**, *edited by Richard A Rempel, Louis Greenspan, Beryl Haslam, Albert C Lewis, Mark Lippincott, Routledge, 1995, pages 375-377*

The German Peace Offer
(1918)

The more we hear about the Bolsheviks, the more the legend of our patriotic press becomes exploded. We were told that they were incompetent, visionary and corrupt, that they must fall shortly, that the mass of Russians were against them, and that they dared not permit the Constituent Assembly to meet. All these statements have turned out completely false, as anyone may see by reading the very interesting despatch from Arthur Ransome in the *Daily News* of December 31st.

Lenin, whom we have been invited to regard as a German Jew, is really a Russian aristocrat who has suffered many years of persecution for his opinions. The social revolutionaries who were represented as enemies of the Bolsheviks have formed a connection with them. The Constituent Assembly is to meet as soon as half its members have reached Petrograd, and very nearly half have already arrived. All charges of German money remain entirely unsupported by one thread of evidence.

The most noteworthy and astonishing triumph of the Bolsheviks is in their negotiations with the Germans. In a military sense Russia is defenceless, and we all supposed it a proof that they were mere visionaries when they started negotiations by insisting upon not surrendering any Russian territory to the Germans. We were told that the Germans would infallibly insist upon annexing the Baltic Provinces and establishing a suzerainty over Poland. So far from this being the case, the German and Austrian Governments have officially announced that they are prepared to conclude a Peace on the Russian basis of no annexations and no indemnities, provided that it is a general Peace, and they have invited the Western Powers to agree to these terms.

This action has placed the Governments of the Western Powers in a most cruel dilemma. If they refuse the German offer, they are unmasked before the world and before their own Labour and Socialist Parties: they make it clear to all that they are continuing the war for purposes of territorial aggrandizement. If they accept the offer, they afford a triumph to the hated Bolsheviks and an object lesson to democratic revolutionaries everywhere as to the way to treat with capitalists, Imperialists and warmongers. They know that from the patriotic point of view they cannot hope for a better peace by continuing the war, but from the point of view of preventing liberty and universal peace, there is something to be hoped from continuation. It is known that unless peace comes soon there will be starvation throughout Europe. Mothers will be maddened by the spectacle of their children dying. Men will fight each other for possession of the bare necessaries of life. Under such conditions the sane constructive effort required for a successful revolution will be impossible. The American Garrison which will by that time be occupying England and France, whether or not they will prove efficient against the Germans, will no doubt be capable of intimidating strikers, an occupation to which the American Army is accustomed when at home. I do not say that these thoughts are in the mind of the Government. All the evidence tends to show that there are no thoughts whatever in their mind, and that they live from hand to mouth consoling themselves with ignorance and sentimental twaddle. I say only that if they were capable of thought, it would be along such lines as I have suggested that they would have to attempt to justify a refusal to make Peace on the basis of the German offer, if indeed they do decide to refuse.

Some democrats and Socialists are perhaps not unwilling that the war should continue, since it is clear that if it does it must lead to universal revolution. I think it is true that this consequence must follow, but I do not think that we ought on that account to acquiesce in the refusal to negotiate should that be the decision at which our Governments arrive. The kind of revolution with which we shall in that case be threatened will be far too serious and terrible to be a source of good. It would be a revolution full of violence, hatred and bloodshed, driven by hunger, terror and suspicion – a revolution in which all that is best in Western civilization is bound to perish. It is this prospect that our rulers ought to be facing. It is this risk that they run for such paltry objects as the annexation of African Colonies and Mesopotamia. Labour's war aims accepted almost unanimously on December 28th are on the whole very sane, and might easily form the basis for the immediate initiation of negotiations. Labour at the moment has enormous power. Is it too much to hope that it will use this power to compel some glimmer of sanity on the part of the blinded and maddened rulers of the Western Powers? Labour holds the key. It can if it chooses secure a just and lasting peace within a month, but if this opportunity is allowed to pass by, all that we hold dear will be swallowed up in universal ruin.

This was the article for which Russell was imprisoned in 1918. It was published in The Tribunal, *the journal of The No-Conscription Fellowship, on 3 January 1918.*

Source: **Pacifism and Revolution, Volume 14, The Collected Papers of Bertrand Russell,** edited by Richard A Rempel, Louis Greenspan, Beryl Haslam, Albert C Lewis, Mark Lippincott, Routledge, 1995, pp 398-399

Draft of Defence
(1918)

I am being prosecuted on the charge of having made a statement 'intended and likely' to prejudice the relations of this country with the United States.

I desire to assert with the utmost emphasis that I had no such intention, and that, when account is taken of the context in which the sentence in question occurred, it must be obvious to any candid reader that my intention was the exact opposite.

The charge is based upon a single sentence, in an article which otherwise contained no mention of America, being concerned with the negotiations between Russia and Germany. I, like every pacifist, wish to see good relations between all nations, and certainly not least between ourselves and the United States. I realize to the full the idealism which inspires many advocates of the present war in America, and especially those who have shown readiness for the ultimate sacrifice by willingly entering into the new army which is being sent to France.

But I remember the high idealism of many among ourselves who enlisted voluntarily in 1914, and I know, better than those whose knowledge is only derived from newspapers, how bitter has been the disillusionment which has come to the more thinking portion of these brave men when they have discovered the ends for which they were being asked to sacrifice their lives. I know also, what is less visible across the Atlantic, the misery and ruin which is overtaking the civilian population of Europe, belligerent and neutral alike, owing to the rapidly growing scarcity of all the necessaries of life, and I know how revolutionary feeling, emanating from Russia, is replacing ardour for the war in one nation after another.

The article in which the sentence in question occurred was concerned to point out the extreme likelihood of revolution everywhere, if the war is prolonged much beyond the present year. There is reason to think that, in nation after nation, the war of governments will be replaced by a class-war. This has happened in Russia, where the privations have been greatest. It all but happened in Austria, and was only prevented – perhaps not for long – by the capitulation of the government to the working-classes. The German strikes show that the same result is not a very remote contingency even there. And among ourselves, though the movement towards a class-war is less advanced, it is rapidly gaining ground, and will become irresistible if the war continues through next year and the food shortage grows worse, as, in that case, it is bound to do. The class-war cuts across the old divisions. Thus the Ukrainian Rada has been supported against the

Bolsheviks both by the Allies and by the Central Powers. *The Nation* (Feb. 16) comments on this act as follows: 'What, finally, becomes of the money and the military mission which the French Republic sent to aid the Rada against the Bolesheviks? The class war in the East is making nonsense of the war of the Great Powers.'

It was the development of this situation with which the article dealt. On the one hand, it pointed out the danger to the Governments of the world. On the other hand, in its concluding paragraph, it pointed out to those ardent spirits who view the prospect of revolution with equanimity, that a revolution brought on by hunger is likely to be very terrible, full of violence, and destructive of much that we should wish to preserve. In the course of adumbrating the consequences to be feared in such an eventuality, I suggested that our Government might, in such circumstances, use American troops 'to intimidate strikers'. This might happen without any complicity of the American people, or even of the American Government. American troops in this country will, as a rule, be stationed where our authorities recommend that they should be placed. It is obvious that if these troops, in increasing numbers, were drafted into disturbed areas such as the Clyde, their mere presence would intimidate strikers, or men contemplating a strike. In this suggestion there is nothing to jeopardize our relations with the United States. On the contrary, the actual use of American soldiers in this way, with however little complicity on the part of America, might cause bad blood with British Labour, and thus produce the very evil which I am falsely accused of intending. For this reason, it appeared to me a public duty, in the interests of good relations between the two nations, to utter a warning; and I am glad that, at whatever cost to myself, the prosecution have given a publicity to my warning which it could not otherwise have obtained, since by this publicity the danger is likely to be averted.

One phrase in my article has been distorted by the prosecution into a criticism of the military excellence of the American army. I had set forth in an earlier passage the view, which I share with Mr. Lloyd George, that the opposing armies in the West constitute an 'impenetrable barrier', and that, as an instrument for breaking through this barrier, where the British army has failed, there is no reason to suppose that the American army will succeed. In the sentence upon which I am being prosecuted, I summed up this discussion in the phrase 'whether or not they (the American troops) will prove efficient against the Germans'. By 'efficient' I meant 'efficient for the purpose of breaking through'. I did not mean to suggest any less efficiency than has been shown by our troops; and surely it is not illegal to regard the troops of one's own country as no less efficient than those of an Ally.

Liberal-minded Europeans look to America, and in particular to the

President, to prevent the war from being prolonged for imperialistic aims, and to keep alive the idealism inspiring very many of those who are fighting. This hope I fully share. But I am conscious of the power of the military machine, and of its indifference to higher moral aims in comparison with victory in battle. I know how easily the best men can be used, without their knowledge, to further ends which they would detest. The publication of the secret treaties by the Russians has shown the reality of this danger. I think it is important that America should realize this danger. If I had not been prosecuted, my words would not have been heard across the Atlantic. As they have been heard, I beg that they may be read as they were intended, as at once a warning to our Government, and an appeal to the love of liberty and the democratic ardour which animates the American nation.

Russell wrote this statement in preparation for his defence against charges brought against him under the Defence of the Realm Act in 1918. It was not published during his lifetime. He gave the typescript to Ottoline Morrell and it was preserved among her papers.

Source: **Pacifism and Revolution, Volume 14, The Collected Papers of Bertrand Russell,** *edited by Richard A Rempel, Louis Greenspan, Beryl Haslam, Albert C Lewis, Mark Lippincott, pages 403-405.*

Bertrand Russell from Routledge

The Selected Letters of Bertrand Russell, Volume 1
The Private Years 1884–1914
Edited by **Nicholas Griffin**, McMaster University, Canada

'With the appearance of *The Selected Letters of Bertrand Russell*, the non-specialist reader is given the run of that extraordinary headpiece as it applied itself to more accessible topics like sex, love and marriage.' – Stefan Collini, *Times Literary Supplement*

'Full of interest, both human and philosophical.' – *Evening Standard*

'A most enjoyable introduction to a man whose exceptional brain lit almost a century with philosophical ideas.' – *The Spectator*

'The combination of Russell's letters and Griffin's editing provides an enthralling introduction to one of the most remarkable and bizarre figures of the 20th century.' – *The Sunday Telegraph*

August 2002: 234x156: 548pp:illus. 31 b+w photographs

The Selected Letters of Bertrand Russell, Volume 2
The Public Years 1914–1970
Edited by **Nicholas Griffin**, McMaster University, Canada

'The most useful and accessible introduction to Russell's life that any reader could possibly wish for.' – Noel Malcolm, *The Sunday Telegraph*, London

'Anybody who reads this splendid and revealing selection of letters will soon feel that he knows Russell. Nicholas Griffin completes a two-volume epistolary biography unrivalled for its scholarship.' – *The Economist*

'At times one feels that if Russell had not existed, Nancy Mitford or Evelyn Waugh would have had to invent him.' – *The Times*

'A markedly perceptive, sympathetic and accurate biography. Nothing else written about Russell's life, including recent biographies, comes near it in value.' – A. C. Grayling, *Literary Review*

August 2002: 234x156: 688pp

www.routledge.com

THE COLLECTED PAPERS OF BERTRAND RUSSELL

The McMaster University Edition

Volume 1 *Cambridge Essays, 1888–99*
Volume 2 *Philosophical Papers, 1896–99*
Volume 3 *Toward the "Principles of Mathematics", 1900–02*
Volume 4 *Foundations of Logic, 1903–05*
Volume 5 *Toward "Principia Mathematica", 1905–08*
Volume 6 *Logical and Philosophical Papers, 1909–13*
Volume 7 *Theory of Knowledge: The 1913 Manuscript*
Volume 8 *The Philosophy of Logical Atomism and Other Essays, 1914–19*
Volume 9 *Essays on Language, Mind and Matter, 1919–26*
Volume 10 *A Fresh Look at Empiricism, 1927–42*
Volume 11 *Last Philosophical Testament, 1943–68*
Volume 12 *Contemplation and Action, 1902–14*
Volume 13 *Prophecy and Dissent, 1914–16*
Volume 14 *Pacifism and Revolution, 1916–18*
Volume 15 *Uncertain Paths to Freedom, 1919–22*
Volume 21 *How to Keep the Peace: The Pacifist Dilemma, 1935–38*
Volume 28 *Man's Peril, 1954–55*
Volume 29 *Détente or Destruction, 1955–57*
Bibliography, Volume I: *Separate Publications, 1896–1990*
Bibliography, Volume II: *Serial Publications, 1890–1990*
Bibliography, Volume III: *Indexes*